Don't Reinvent the Wheel Just Paint it

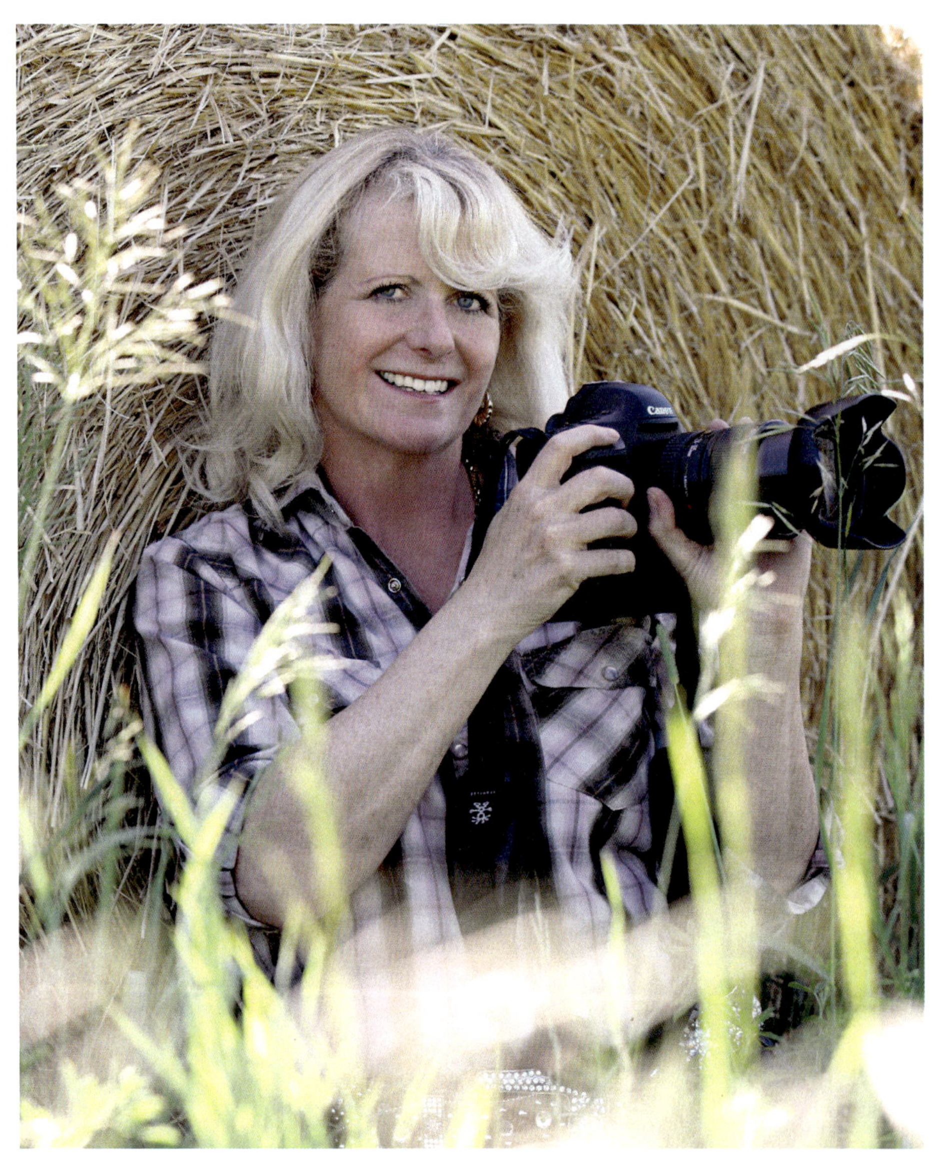

Artist - Author - Fine Art Photographer
Linda Finstad

Cover art by Marjorie Shannon-Graham

ISBN - 978-1-9995545-4-5

Dedication

I never met a child yet that didn't like
to crayon, colour and make art
This book is dedicated to the artist that lives within everyone.

You may have to dig a long way back to find that child artist.
My hope is that you will be inspired to
allow him or her to once again play with all
the colours in the paint box.

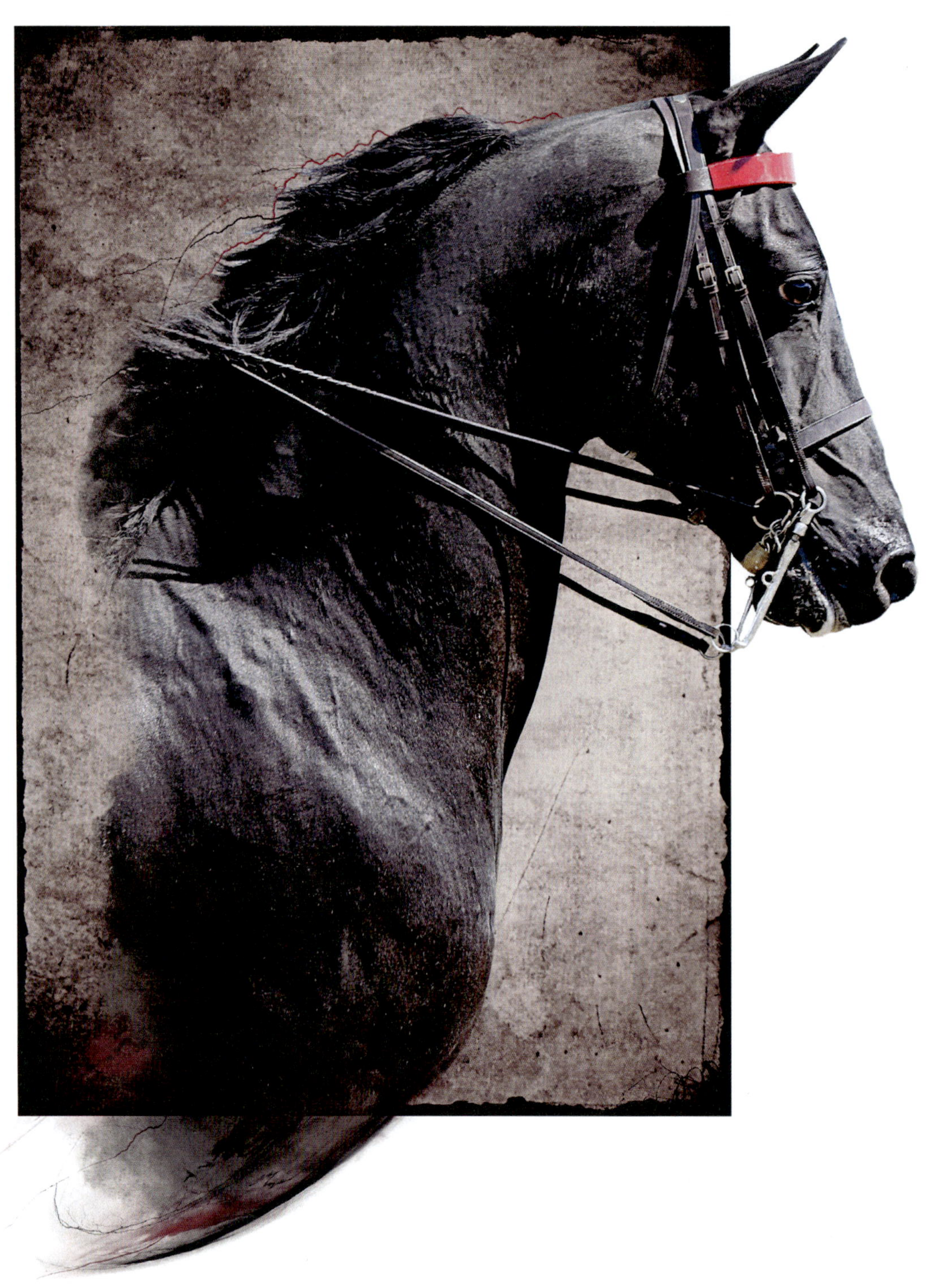

Table of Contents

Why paint photographs? 7

Choosing the right photograph 13

Print methods and papers 19

Mixing colours 22

Painting versus tinting 27

Acrylic paints includes Q-tip art 29

Art by Linda Finstad 37

Watercolour paints and inks 41

Getting Started 43

Pastels 47

Watercolour pencils and crayons 57

Marshall's Photo Oils 65

Pencil crayons and coloured markers 73

Congratulations 83

Guest artist gallery 85

Choosing the right mat 102

Preserving and framing your work 103

About the author 107

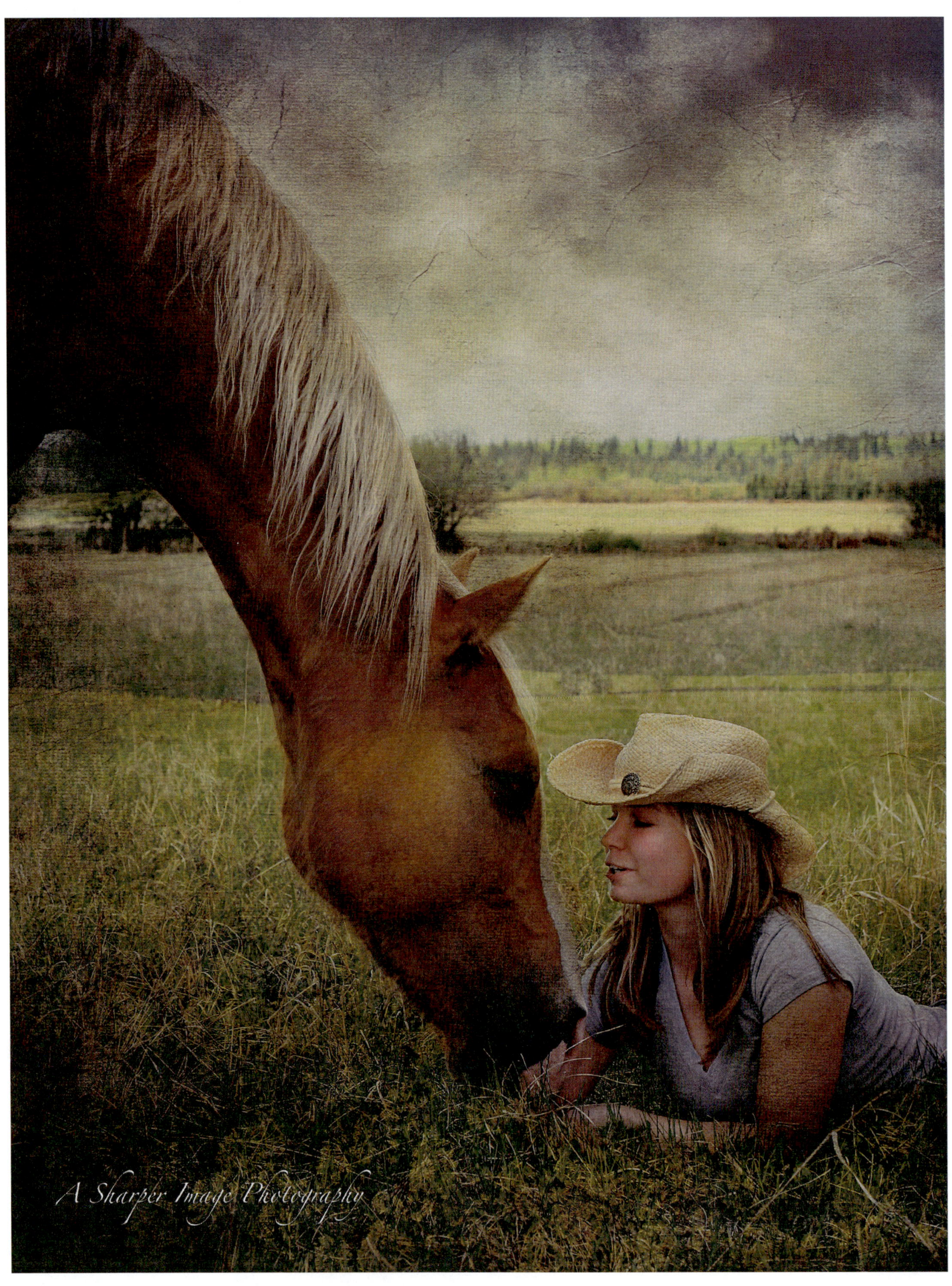
A Sharper Image Photography

Why paint photographs?

Greetings! My name is Linda Finstad and for over 15 years I earned my living as an equine photographer. This truly was a dream job, spending time outdoors photographing beautiful horses and their owners. In all honesty it was hard to call it a job, plus equine photography was extremely lucrative. However, all good things come to an end. With the introduction of sophisticated cell phone cameras and user-friendly DSLR cameras my clients were able to capture their own images.

To stay in business would mean creating images with a "holy crap" factor. These were images that amateur photographers would not be able to capture for themselves with a cell phone or auto settings on their expensive cameras. This meant developing my Photoshop skills and spending many hours at the computer transforming photos into digital art.

This plan worked like a charm. Sales of "edited" photos resurrected my failing photography business. However there was one massive downside to offering manipulated photos. My clients saw them as exactly that (manipulated photos) and they did not view them as works of art.

It was very frustrating. When exhibiting at trade and art shows, people would admire my work and ask "Is that a painting?" On discovering the image they were admiring was digital art — they would rudely comment "Oh, you just Photoshopped it" and walk away.

Hmm. My clients were genuinely disappointed when they discovered that the image was not hand painted. The mention of computer generated art seemed to turn them off and cause them to walk away.

Learning Photoshop had been hard but with many YouTube video tutorials, perseverance and practice I had been able to master it.

If my clients wanted paintings, perhaps I could learn to paint?

I dedicated a full year to learning and developing painting skills, experimenting with different paints and mediums. During that time immersed in painting something amazing happened.

Number one, I fell in love with painting and number two, I developed a very distinct style. I call my style Prism-Equus. This made-up word means equine personality depicted in colour. My paintings were all of horses (of course), however they were brightly coloured and definitely NOT photorealistic.

To my great joy and somewhat surprise these abstract horse paintings sold like hot cakes. Perhaps the reason was that no one had ever seen horses painted in this fashion. Prism-Equus style was fresh and new. Or was the real value in the fact that they were hand painted and not computer generated?

Now I can add artist to my resume. Yea me!

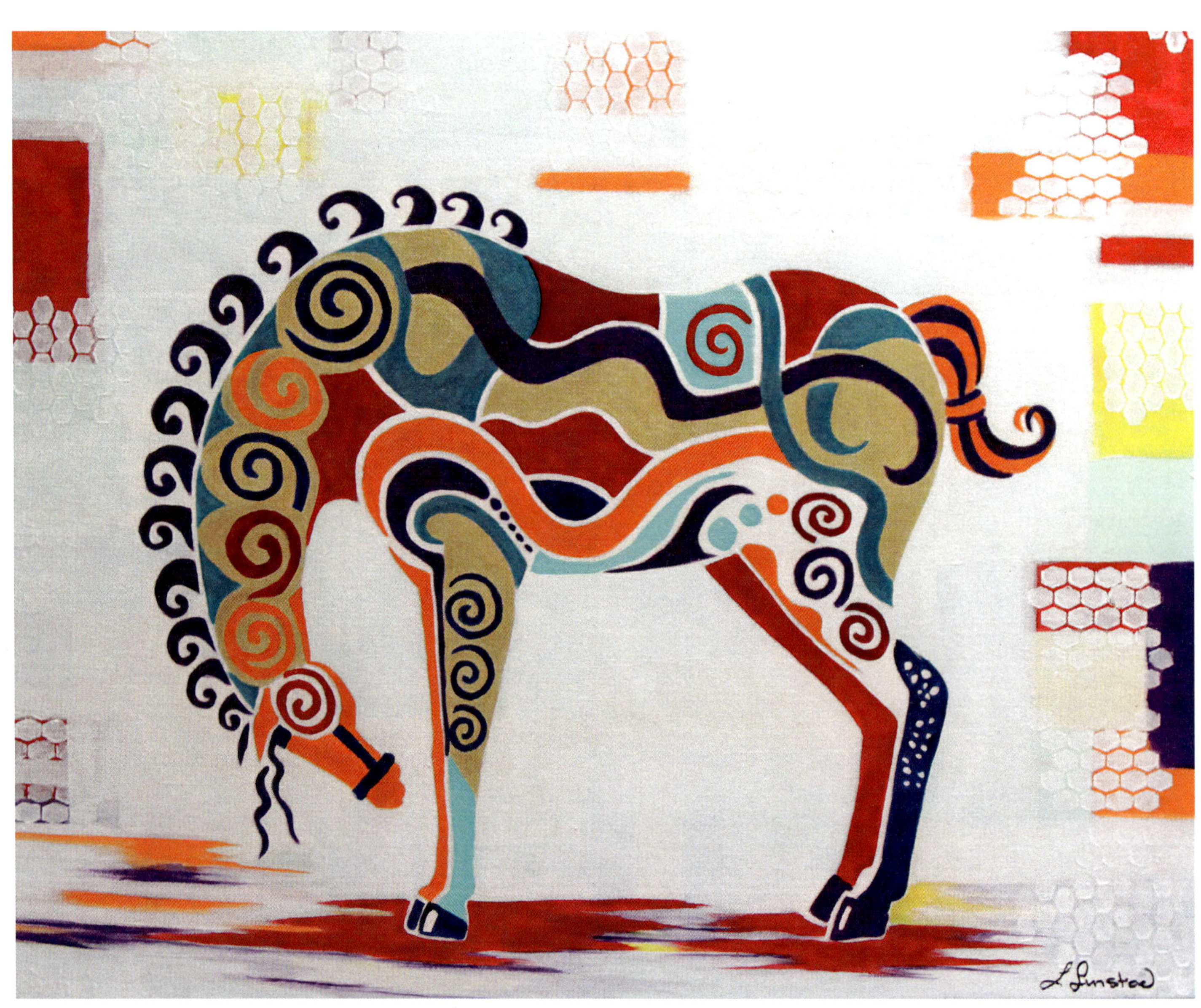

Painting was lots of fun but my first love was for photography. So I decided to combine the two and hand colour my photographs turning them into original art.

There is nothing new about this idea; it was probably thought of two minutes after the very first black and white print was made. But the goal was not to re-create vintage looking hand tinted images. If this vintage method of colourizing photos was to generate new income it too must be fresh and modern.

If you want to restore and hand tint old photos the techniques featured in this book will definitely help you achieve that goal, but that is not the true purpose of this book.

The focus is to combine two art forms - photography and painting to create new and exciting works of art that wow the viewer and hopefully generate sales.

How do you create new and exciting ideas and images?

The easiest way to come up with interesting alternatives to what has gone before is to take a long, hard look at what has gone before and pick it apart.

What does that mean?
The easiest way to do that is to look at a selection of photographs which have been hand tinted / painted and objectively critique them.
On a piece of paper create two columns and on one side list all the attributes you like.
On the other side what you don't like or what you feel could have been done better.

Repeat this process with 4 or 5 different hand tinted photos (different subjects).
This is a great starting point because now you know what you don't like.

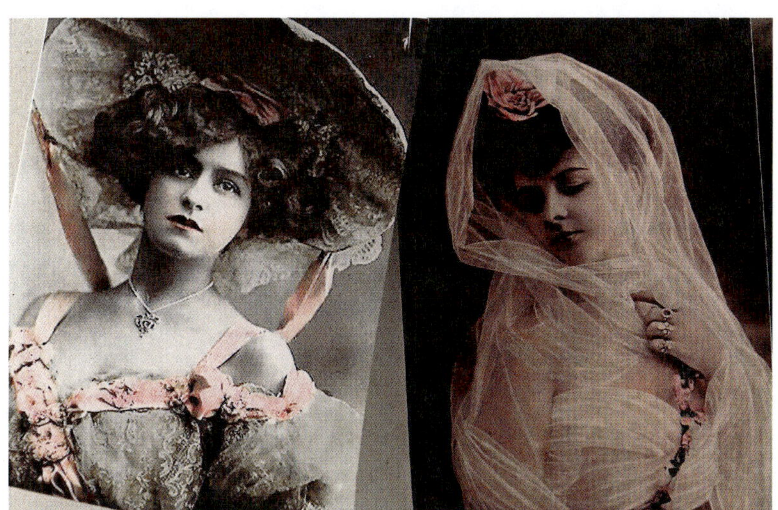

The following images were carefully chosen examples of vintage hand coloured photographs. As you can see the skill of the artist varies greatly from image to image. Looking at beautifully executed hand colouring can be a little intimidating especially as you learn this new skill. This is why it was important to include a few images that show what not to do.

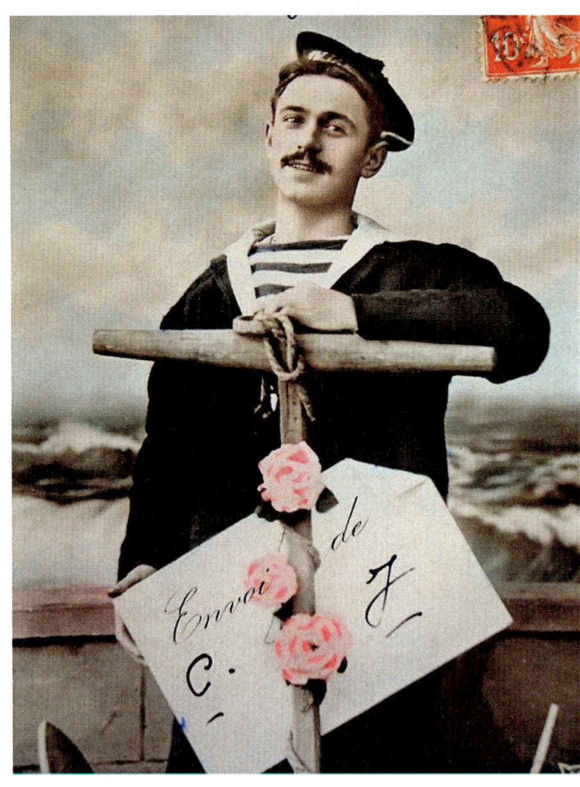

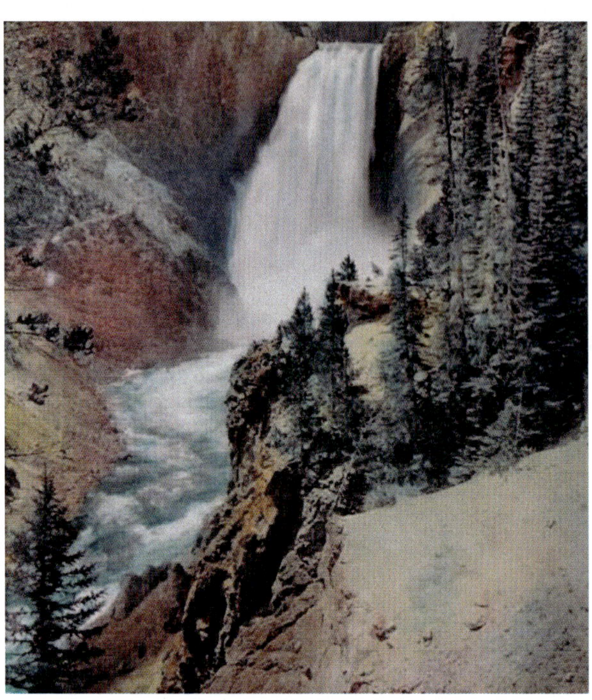

Ask yourself the following questions:
Do you prefer bold or subtle colours?
Are you drawn to landscapes and nature?
Perhaps you prefer portraits of people.
Which of these 4 photographs do you like best?
Which is your least favorite and why?

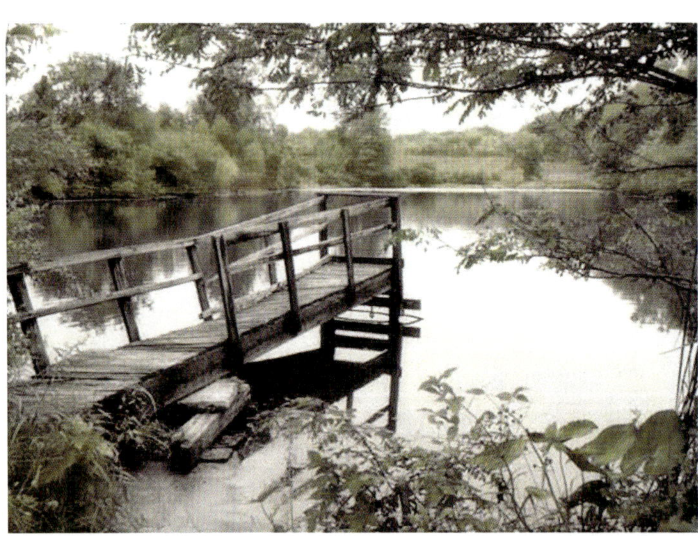

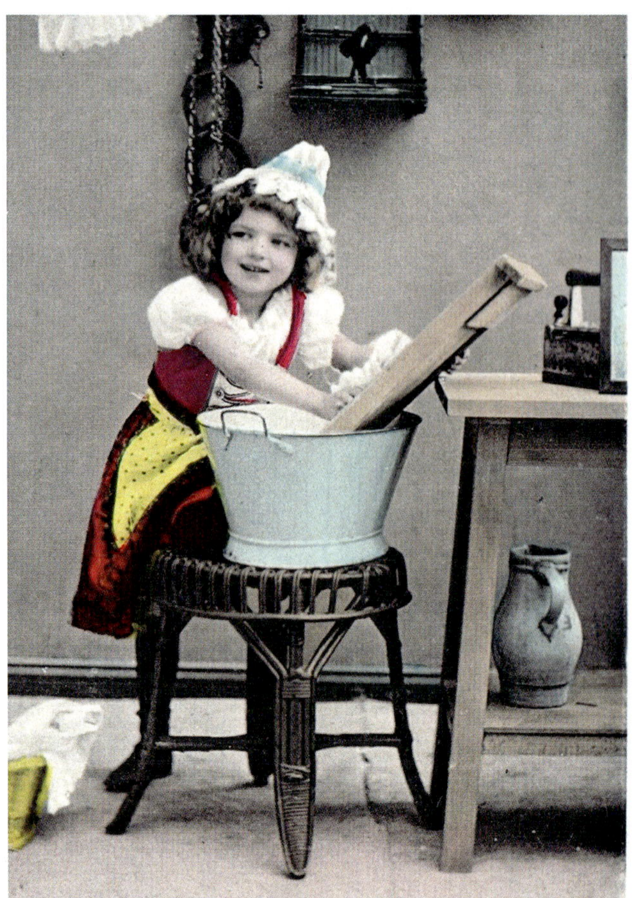

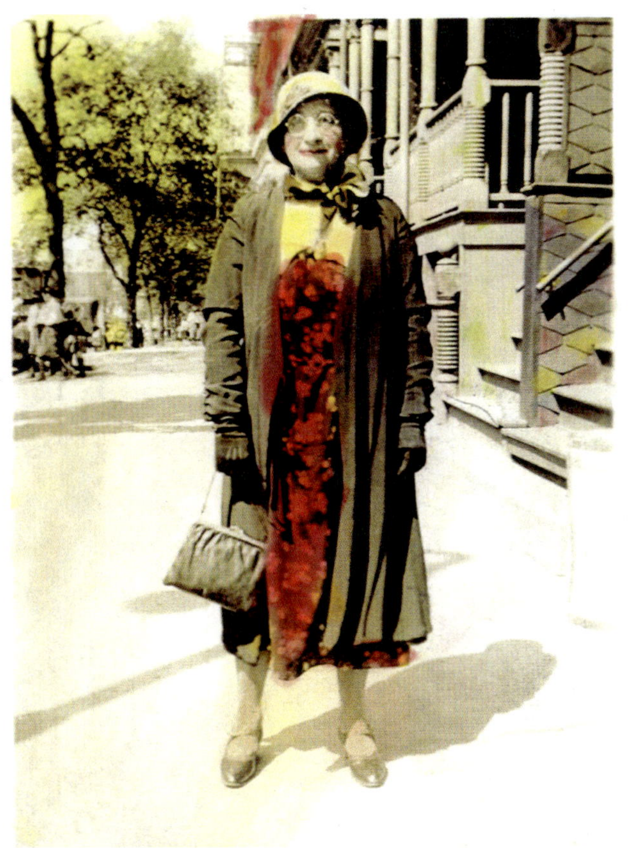

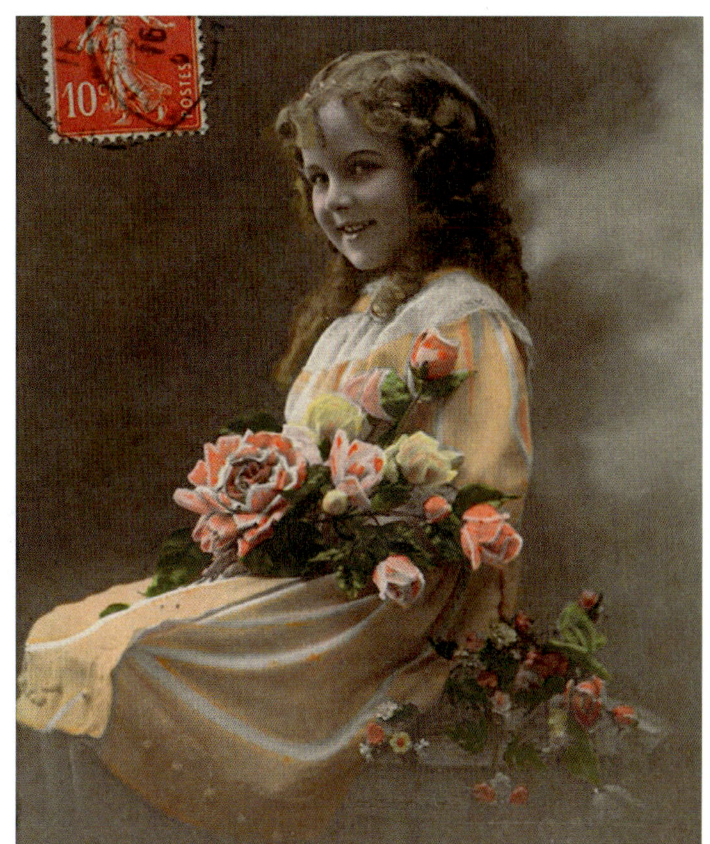

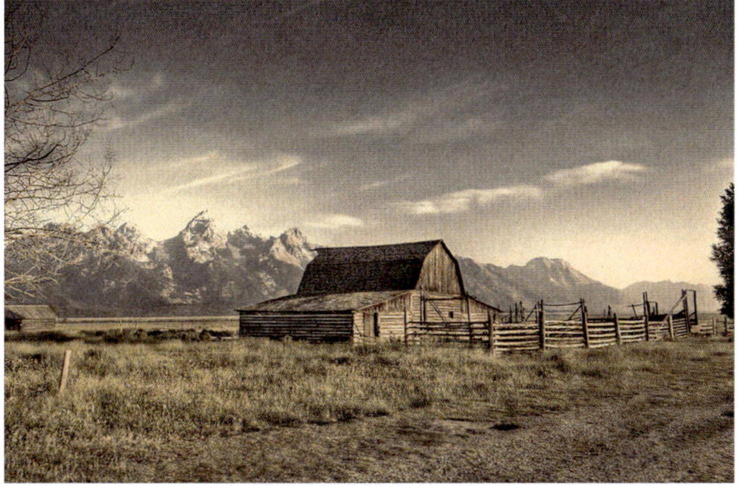

After completing this little exercise I discovered landscapes and urban architecture don't turn my crank, which is very helpful to know. I prefer to photograph animals rather than people, again good to know.

Another personal discovery was a preference for bold vibrant colours with high contrast.

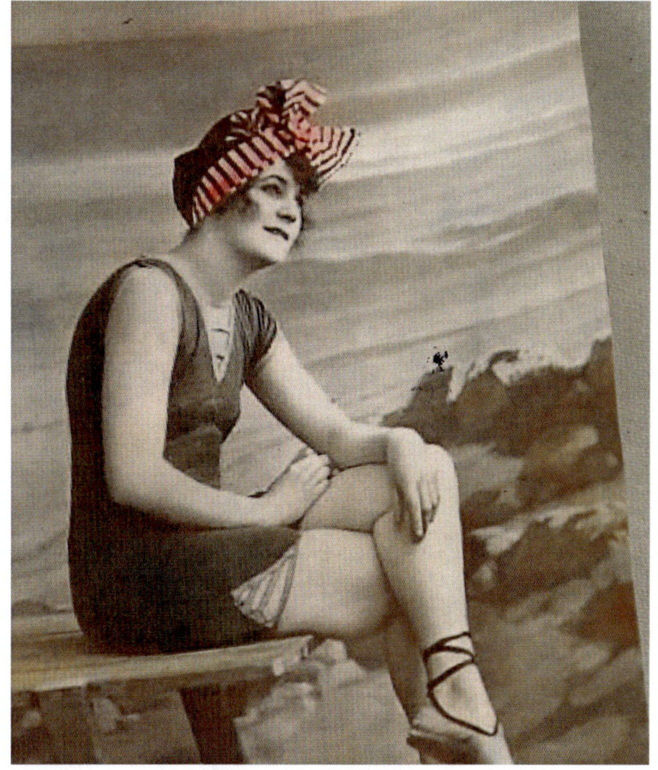

There is no right or wrong,
just what is right for you.
It is more likely that you will create an exciting piece of art when you are excited about the subject and the colour palette.

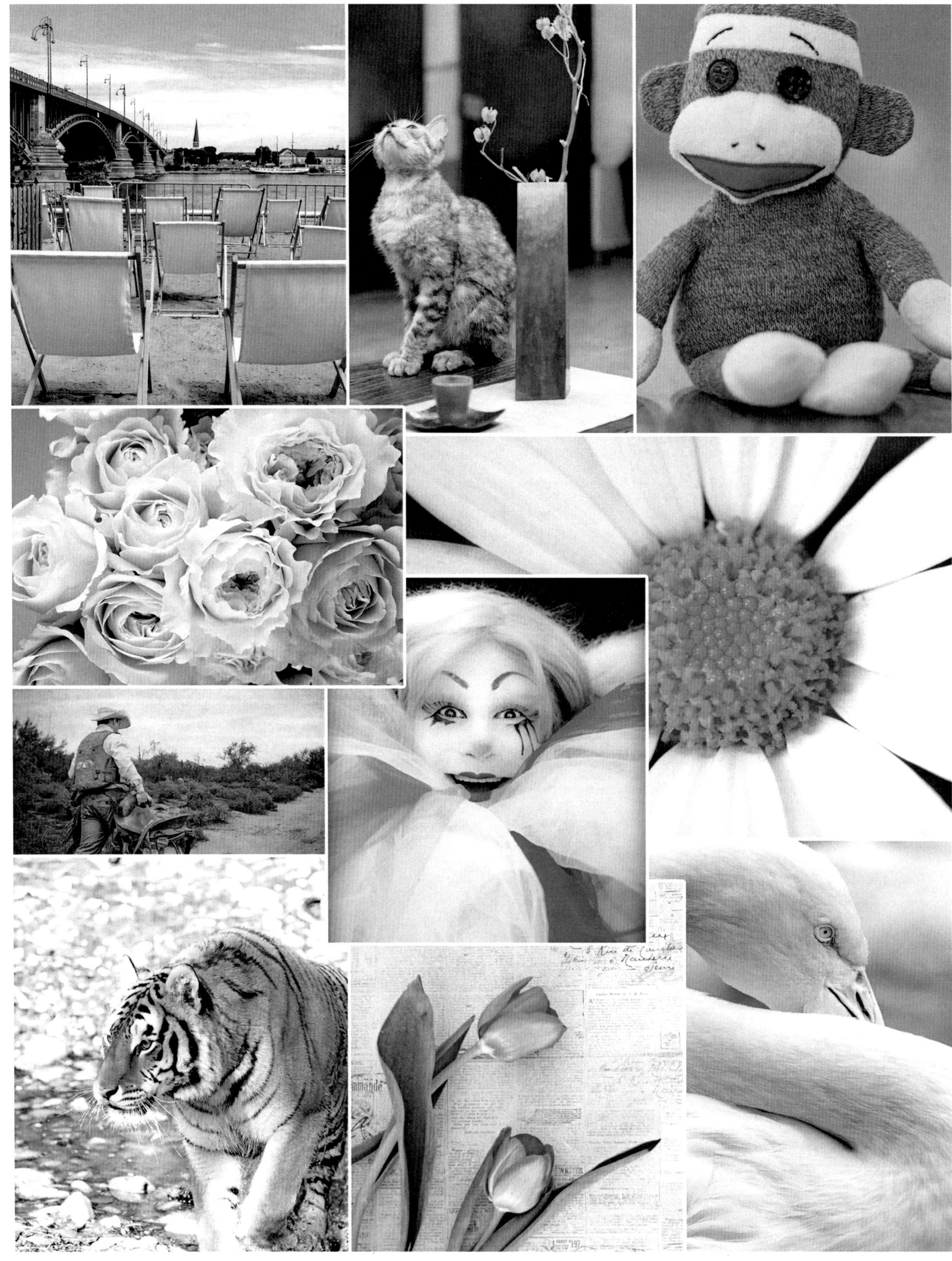

Choosing the right photograph

Before we can get into a discussion about choosing the right photograph for hand colouring and painting let's take a few moments to learn how to take a good quality, tack-sharp photograph.

First and foremost when printing your photographs to hand colour I would recommend printing them at least 8x10 inches. This will give you more room to work and also a nice sized finished art piece should you want to frame it. In order print a photograph at that size it must have enough information contained within each square inch of the image. The technical term is DPI meaning, dots per inch.

Cell phone cameras usually capture images at 72 DPI which is perfect for uploading to Facebook or Instagram but will only produce a very small print before losing clarity.

Most DSLR cameras output images at 225 DPI which is perfect for printing and very often can be expanded to 300 DPI which is the requirement for commercial printing such as magazines or books.

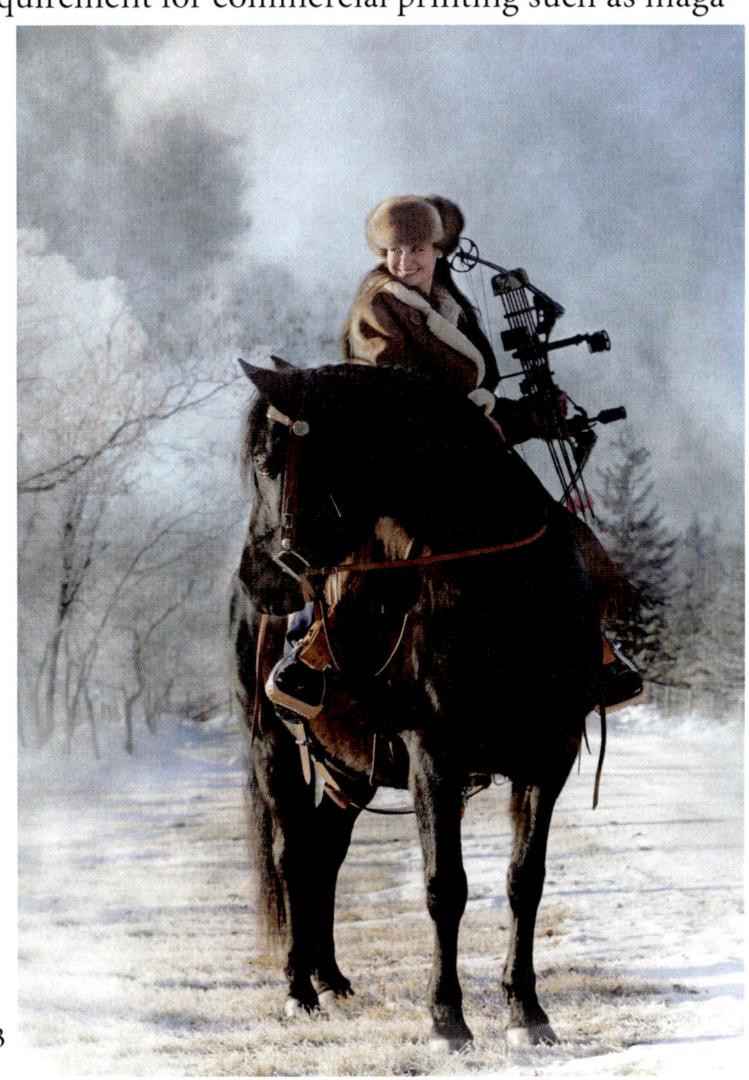

I have been a professional photographer for over 20 years and in my experience there are two basic scenarios. Your subject is either moving or standing still. It's as simple as that.

This means to master the art of photography all you need to know is how to set your camera for either action shots or still life (which can include architecture and landscape).

OK, that is a very simplified analogy and there is a lot more to photography than just two settings, but for the sake of keeping it simple we will take a look at how to master those two basic areas.

Action photography

This means anything that is moving whether it's moving slowly like a flower gently wafting in the breeze or a cheetah chasing a gazelle on the Savannah. The principles are the same for both.

The way to capture tack-sharp action shots it to set the shutter speed fast enough to stop the action. It's that easy and the opposite is also true. If you are photographing a child running across a playground and you don't have the shutter speed set fast enough you will produce blurry photographs.

How do you set the shutter speed?

Most DSLR cameras have similar settings which include automatic, semi-automatic and manual. Forget the automatic setting because nine out of ten times your camera will not select a fast enough shutter speed. You are going to be using the semi-automatic setting, shutter speed priority. By selecting this mode you will have the ability to change the shutter speed and the ISO, the camera will select the third component that makes up a photograph which is the aperture.

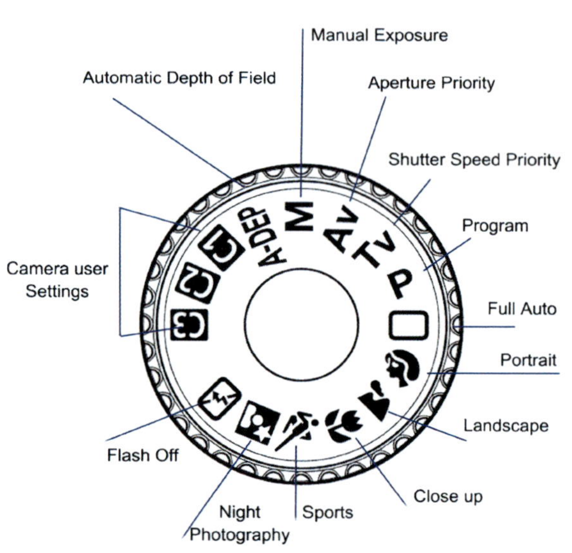

How do you know how fast, will be fast enough?

A general rule of thumb is the faster the subject is moving the faster the shutter speed needs to be to stop the action. For a person walking you will need a shutter speed of at least 125/th of a second to stop the action. A cheetah running after a gazelle will require a shutter speed of 4000th/of a second. Of course there are lots of variables in between. I typically photograph horses outdoors so at the start of a photo shoot I will set my shutter speed to around 500th/ of a second. However if the horse is galloping really fast I will increase that speed to 800th/ of a second.

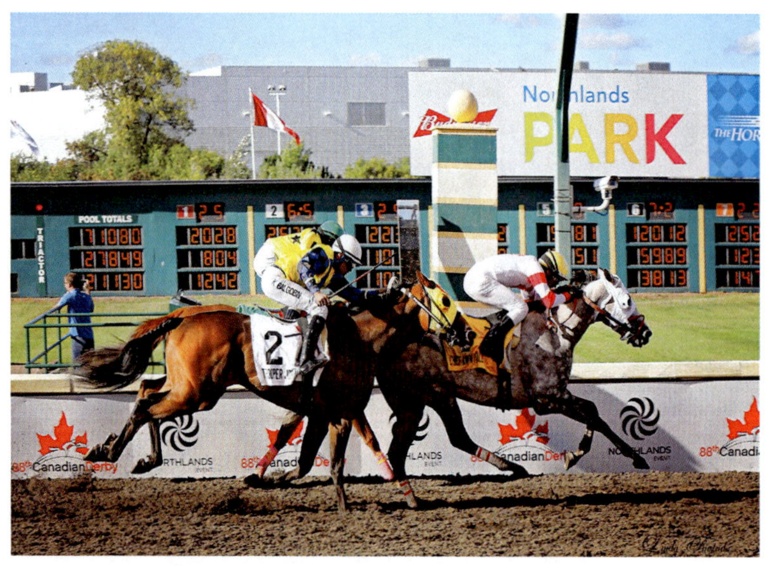

You may be wondering why not just crank the shutter speed as high as it will go? Would that not ensure any and all action would be captured? The answer is all about the light. When the shutter slams shut really fast there is very little time for light to hit the sensor and create a well exposed image. This means the faster the shutter speed the more (brighter) light is required to get an exposure.

This is where the ISO comes into play. I won't go into complicated detail about how the ISO works. The simple explanation is the ISO allows more light into the camera. This means in low light situations you can increase the ISO setting to achieve a good exposure.

Hmm. So if that is the case why not just crank the ISO to the highest setting and then you will always have enough light no matter the situation? Oh, if it were only that simple! True the ISO does allow more light into the camera but it also effects the quality of the picture. The higher the ISO setting the more grainy your finished print will be. It is a delicate balance between exposure and quality. For example, 100 ISO will result in the best quality photographs with no grain - 10,000 ISO may allow you to shoot in low light situations but the resulting photographs will be grainy.

Portraits (humans and animals)

When you want to shift the focus just onto your subject and push the background out of focus you need to select the other semi-automatic setting which is Aperture Priority. This camera mode gives you the ability to change the aperture and the ISO and the camera selects an appropriate shutter speed to produce an exposure.

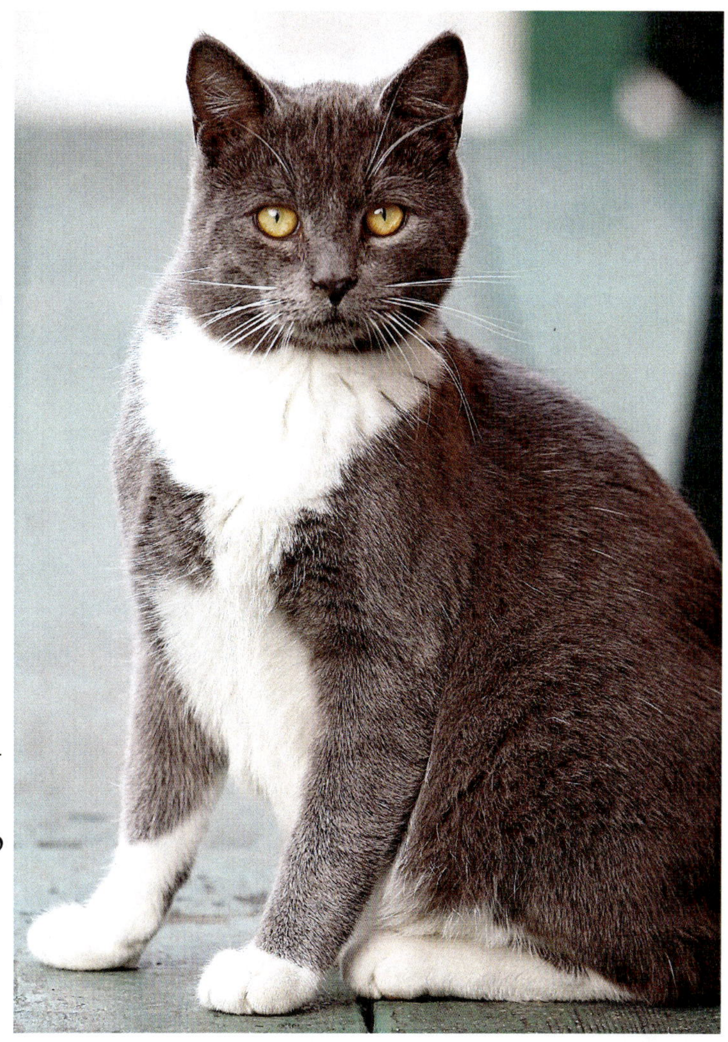

What is Aperture?

Aperture describes the size of an opening within the camera lens that allows light to pass through the lens. The aperture works with the shutter speed to control the amount of light striking the sensor. It also affects the depth of field within an image.

A lower aperture number such as 2.8 produces a shallow depth of field and blurs the back ground. Aperture is also referred to as F-stop and is one of the most confusing aspects of photography for new photographers to understand, so please bear with me.

Landscape and architecture

If your goal is to capture a scene where everything is in focus, for instance a building or a beautiful view, you will still need to have your camera set to Aperture Priority. This time you will select a higher number such as 8 or16. This will push the depth of field much further out and ensure you capture all the details in the scene. Again you get to choose the ISO and the camera will choose the appropriate shutter speed to create an exposure. Be careful though, because to let in enough light your camera may need to select a slow shutter speed if your aperture is very narrow (higher number). This means you might produce a blurred photograph due to camera-shake if you hold your camera by hand. Best to use a tripod and trigger your shutter remotely.

Choosing the right photograph

After the brief lesson on how to set up your camera to achieve the best results, now it is time to think about what kind of photographs work well for hand colouring.

The subject matter is entirely up to you, but one thing to keep in mind is how detailed the image is. When starting out it is best to choose photographs with large areas to colour. Cars and close ups of flowers are easy to colour and those subjects can be coloured with any hue. They do not have to be true to life, as opposed to hand colouring a portrait of a loved one .

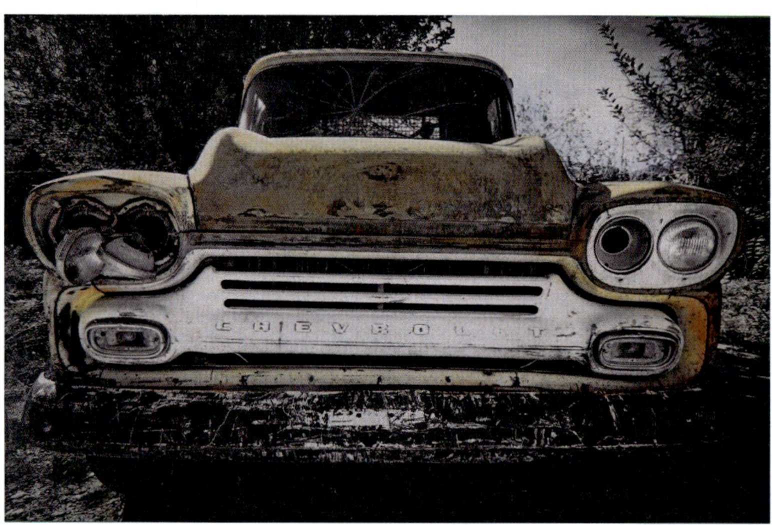

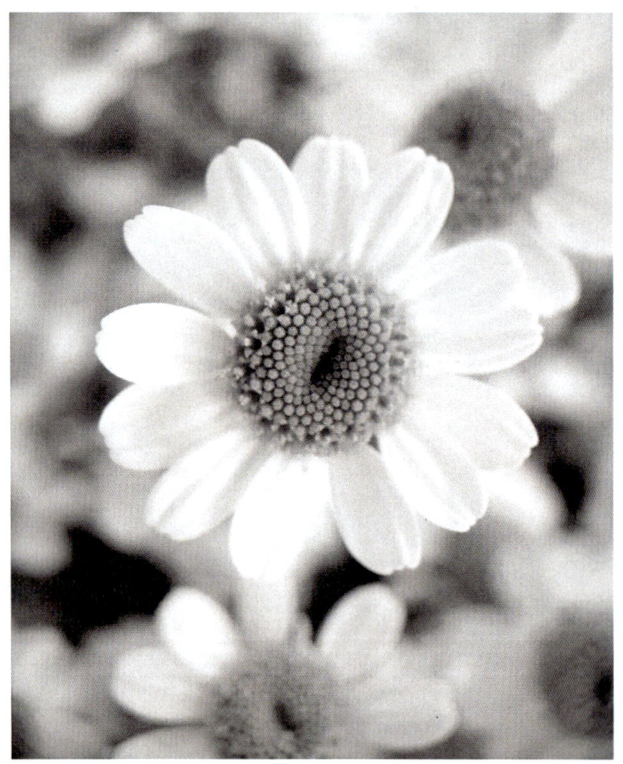

Choose photographs with lighter tonal values. These will take colour much better than areas of the photograph that look almost black.

This is especially important when photographing landscape scenes.

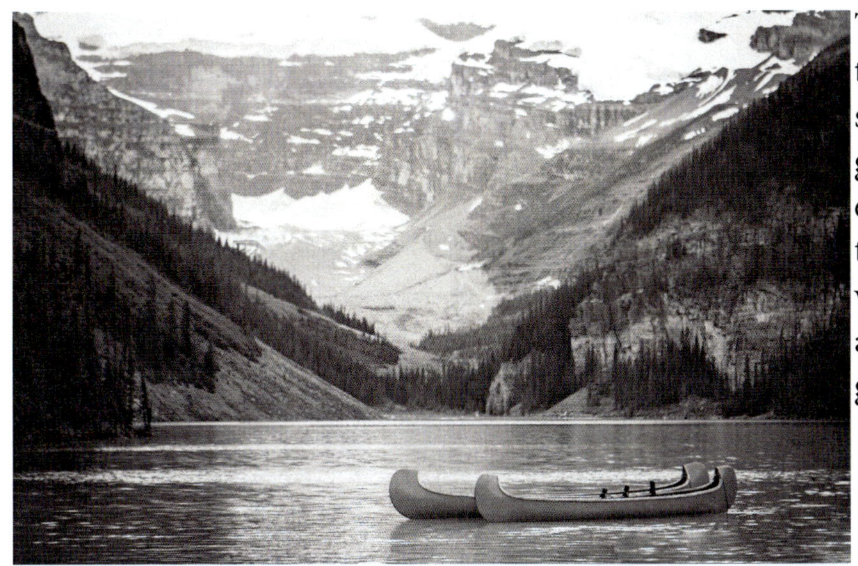

The original colour photograph of this mountain view was absolutely stunning with rich hues of blue and green. However once it was converted to black and white the trees along the mountainside and water turned very dark. Much of the detail was lost and those dark areas of the photograph and will not take colour well.

I enjoy photographing horses and animals but not all those shots are suitable for hand colouring. Take the photograph on the right, a lovely image of a horse galloping in the snow, yet I just did not know where to start colouring this picture.

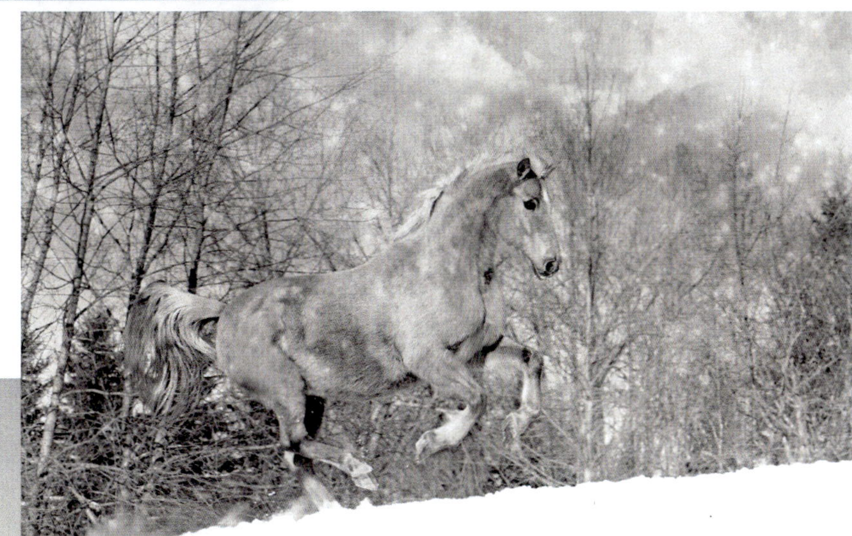

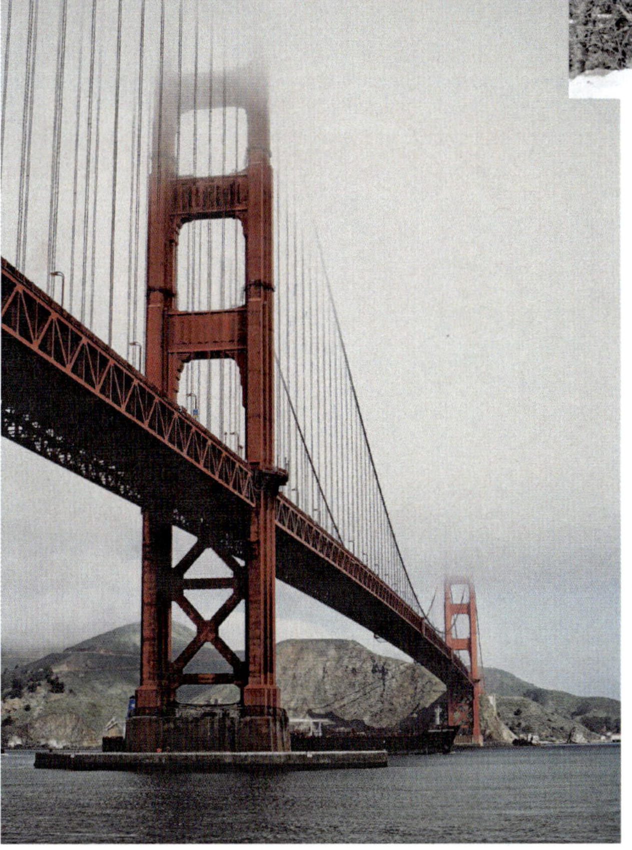

On the other hand, bridges are perfect for colouring or painting because they are well defined and it is easy to see where a splash of colour would enhance the image. Using your creativity you can make the bridge any colour you like.

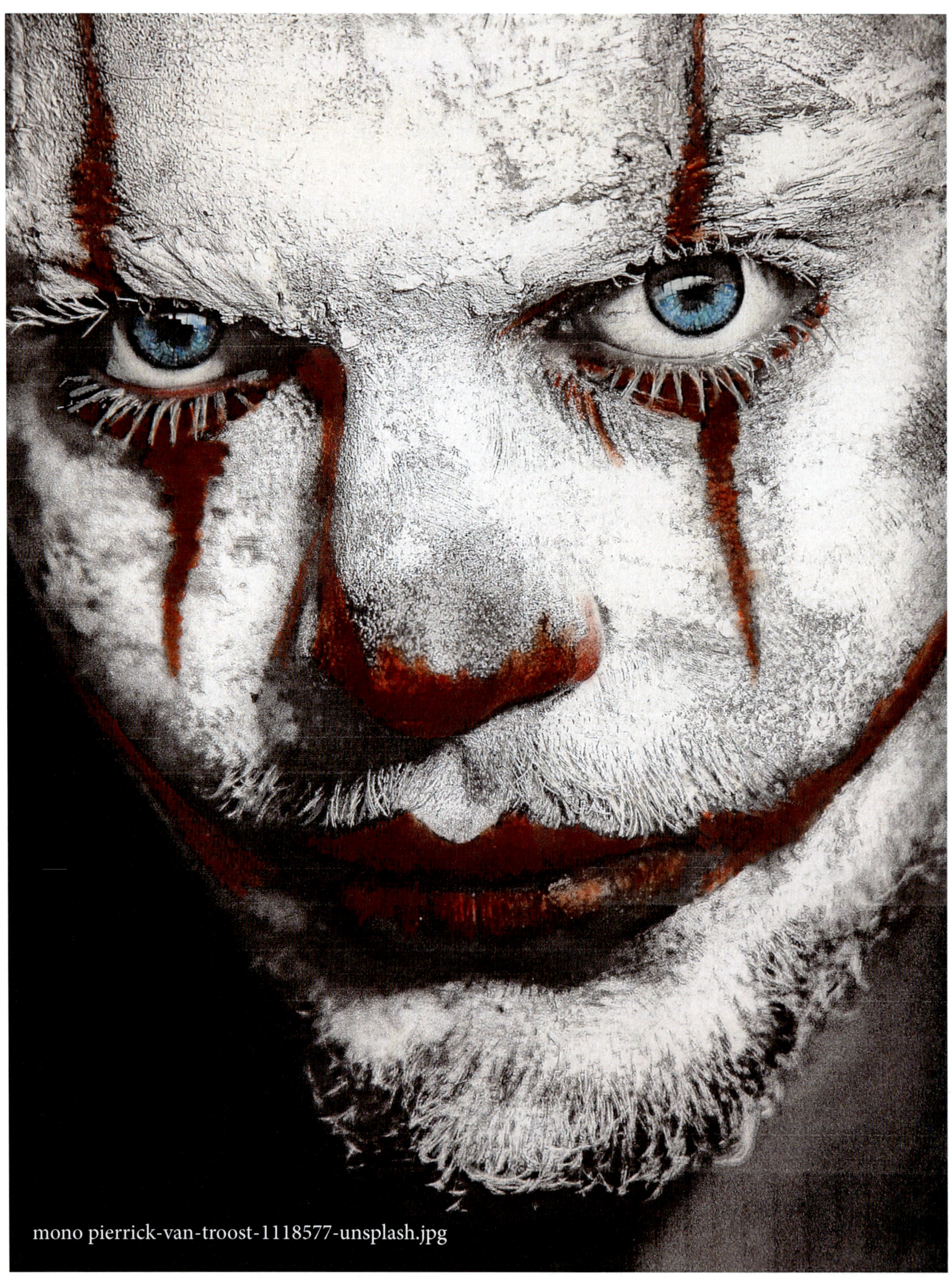
mono pierrick-van-troost-1118577-unsplash.jpg

Print methods and papers

Choosing the right photo paper and print process required much trial and error. Only by extensive experimentation was I able to reveal the types of paper and printing methods suitable for hand painting. This research was both costly and time consuming. I have done the leg work and discovered what works and what doesn't work - so you don't have to.

This information alone is worth the price of the book.

Don't reinvent the wheel
Just paint it

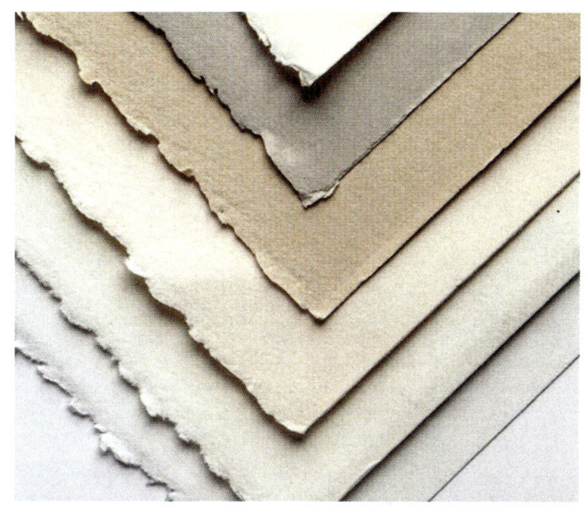

This book takes a modern look at a vintage technique. This means you are not limited to specialty photographic papers, toxic chemicals and darkroom photo development. You are free to explore modern printing methods and the whole array of art papers that are available for print. This is good news because many of those materials are no longer available or deemed safe to use.

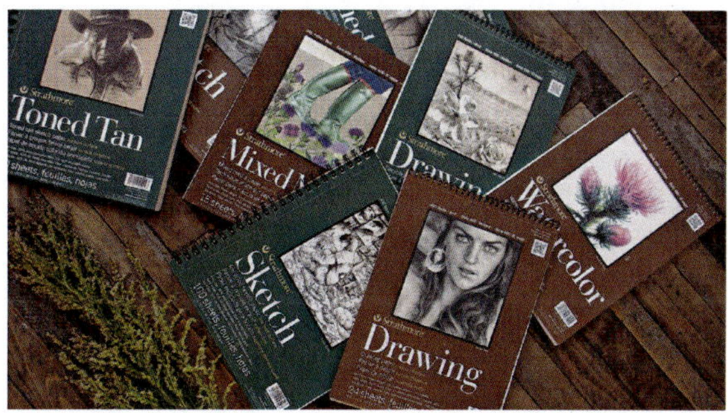

Once you have your digital photograph cropped, sized, edited, converted to black and white and ready to print it's time to decide what kind of paper on which to print. Your choice of paper will vary depending on which artists' materials you intend to use in hand colouring. We will discuss the merits of a variety of these papers as we explore different art mediums and paints.

Typically when you order photographic prints from big box store photo printing labs such as Costco or Walmart you only have two basic photo finishes to choose from, glossy or matte. Specialized photo labs may offer more finishes and different papers but these labs are few and far between as they too have felt the pressure of the digital age.

Glossy photo finish is smooth and reflects light. Only acrylic paints will adhere to this surface, but it is not the best choice because acrylics dry to a matte finish making the contrast between the paint and the photographic finish very distinct.

Matte photo finish has a dull surface and offers a little more texture and will hold oil paints and pastels slightly better.

However, you are not limited to glossy or matte as it is possible to print your photos from your home printer using a variety of specialty art papers, available from art and craft stores.

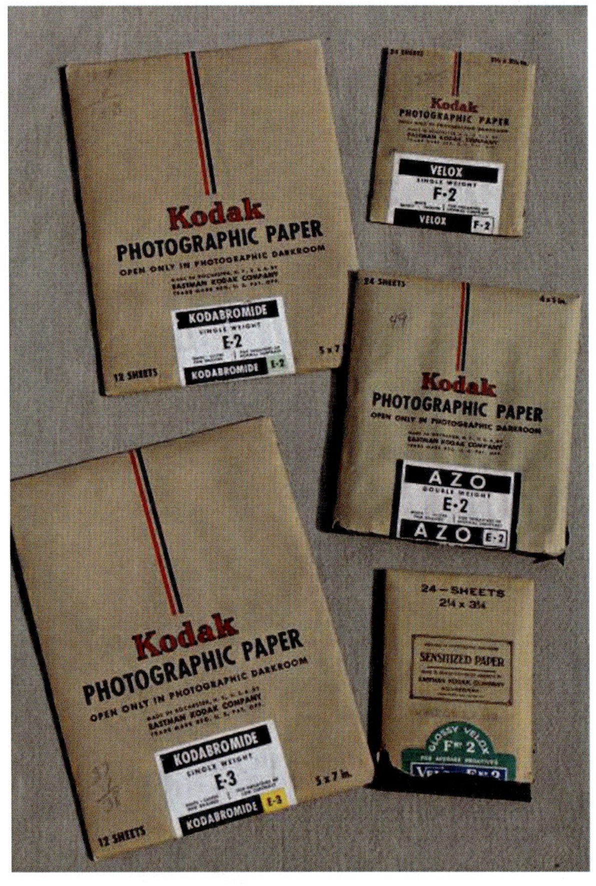

Vintage photographic papers would be fun to experiment with if you can find them.

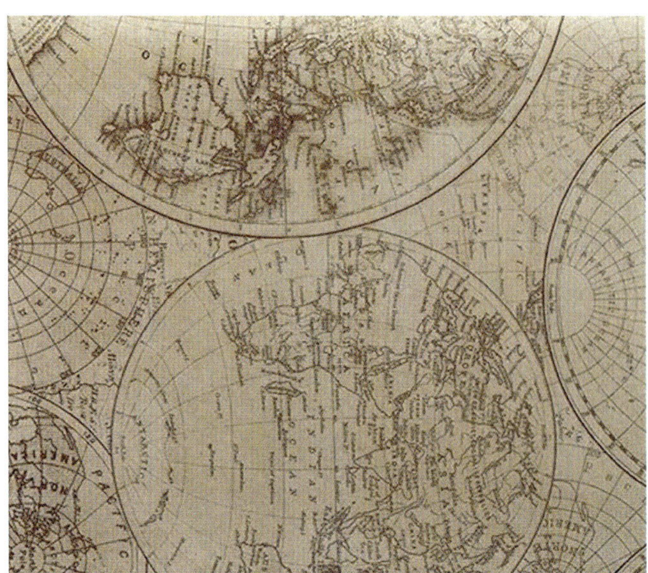

Old maps can make very interesting backgrounds for your black and white photographs.

Just photocopy the map onto the art paper of your choice prior to printing the photograph onto it.

Tea stained paper

A very interesting anitiqued effect can be achieved by using tea to stain your mixed media paper before printing the photograph on it.

Soak three bags of black tea in two cups of hot water.When the tea is ready, apply it by dabbing the paper with the tea bag or by dipping a paintbrush into the tea and brushing it onto the paper. Once you have stained the paper to the desired colour, set it out to dry. Put a pane of glass or a nylon screen on top of the paper to ensure it will dry flat. This will prevent the edges from wrinkling or warping. Once your stained paper is completely dry, you can print your black and white photograph onto it.

Mixed media paper This general purpose paper provides the best choice for most paints, pencil crayon and pastels. The fine textured paper with heavy sizing is perfect for both wet and dry media. These acid-free, large pads of art paper are relatively inexpensive.

Watercolour paper If you want your watercolour paints to "bloom" by wetting the paper before applying the colour please buy the best watercolour paper available. My personal favourite is Arches 100% cotton 140 lb. Although a little more expensive than the student grade watercolour paper, the results are definitely worth the money.

Canvas paper Yes, you can buy sheets of canvas paper that will fit into your home printer. Canvas paper is perfect for acrylics or regular artist oil paints and gives your photo a very painterly feel. Note: The canvas paper is a buff colour not white which means when you print your photograph onto it there will be no white highlights. This is not necessarily a bad thing but definitely something to take into consideration when choosing a suitable image to print.

Giclee art canvas Giclee canvas prints have a protective finish applied to them, which is a great feature when hanging them in your home. The finish allows you to wipe them over with a damp cloth when they get dusty. The down side is they are smooth and non-porous which means most art mediums will not adhere to the finish.

However, I have had incredible results transforming giclee canvas prints of my photos into hand finished works of art using acrylic paints and a gel medium. Giclee art canvases are the most expensive of the options mentioned, so I would urge you to hone your skills and practice a little before risking a large giclee.

Of course there are many more specialty art papers available. If you want to get really creative take a walk through the scrapbook section of the art and craft store. You will be amazed at the wide selection of papers. Or think entirely outside the box and cut textured wall paper to printable sizes and print your black and white photo on it. Perhaps newsprint, wrapping paper or even translucent parchment paper would give you interesting results. Creating art is all about having fun and experimenting with different ideas and techniques. The ideas contained in this book are designed and intended to set you on your own creative journey.

Mixing colours

Colour theory is the science and art of using colour. It takes an in-depth look at how we perceive colour and hues, along with how to mix colours. It examines which colours harmonize or contrast with each other and how those colours convey subtle messages by communicating an emotional response when used in art or design. There are countless books and huge volumes devoted to the art and science of colour theory if you would like to study it more thoroughly.

For the purpose of hand tinting, colouring or painting photographs it would be extremely remiss not to take a little time to review the basic principles of colour theory.

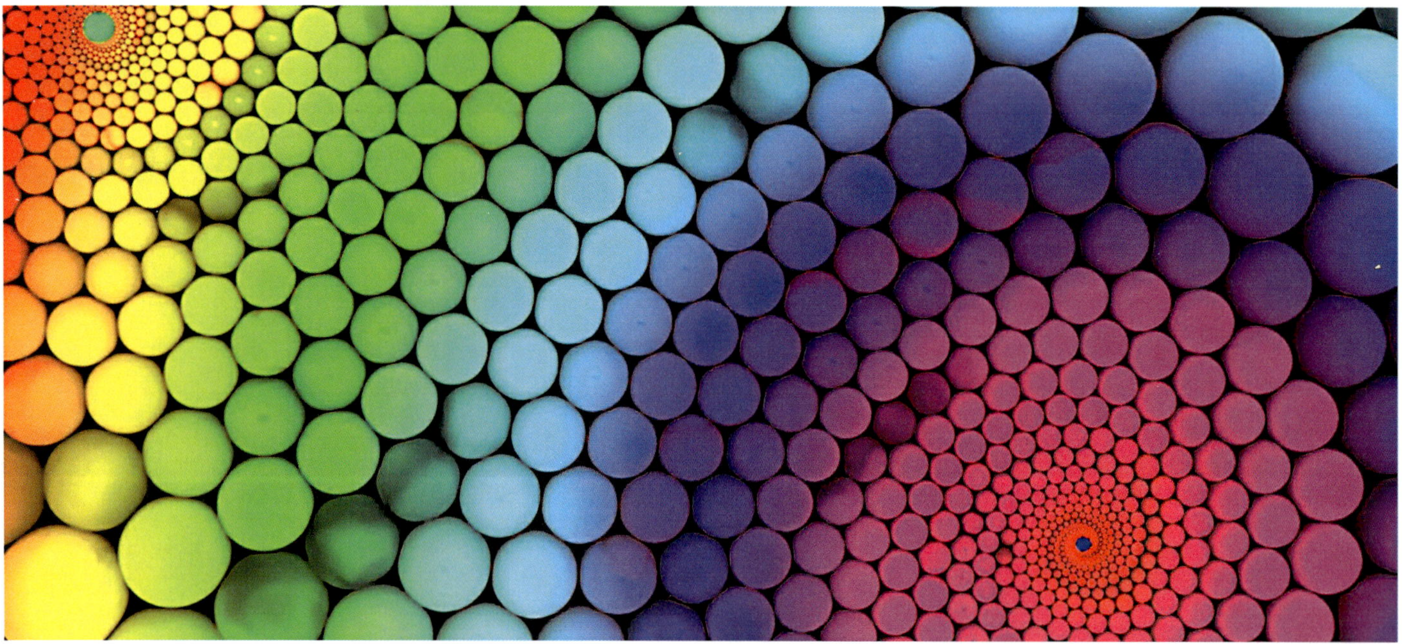

Choosing colours for your art can be the hardest and yet most enjoyable part of hand colouring. The colours and hues that you select will establish a mood or feeling for your finished work which means that it is important to know what that emotional response to the color will be and also if that will work well with the subject matter of the photograph.

Warm colours are generally associated with energy, brightness, and action, whereas cool colours are often identified with calm, peace, and serenity.
When you recognize that color has a temperature, you can understand how choosing all warm or all cool colors in your art can dramatically impact the message your painting conveys to the viewer.

Photocopy this page and using acrylic paints create your own colour wheel.

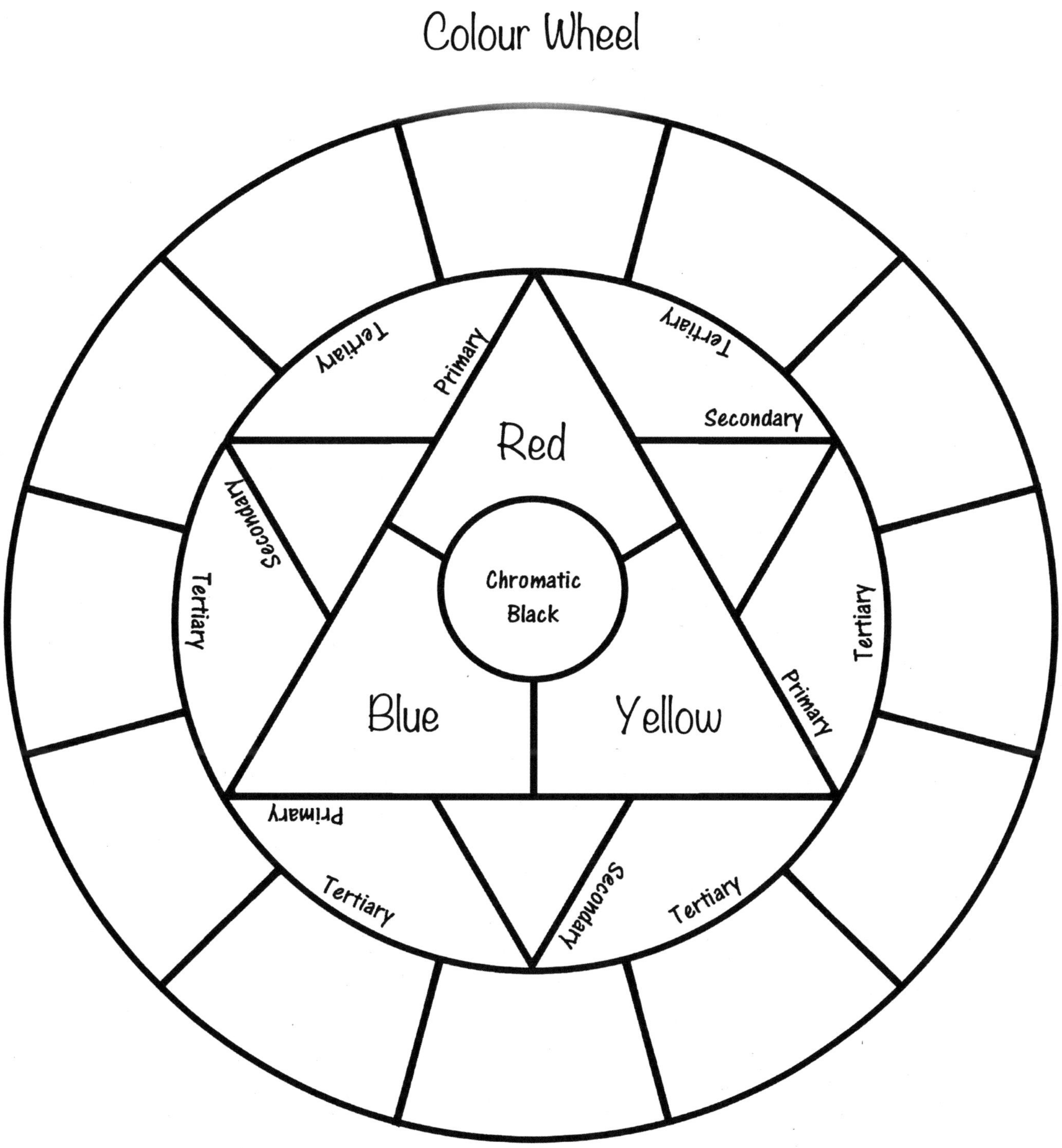

You can buy colour wheels from art and craft stores but the magic of mixing colours really makes sense when you create your own colour wheel.

We are going to start at the very beginning by taking a look at the colour wheel - I am sure for many people this not new, but if you have never experimented with mixing colours or creating your own colour wheel this little exercise will be a valuable step in furthering your understanding of colour.

The first colour wheel was designed by Sir Isaac Newton way back in 1666. It was such a valuable tool that artists and designers still use it today.

At the centre of the wheel are the three **Primary colours.** You probably learned about primary colours long ago in elementary school. This is a group of three colours—red, yellow, and blue—from which all other colours can be created by mixing. This theoretically means you can mix all the colours in the spectrum from these 3 basic colours.

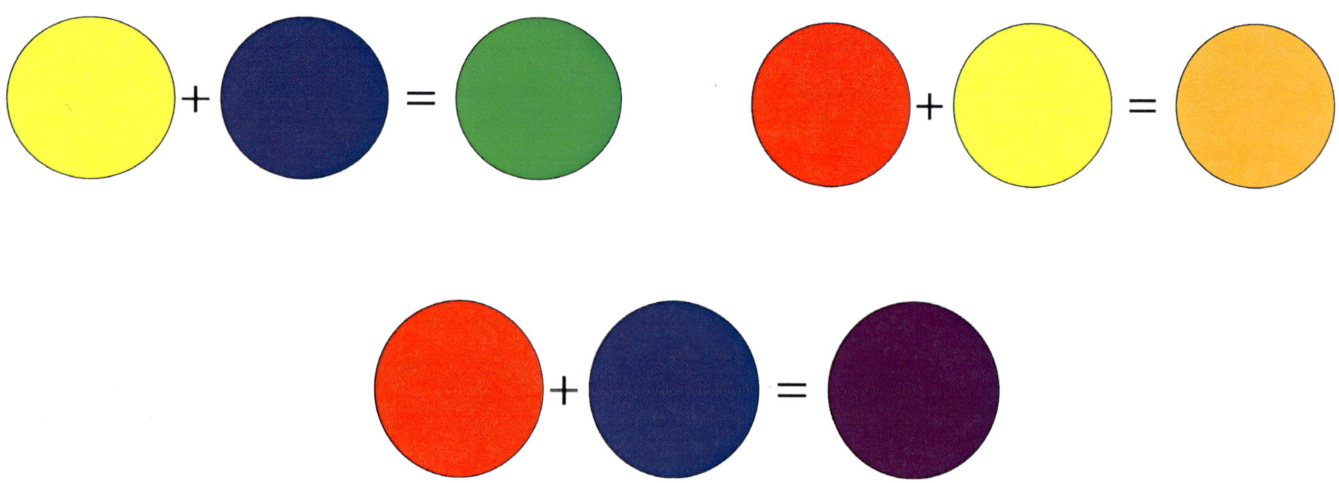

Secondary colours
These are achieved by mixing two primaries:
red and blue produces purple;
yellow and blue make green;
yellow and red yields orange.

Tertiary colours
As the name implies, tertiary colours are made by combining primary and secondary colors.
There are six tertiary colours:
red-orange, yellow-orange, yellow-green, blue-green, blue-violet, and red-violet. These colours can have a lot of variance in them, and you can tweak them to your liking.

What About Black and White?

Black and white can't be made by mixing together other colours, which means they tend to get excluded from colour mixing theory. If you add white to a colour you lighten it and if you add black you darken it.

Something else to consider when choosing which colours to enhance your photographs with is how the colours and hues relate to each other. Colours that are opposite one another on the colour wheel are complementary colours. Red and green, blue and orange, and purple and yellow all represent these special pairings. When placed side-by-side, they make the other appear brighter. There are other ways of viewing the wheel to build complex relationships. Here are a few other examples of combinations you can glean from the colour wheel.

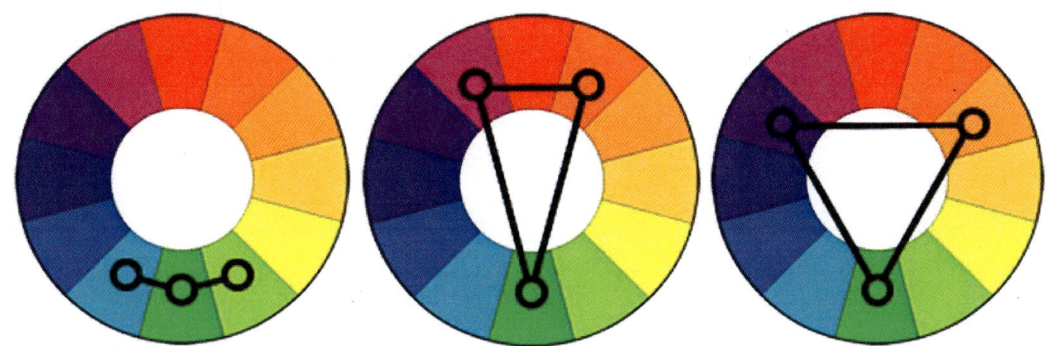

Colour schemes from left to right: analogous, split-complementary, and triadic

Analogous: The analogous arrangement features three colours that are next to each other on the colour wheel. Because of their proximity, they are generally a harmonious combination.

Split-complementary: The split-complementary colour scheme is similar to the complementary arrangement. To make it, you select a hue and find its complement (directly across on the colour wheel). Instead of using that complement, however, you will use the colours on either side of it. This arrangement has the contrast of complementary colours but is more nuanced.

Triadic: This colour scheme is made by selecting colours that are evenly spaced around the colour wheel. The results are often vibrant no matter what colours you select.

Understanding the colour wheel and how colours mix and harmonize with each other is a wonderful asset. However, as you experiment with different art mediums such as pastels, watercolours and pencils you will quickly discover trial and error will be your main source of discovery and understanding.

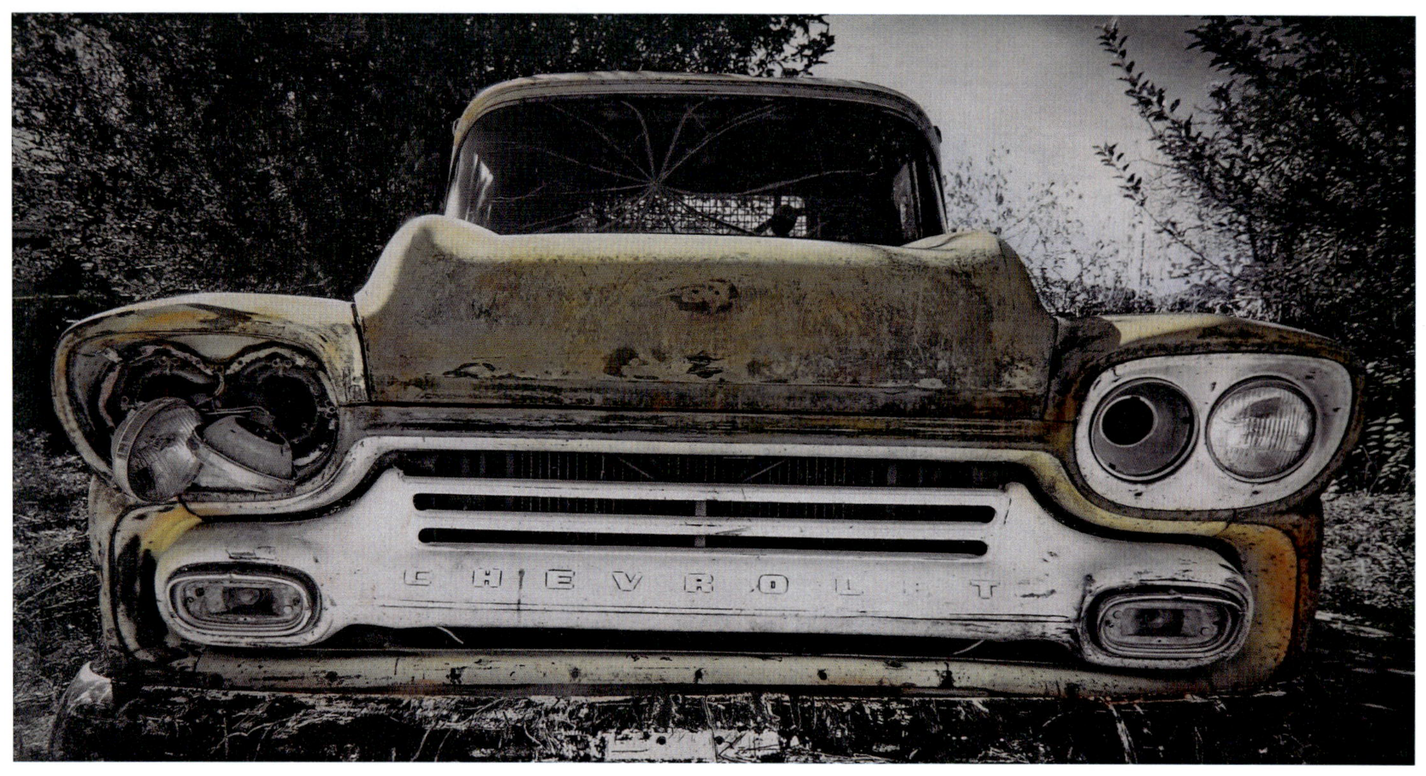

Tinted

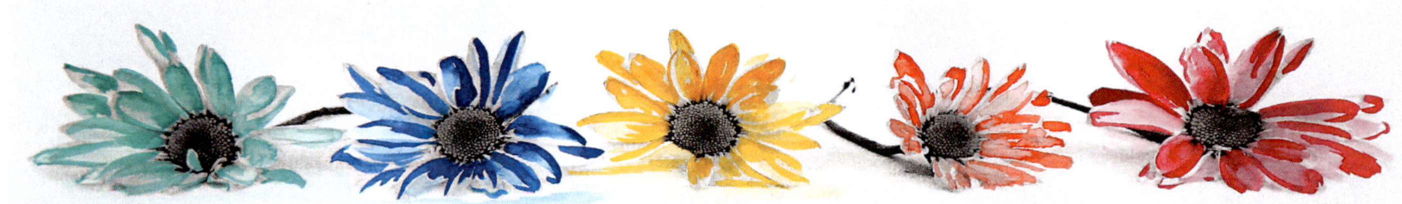

Painted

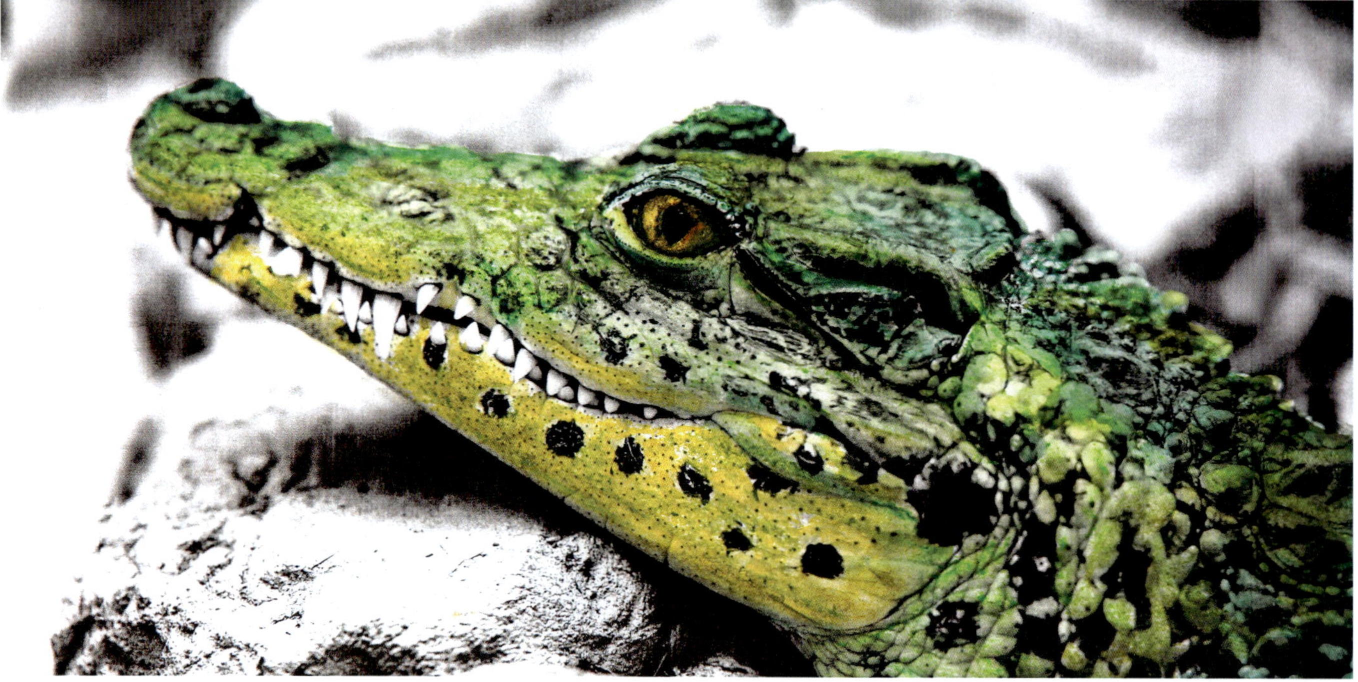

A little of both

Painting versus tinting

What is the difference between photo tinting and photo painting?
The answer lies in the title of each method.

Photo Tinting allows the original black and white photo to show through the colour that is being applied. The colour is also more of a tint than a strong colour, applied in such a way as to give the illusion that it is part of the original photo. The colours are subtle and have a soft dreamy affect on the stark black and white of the photo. This effect can be achieved using Marshall's Photo Oil paints, pan pastels or coloured pencils. These mediums are blended with the underlying photograph using a simple solution of 50% vegetable oil and 50% odourless turpentine which makes the colours more translucent.

Photo Painting is different because most paints tend to be opaque in nature so they cover the original photograph. You may decide to paint a little of the photo, rendering a part of it to be coloured or completely paint over the entire photograph. The choice is yours and will depend on the subject matter and final effect you are trying to achieve.

If you are intimidated by drawing and sketching you will find the process of hand colouring and painting photographs extremely rewarding. It removes the stress of facing a blank canvas, the photograph provides the guidelines and composition for your painting. The highlights and shadows in the photograph are also very helpful when deciding which colours and shades to use. Ideally when creating your original photo art you will use your own photos. be aware that thousands of free photographs are available on the internet that you can use to hone your skills and practice new techniques.

For demonstration and practice purposes many of the images featured in this book were obtained as a free download from www.unsplash.com. The reason for using free photos as examples was to include a variety of photographic styles and subjects.
My personal photographic style is very distinctive and predominantly horses, which to non-horse lovers may get a bit boring. By searching for images to hand colour you will be inspired to take photographs of objects or places you would not normally think of, opening your creativity up to new possibilities.

Disclaimer
If you download free photographs please be respectful of the creator of that photograph and give them photo credits. If you share your work with others or offer your finished art for sale it is always better to use photographs that you have taken yourself.

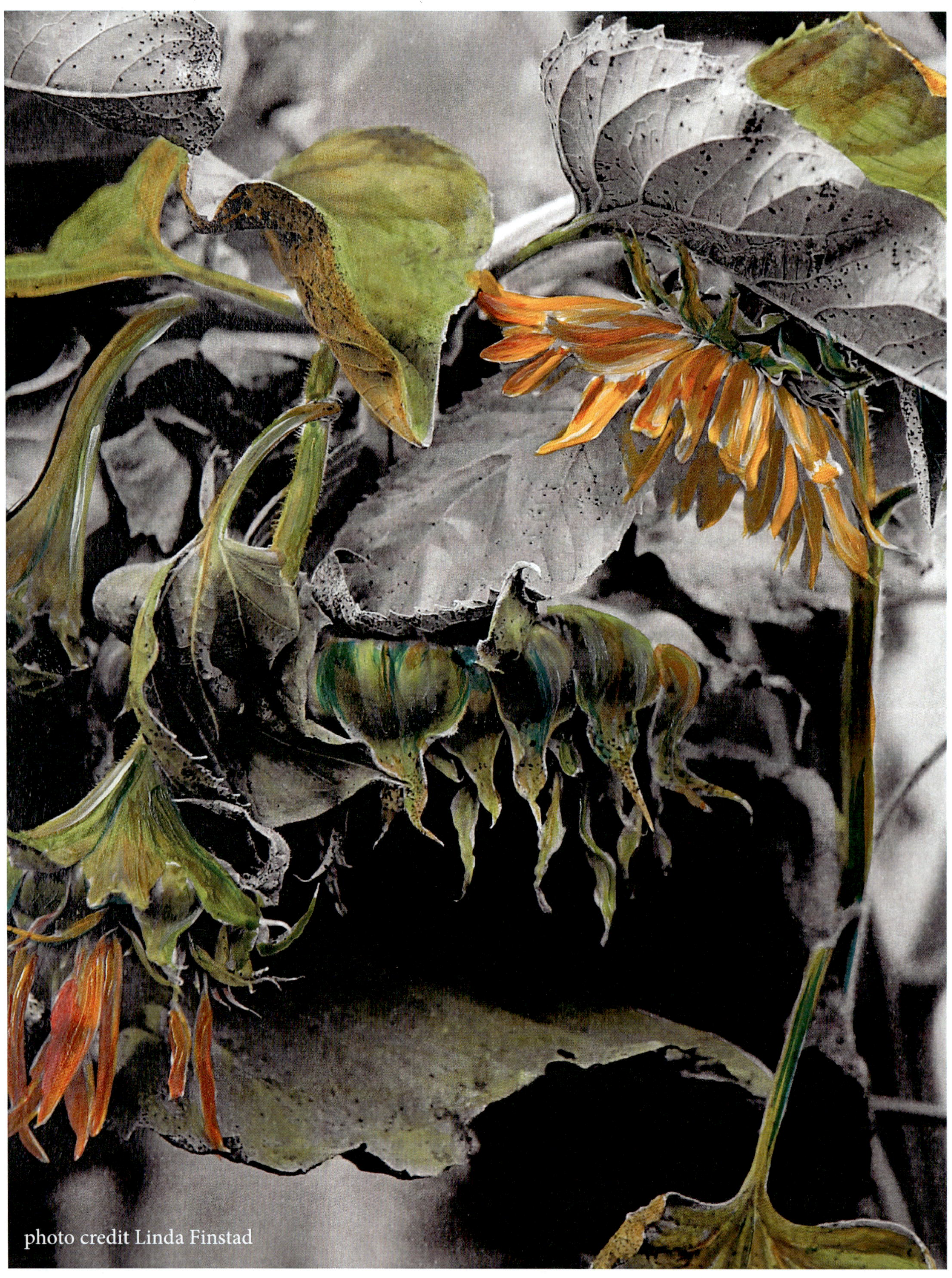
photo credit Linda Finstad

Acrylic paints

When I started my own personal journey into painting acrylics were the obvious choice for several reasons. The lack of odour and easy cleanup and no need for toxic paint thinners to clean brushes made them very appealing. Plus acrylic paints were everywhere from art supply stores to dollar stores, available as fluid or heavy bodied with finishes ranging from matte to metallic and the array of amazing colours seemed endless. An added attraction was that acrylics would adhere to almost any surface including glossy photographs and dry very quickly.

Their fast drying property can be seen as both a pro and also a con. Acrylics are difficult to blend and once applied to the photo are also almost impossible to take off, unlike oil based paints. Another very important quality to take into consideration when applying acrylic paints to photographs, is that acrylics are opaque in nature. The underlying photograph will not be visible through the paint.

Paint applicators

Synthetic artists brushes are the ideal choice for applying acrylic paints. Avoid real hair or natural fibre as they tend to be too soft. You can apply acrylic paint with a variety of other tools such as palette knives, sea sponges and even Q-tips.

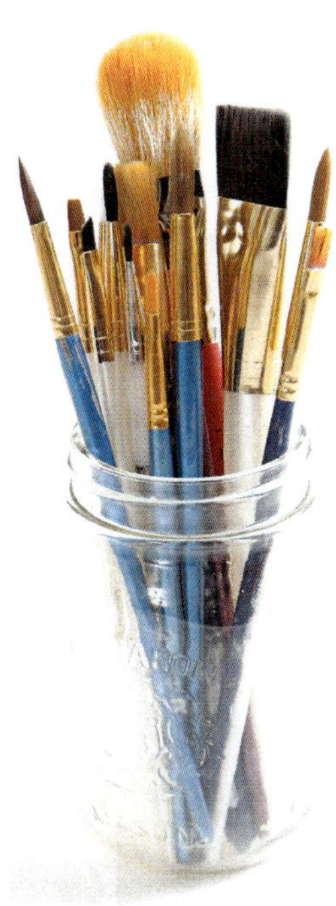

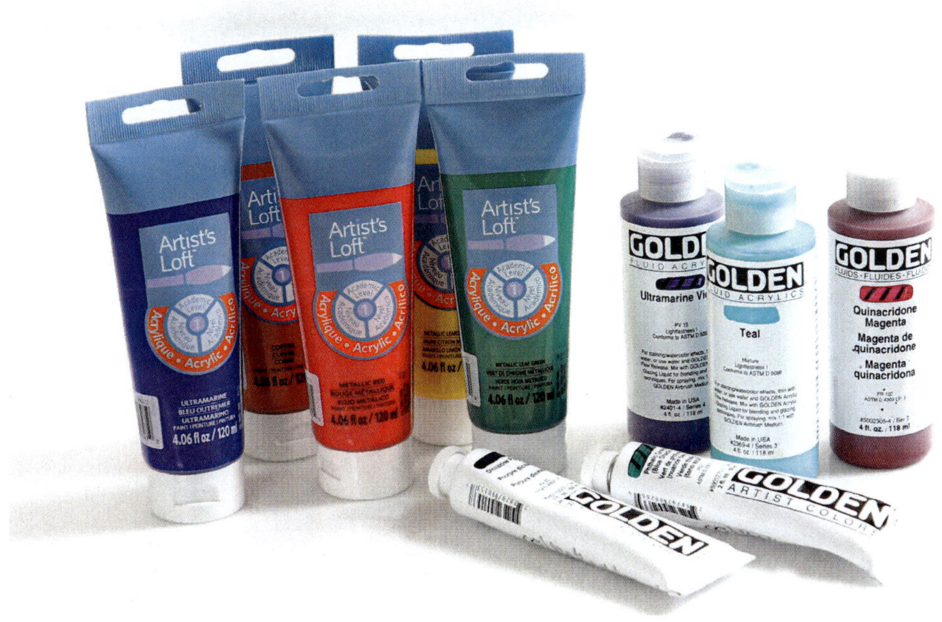

Spot colour

How much or how little paint you apply to your photograph is entirely up to you - there is no right or wrong; after all this is your art. To get the feel for this new art form, start by just applying one colour to your black and white photograph to make a certain area of the image pop.

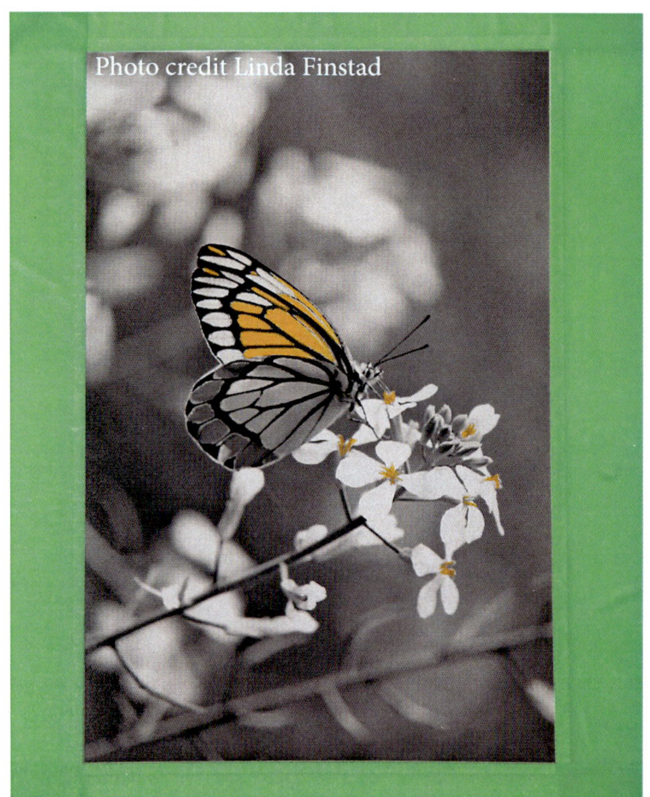

Taping down the photo

To prevent the photograph from moving and warping as you apply paint, tape the photo to a smooth surface. A foam core board will work really well. Green painter's tape found in hardware stores is the perfect choice for this job. Painter's tape is less sticky than masking tape and easier to remove. Attaching your photograph to a board also provides the opportunity to paint at an easel if you prefer to paint upright.

As mentioned acrylic paints dry very quickly, so be sure to assemble everything you need before starting work.

Using a fine round brush I began painting all the areas of the image I wanted to be orange.

Note: This image of a butterfly was printed on glossy paper at Costco photo lab.

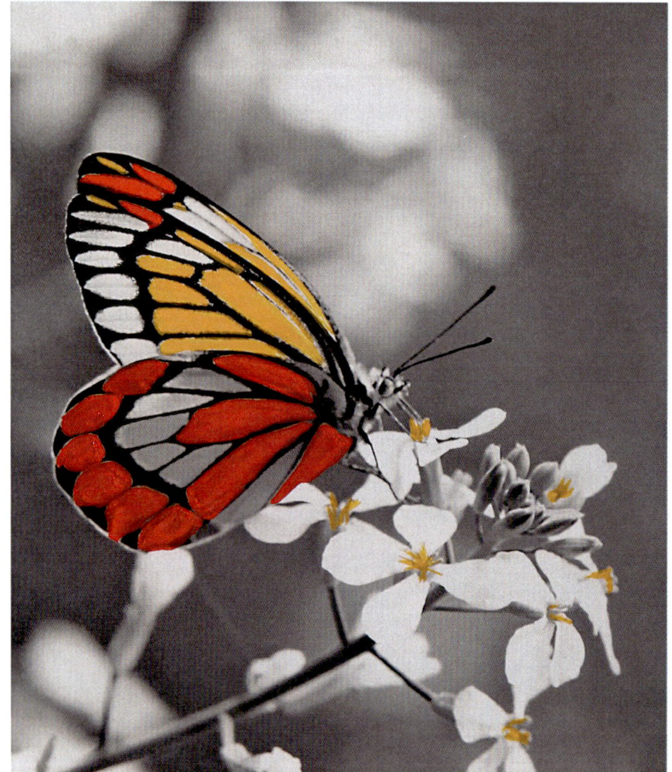

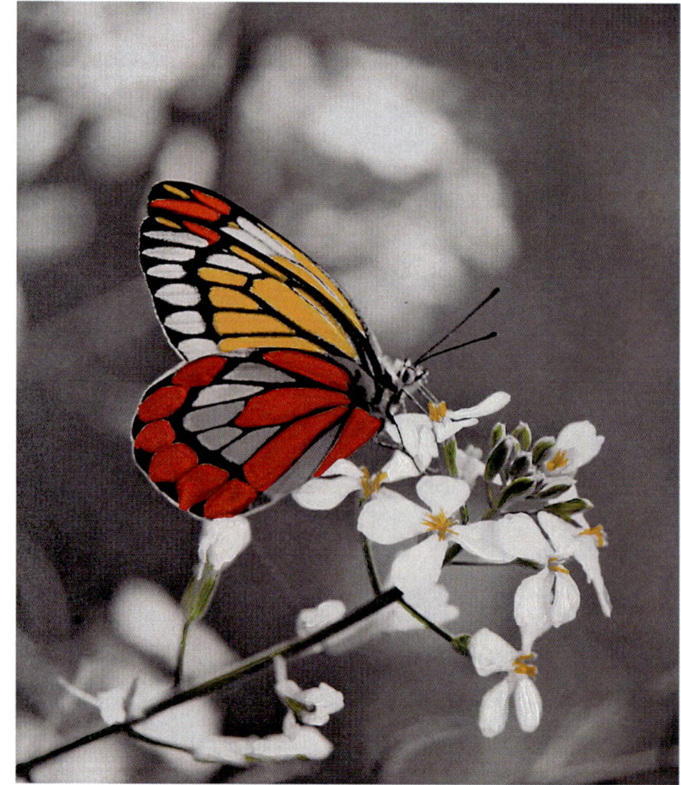

The next step was to add red to the wings and green to the buds and stems.

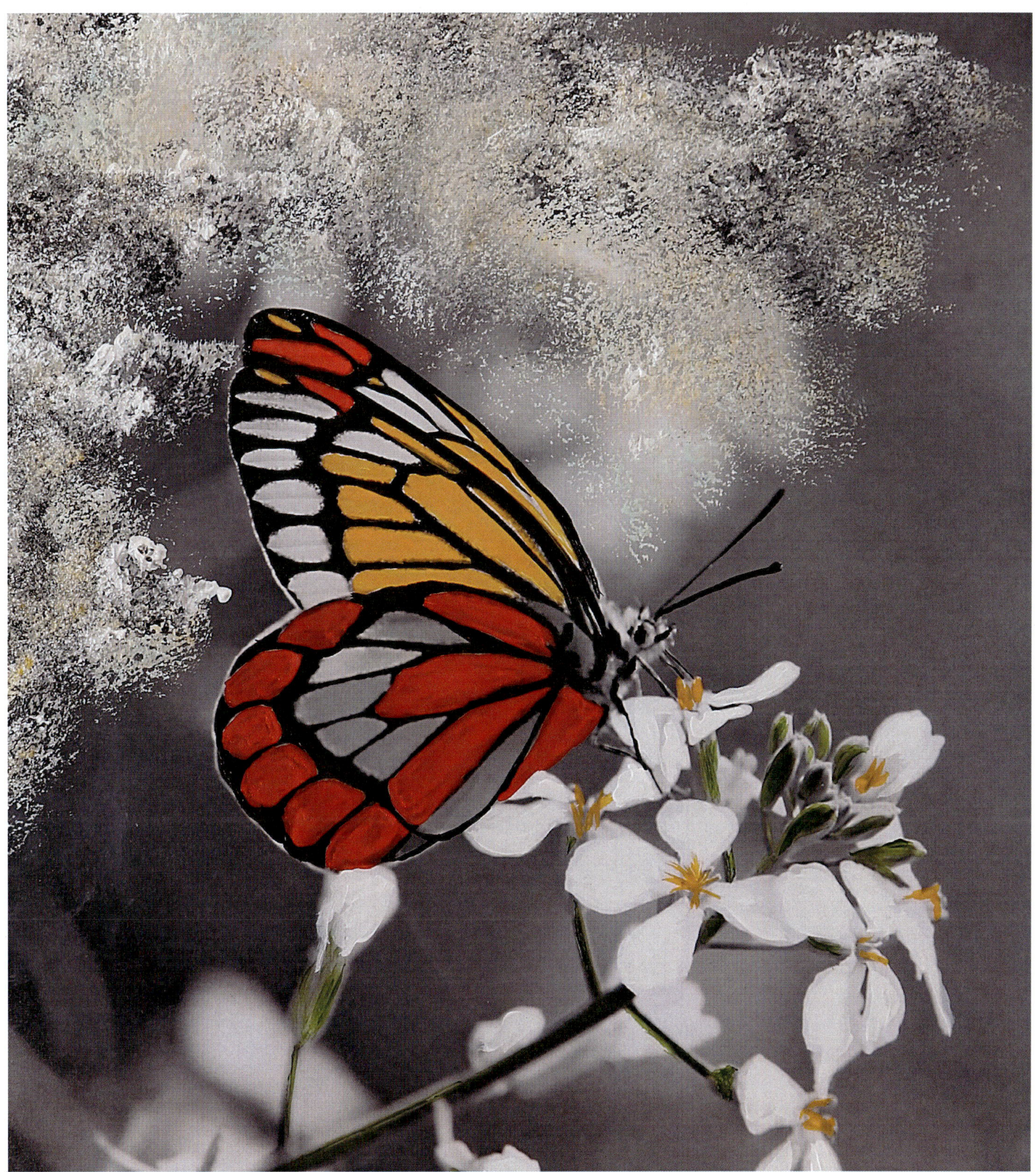

Using black paint and a very fine brush I cleaned around the shapes in the butterfly's wing and enhanced its legs and antenna. The texture was added by dipping a sea sponge in white, orange, pale green and a little black paint and gently dabbing it onto the photograph.

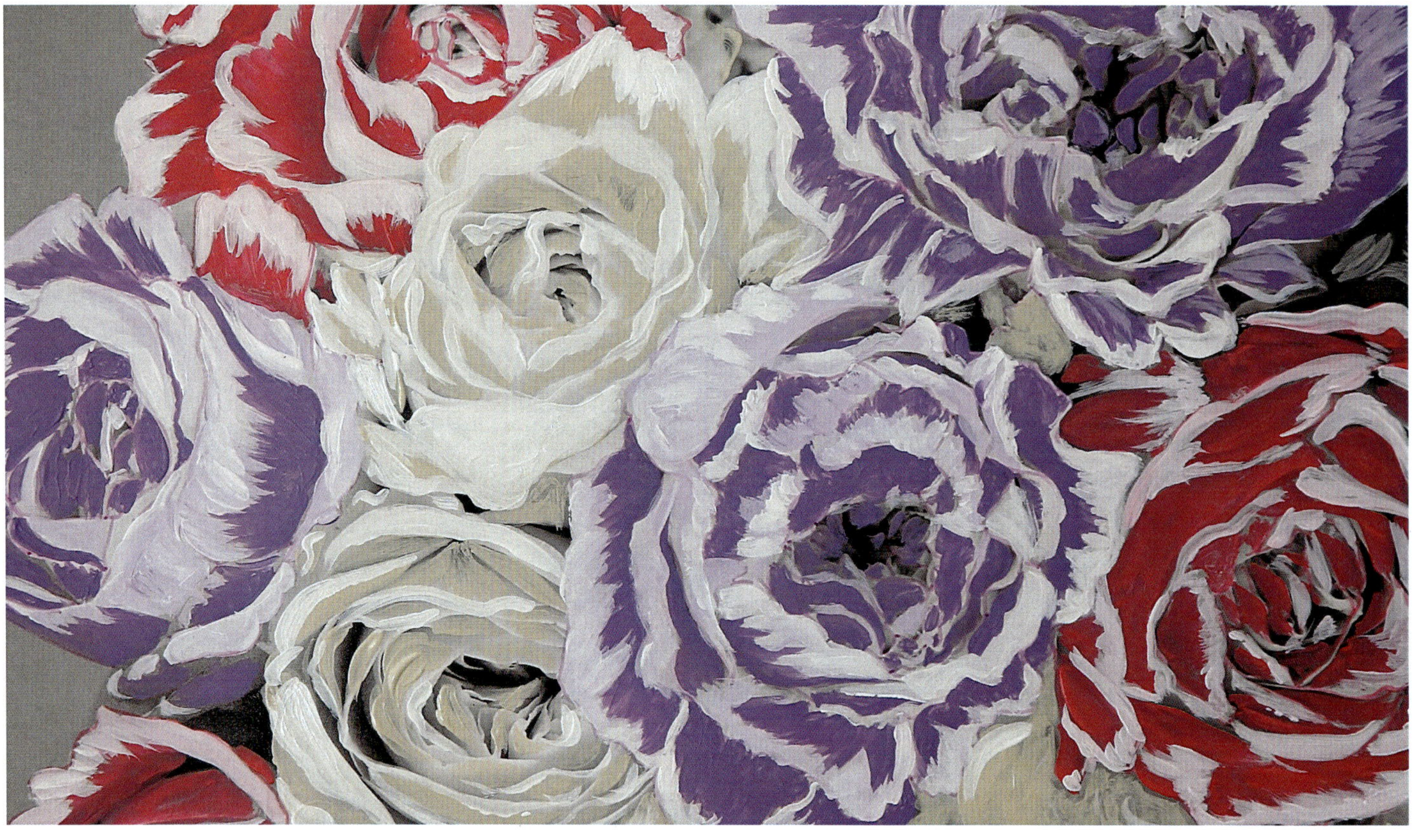

You can treat the underlying photograph as a sketch and completely cover the image with paint. This results in a completely new work of art. The style you choose to do that is again entirely up to you. You may wish to re-create the photo in perfect realism or use a more abstract approach.

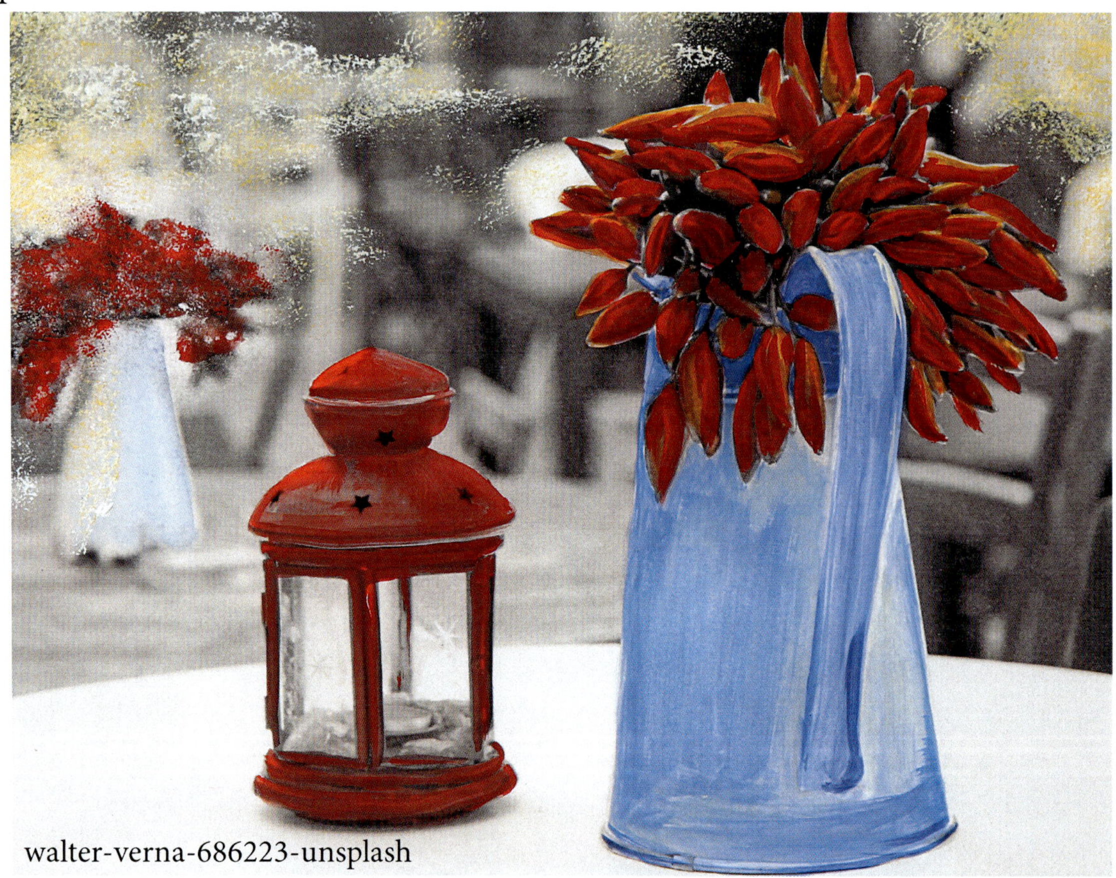

walter-verna-686223-unsplash

Heavy body acrylic paint

Heavy body acrylics have a thick, buttery consistency and allow you to add texture to your painting. You can apply them with either a brush or a palette knife. Personally, I like to add dollops of paint to my art with Q-tips.

That's right, Q-tips! I have used this method of painting to create original art but it works just as well when you are using a photograph as your guide.

With this method of photo painting it is important to print your black and white image on a heavyweight mixed media paper or canvas paper. This process adds a lot of paint (moisture) to the surface and lightweight papers will not retain their integrity.

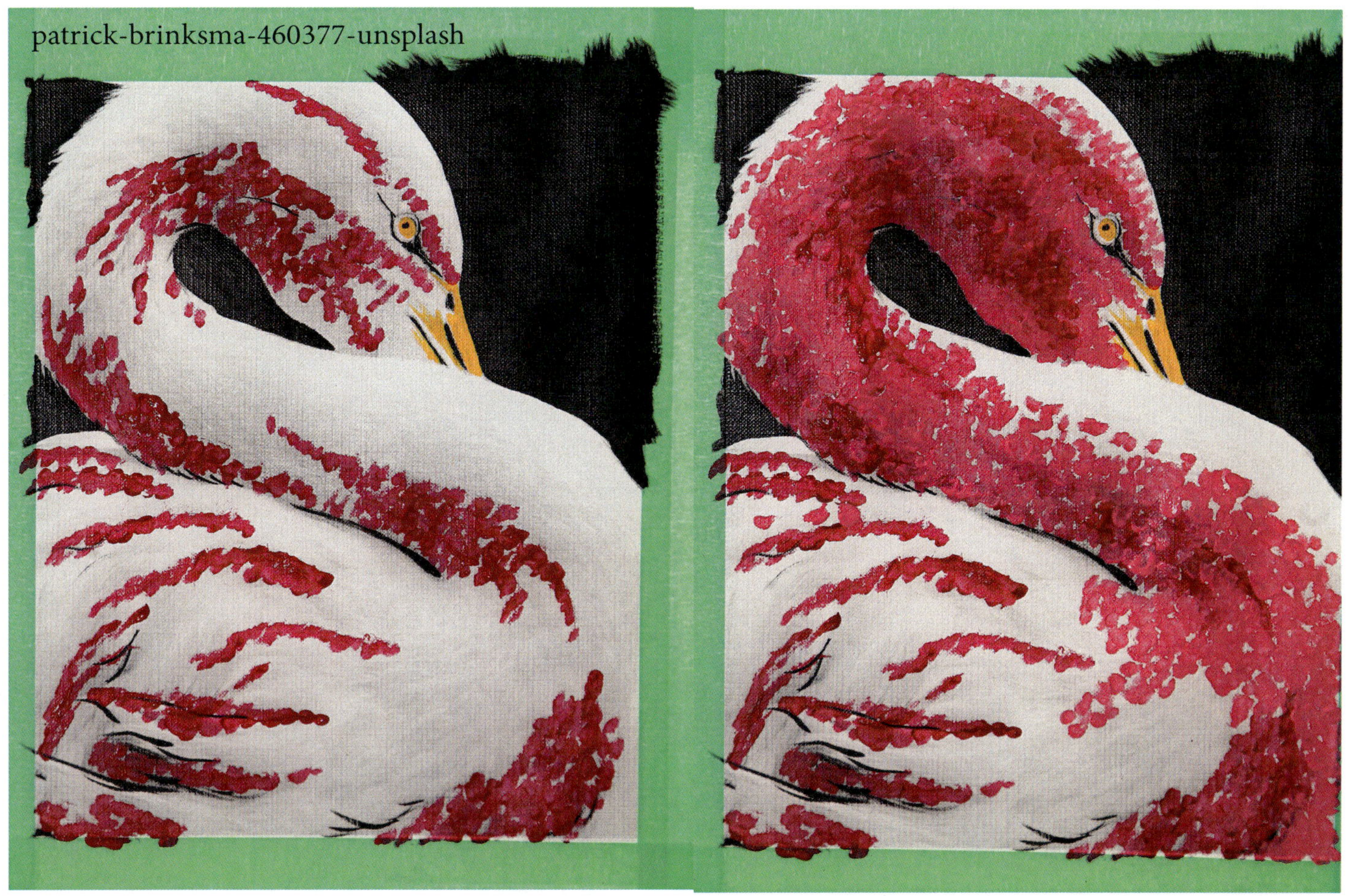

Tape your printed image securely onto a smooth board and begin dabbing on heavy body acrylic paint with your Q-tip. Start with your darkest colour.

Then add the lighter shades on top to create texture and highlights.

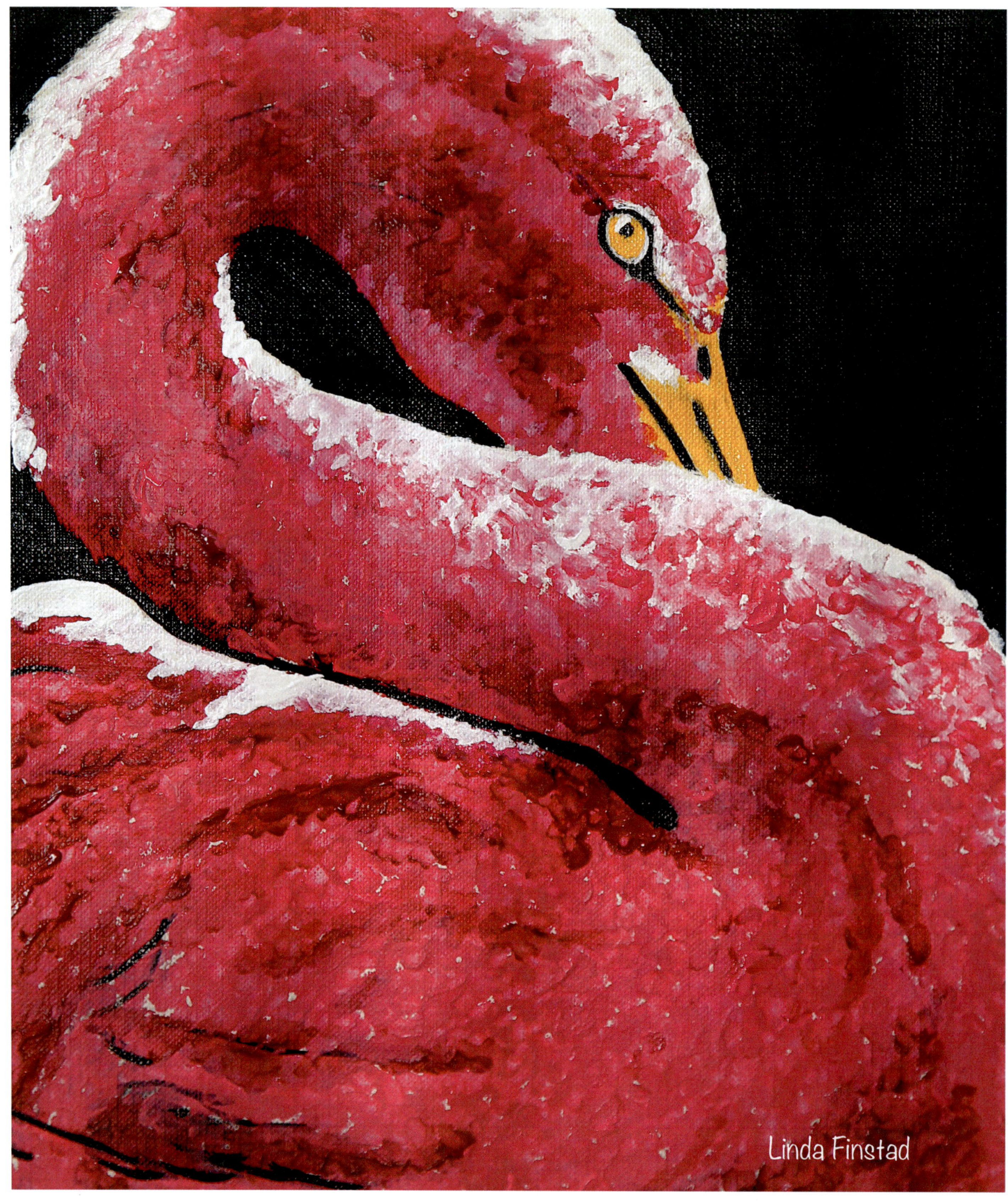

The finishing touches to enhance the bird's beak and eye were painted on using yellow paint and a fine brush.

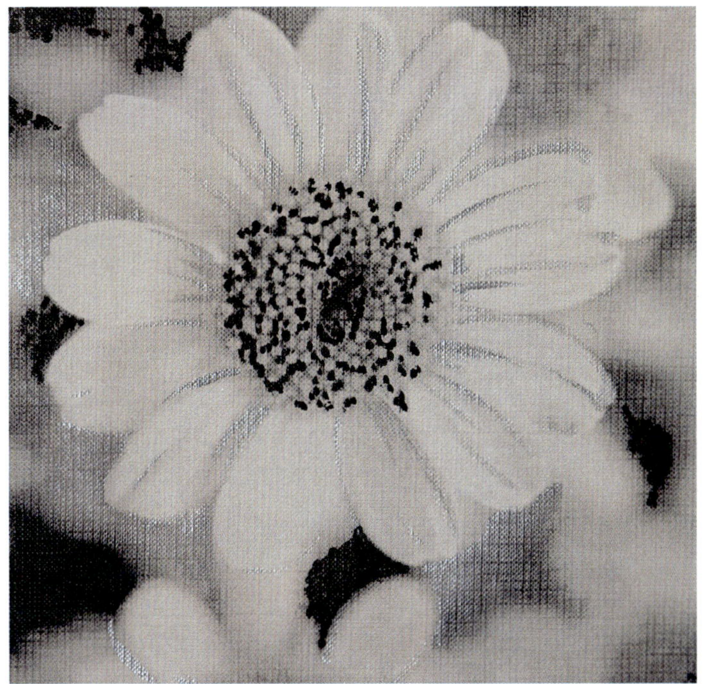

For this image, I loaded a Q-tip with carbon black and using a dabbing motion painted in the shadows.

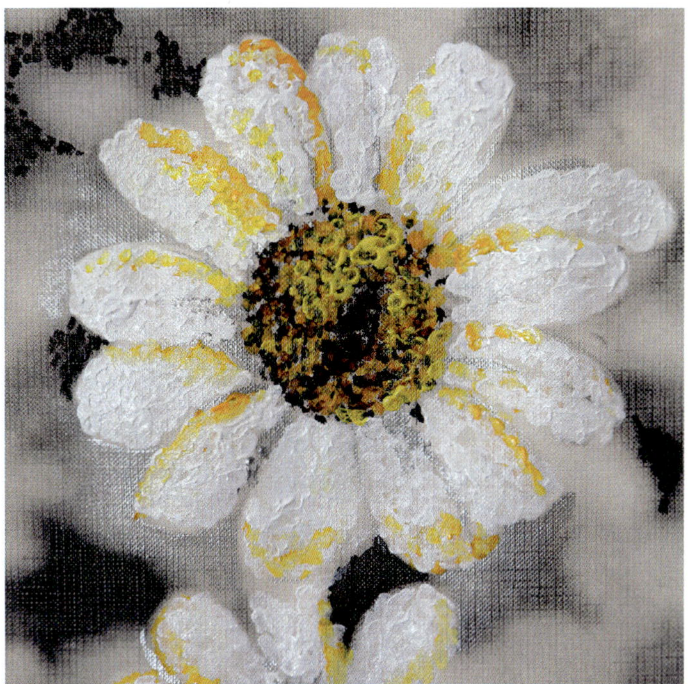

The next step was to dab white to the petals and some yellow and orange accents to the edges.

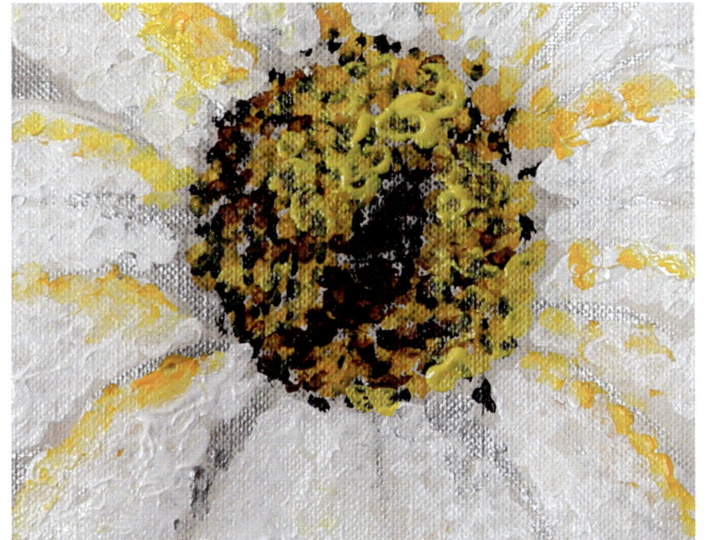

For the centre of the flower start by dabbing on burnt umber which is the darkest colour, then adding orange and yellow to create texture and highlights.

Note: It is not necessary to allow each colour to dry before adding the next.

Q-tip art is fast and fun and perfectly suited to images featuring large blocks of colour such as flowers and flamingos.

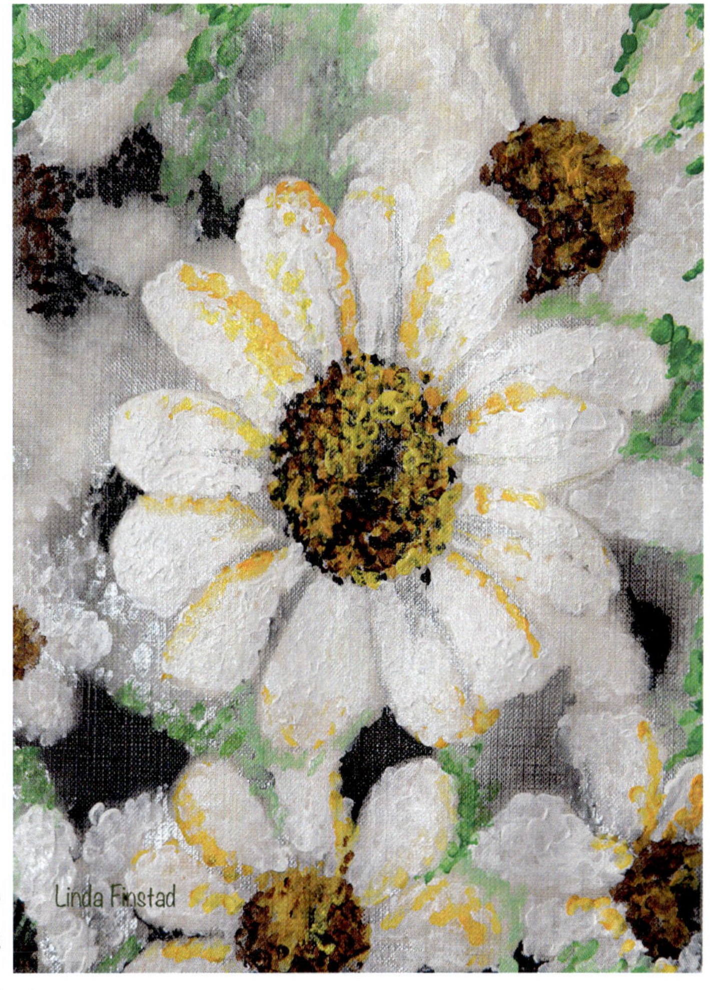

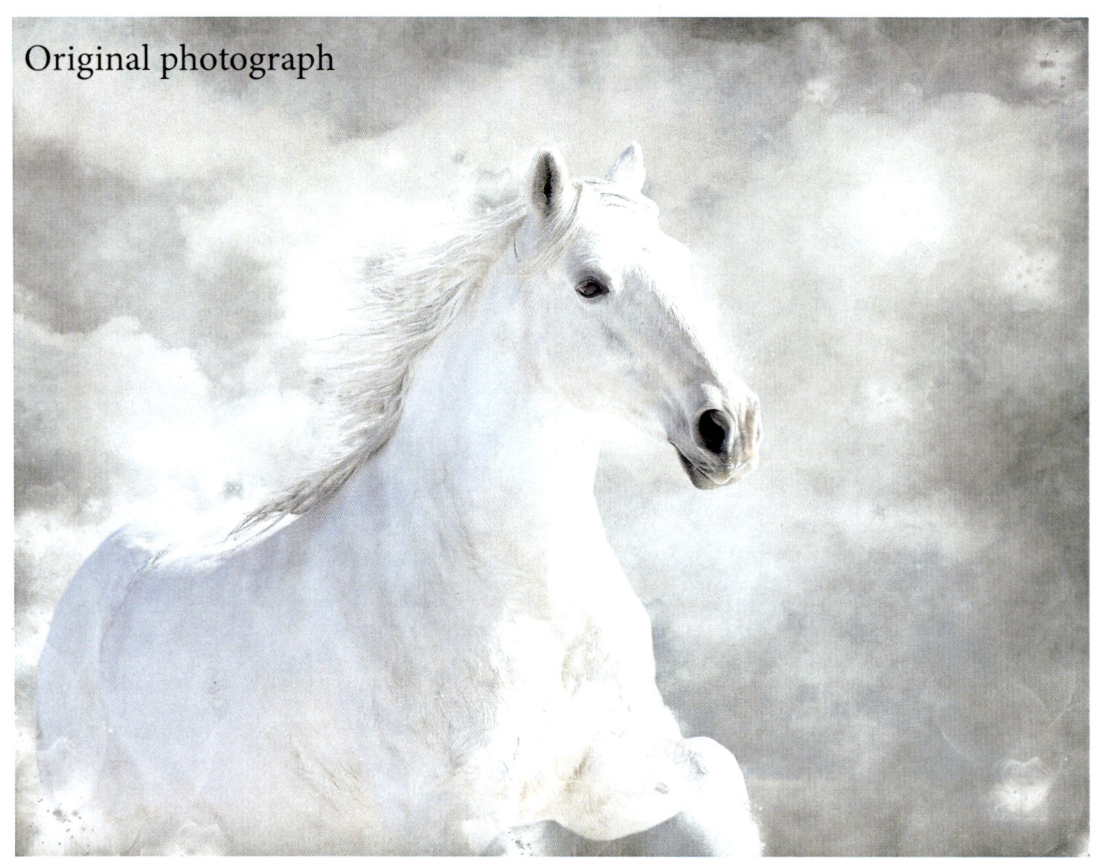
Original photograph

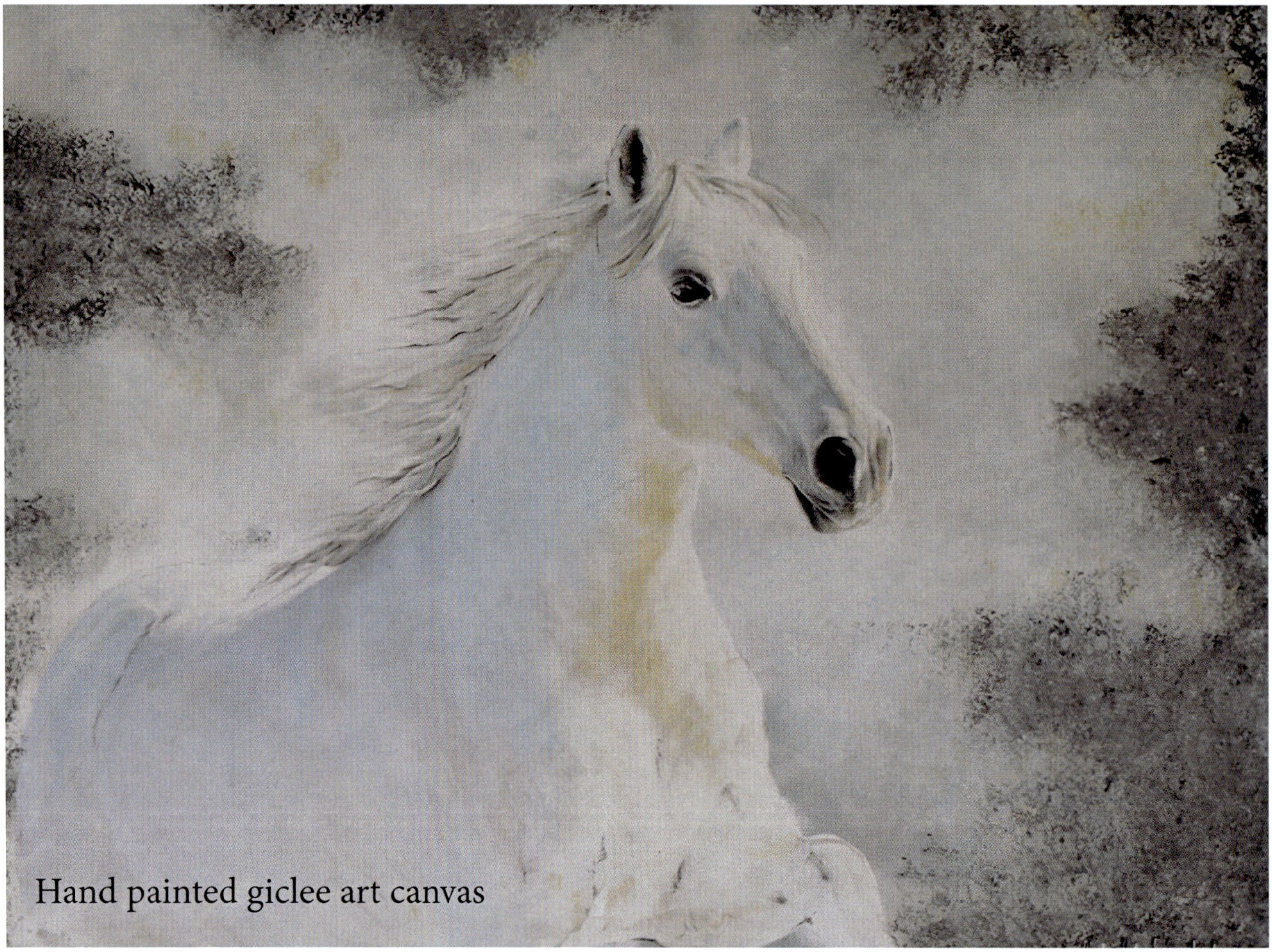

Hand painted giclee art canvas

Art by Linda Finstad

Before we go any farther I would like to share with you how I used hand painting photographs to add not only value but also breathe new life into existing work.

A couple of years ago I wrote a book entitled "How to Identify Your Spirit Horse. " This beautiful little gift book is a compilation of fine art photographs of white horses. Each horse has different characteristics that embody and describe one of 40 different equine spirit horse guides.

The book is available on Amazon (my shameless plug).

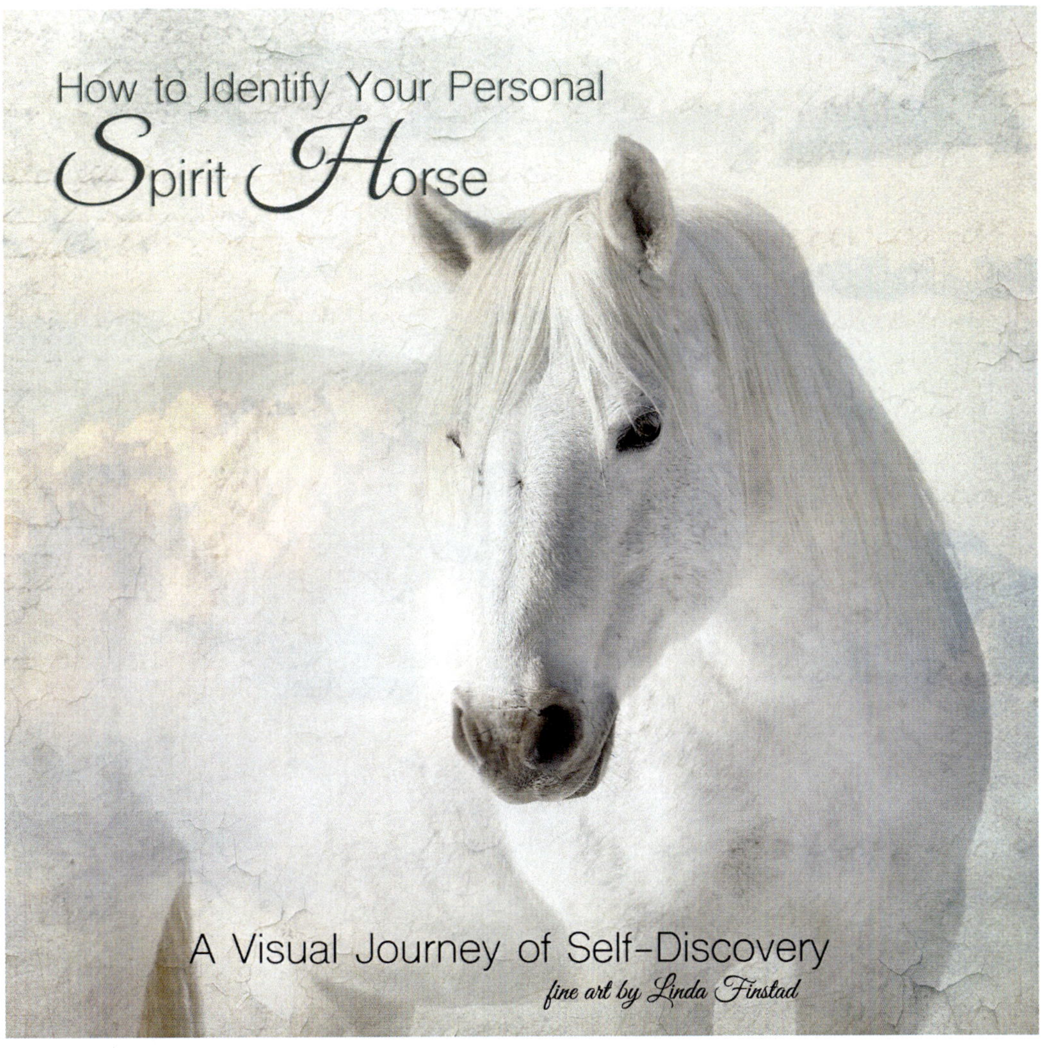

A selection of the images from the book were produced as large format giclee art prints, which I displayed at shows and sales. These were stunning photographs but for some reason just did not sell.

That was until I transformed them into "Hand Painted Giclees" by adding acrylic paint, some gel matte medium and a little glitter. The giclee doubled in its perceived value. It was no longer just a photograph, now it was one-of-a-kind, hand painted art piece.

Just to be clear I didn't double the price but I did add an extra $150 for the extra work.

It took courage to add acrylic paint to that first giclee art print. After all canvas prints are not cheap to have printed and if I messed up, it would be ruined. Acrylic paint is difficult if not impossible to remove. There was no room for error, which meant going very slowly applying only soft, subtle colour. The goal was to enhance not change the composition.

Original photograph

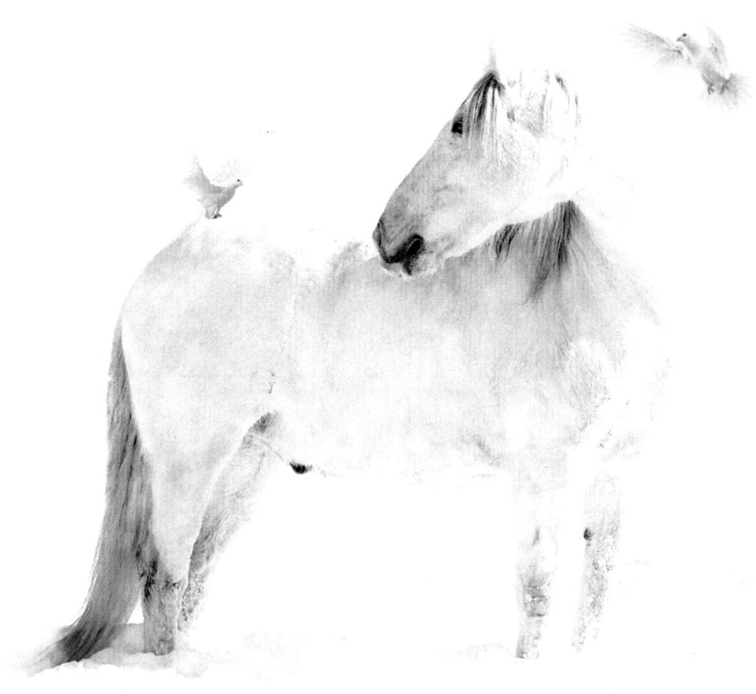

Hand painted giclee art canvas

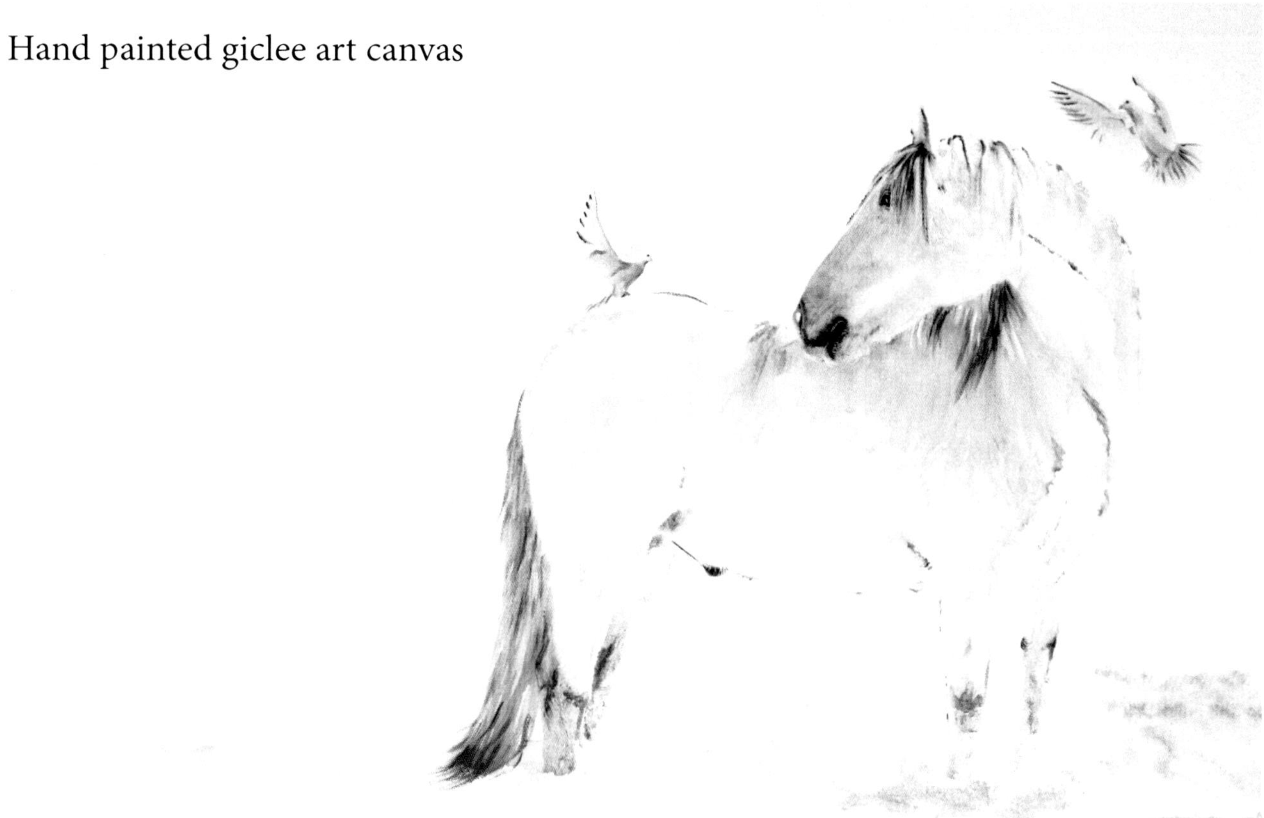

As my confidence grew I decided to add texture into the mane and tail of the horse. So using a palette knife and gel medium I dolloped the thick sticky goo onto the canvas. Gel matte medium is cloudy when you take it from the tub but dries completely clear. Before the gel was completely dry I sprinkled just a little white glitter into the horse's mane. The result was amazing. My spirit horse photograph was now a painting and sold very quickly despite the price increase.

The same enhancement techniques were used on some of my wildlife photos, which also quickly sold as hand painted giclee art canvases.

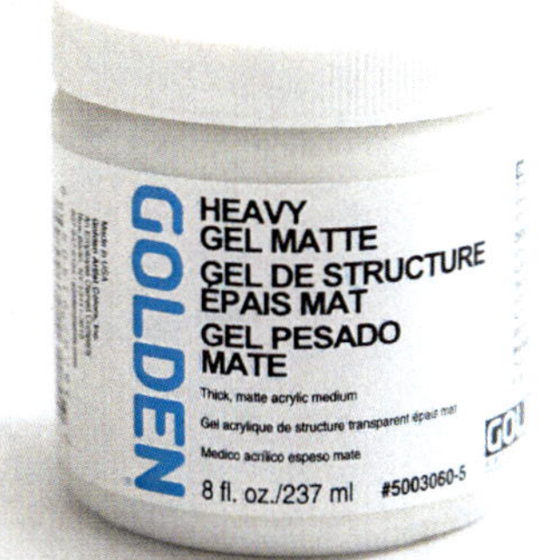

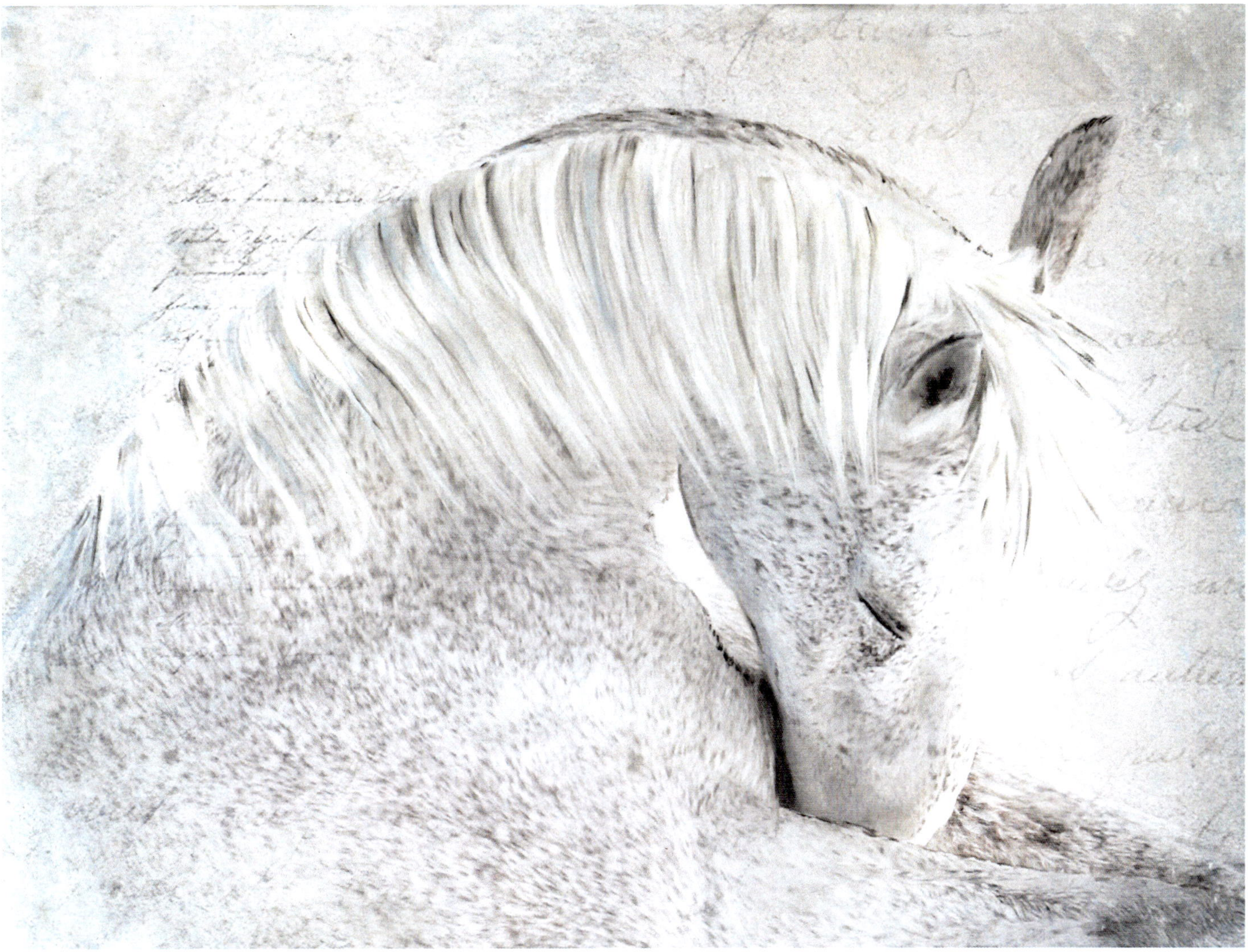

The reason for sharing my success is not to brag but to encourage other photographers to try this simple method of enhancement to add value to their work.

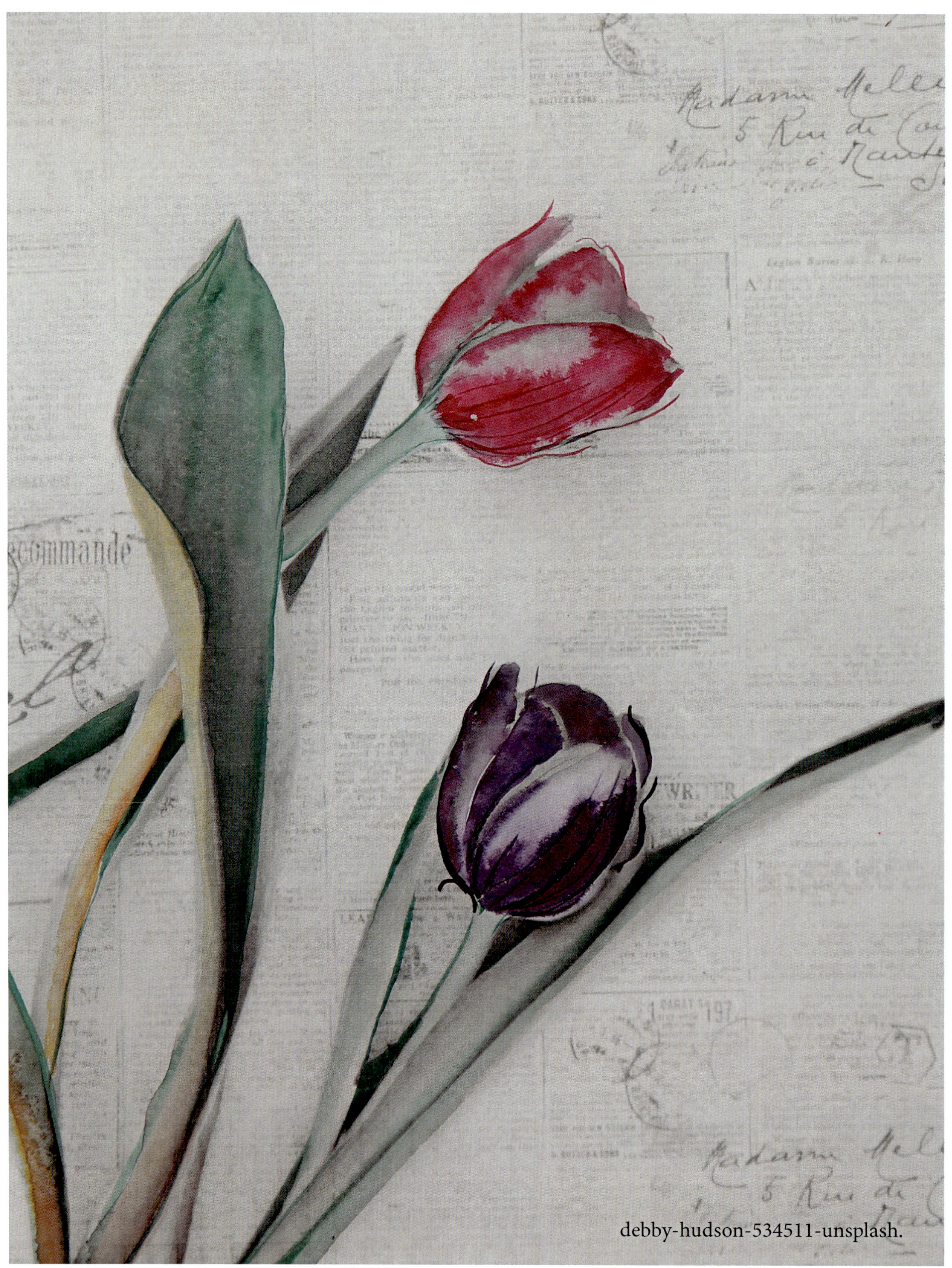

debby-hudson-534511-unsplash.

Watercolour paints and inks

Watercolour paints need expensive specialty paper!

True

If you want your paint to bloom.
Bloom is a term used by artists who first apply water to the paper and then the paint. The wet paper allows the pigment in the paint to spread and bloom. For this to happen it is important to use the best watercolour paper you can get your hands on.

False

The statement is also false because watercolour paints can also be applied to dry mixed media paper and used to create very precise lines and colour. This means the watercolour paint can be both translucent or opaque depending on how you apply it.

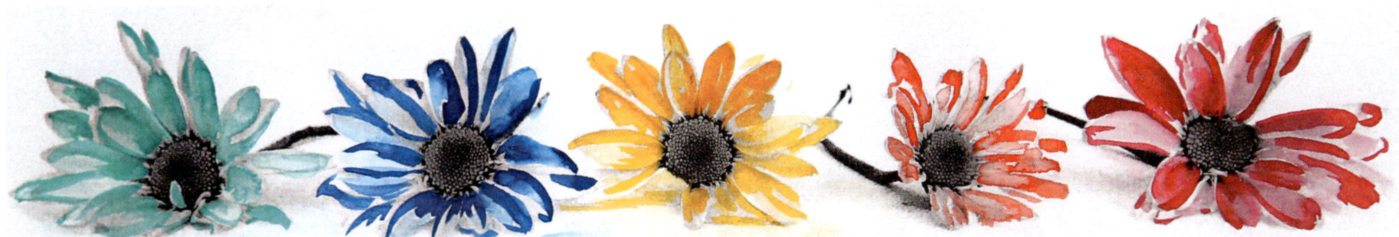

The reason these two mediums are grouped together is because they behave in a similar fashion. Without getting too technical and discussing how inks are produced, the main difference between the two is the intensity of colour.

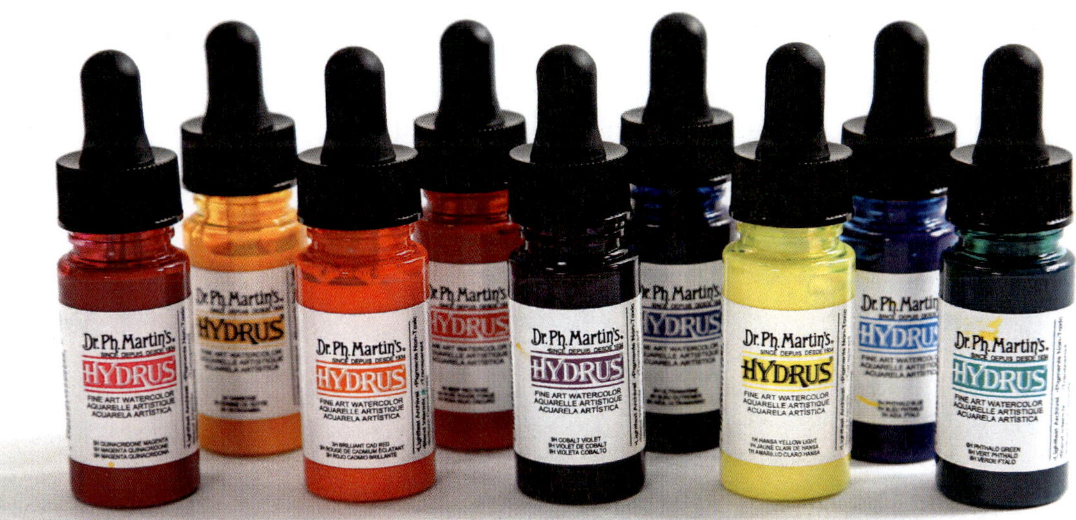

Watercolour paints are available in tubes or pans and just like any other art medium vary in price and quality.

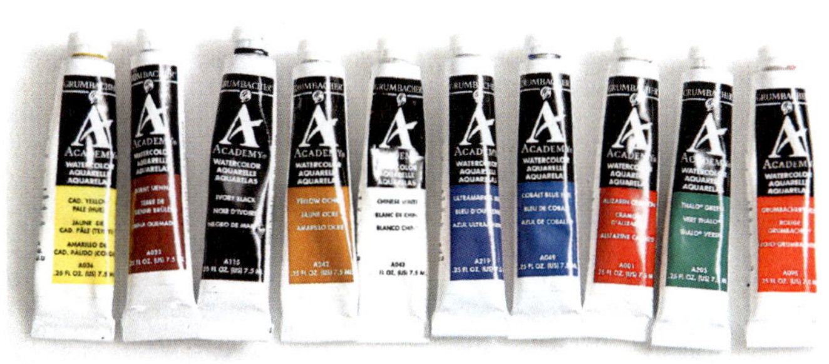

The photograph on the left of Tulips was printed on Mixed media paper and coloured with watercolour inks.

When it comes to paints, watercolours sometimes get a bad rap. They have the reputation of being unforgiving and unpredictable. It's true they can be difficult to control and you sometimes have to be willing to go with the flow and let the paints do their own thing, but they also have a lot of good qualities which make them a perfect choice for hand painting photographs.

Easy clean-up means it's practically impossible to ruin your brushes with watercolor paints. If you forget to wash them, it's not a big deal. You can just rinse them out before you start painting the next time. There is no need to worry about dried paint hardening and ruining your brush. You do need good quality brushes to achieve optimun results.

There is very little waste. If you are using watercolour in tubes and squeeze out too much paint, just let the leftover paint dry on your palette and add water to it the next time you paint.

There are no harsh chemicals. One of my favorite things about watercolours is that they are completely odor-free and they don't involve the use of any harsh chemicals. In a later chapter we will be taking a look at watercolour pencils and crayons which also afford the same qualities.

Due to their transparency, from an artists' perspective, watercolour paint has an inner brilliance and clarity of colour that is often lacking in other types of paint. This is largely due to the fact that it is transparent. Most paints reflect colour directly off the surface of the paint. Watercolours, on the other hand, get their colour as a result of light bouncing off the white paper and reflecting back up through the paint. As a result, the paintings almost look as if they are lit from within.

A single tube or pan of watercolour paint can give you countless different shades of the same colour simply by adding more or less water. You can build colours to add richness, or mix

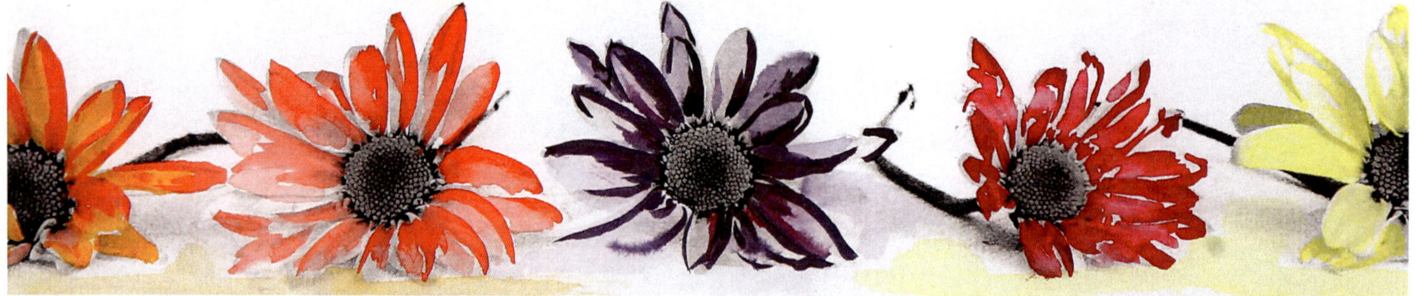

Note: To hand paint your black and white photograph with watercolour paints or inks it is important to print it on either mixed media or watercolour paper.

Watercolours will not adhere to either glossy or matte photographic paper.

Getting started

Set up your space

Keep your work surface, brushes, paint, palette, water for mixing, a paper towel for drying brushes and a piece of scrap paper all at the ready. Make sure that everything is within easy reach, but that nothing is in the way of your dominant hand so that you won't be knocking anything over by accident as you work.

Tape down your project

It is more important than ever to tape down your project when using watercolours. The added water typically causes the paper to warp and buckle. If secured properly the paper should flatten back down when completely dry. Don't panic if it doesn't, you can iron the paper flat again. Place a clean cloth over the painting and apply heat to smooth the paper flat (just don't use the steam setting on your iron).

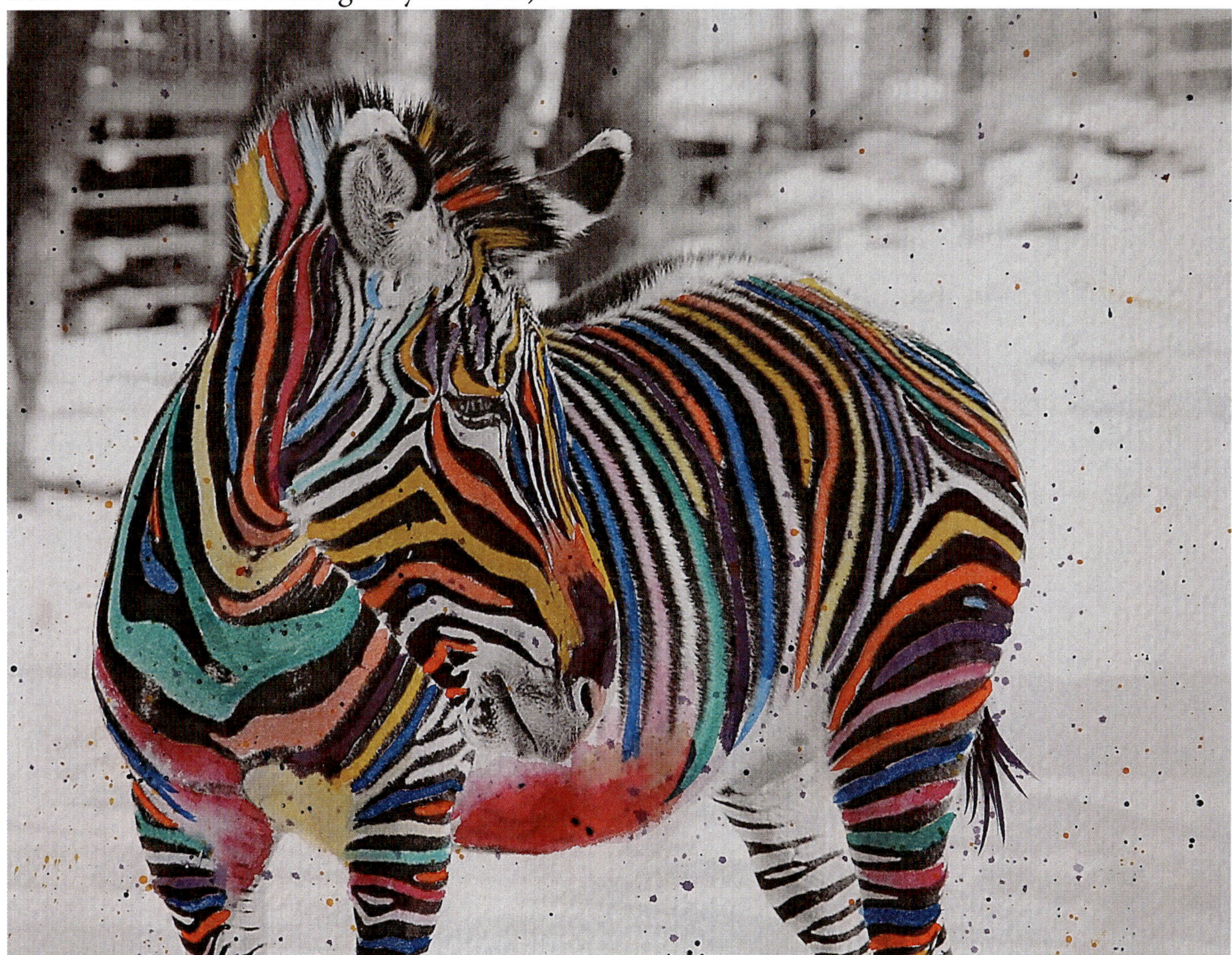

Just because you are hand painting a photograph does not mean your finished art must be photo-realistic. This photograph of a zebra was printed on mixed media paper. To keep the paint from "blooming" it was applied directly to the dry print (no water was added to the paper).

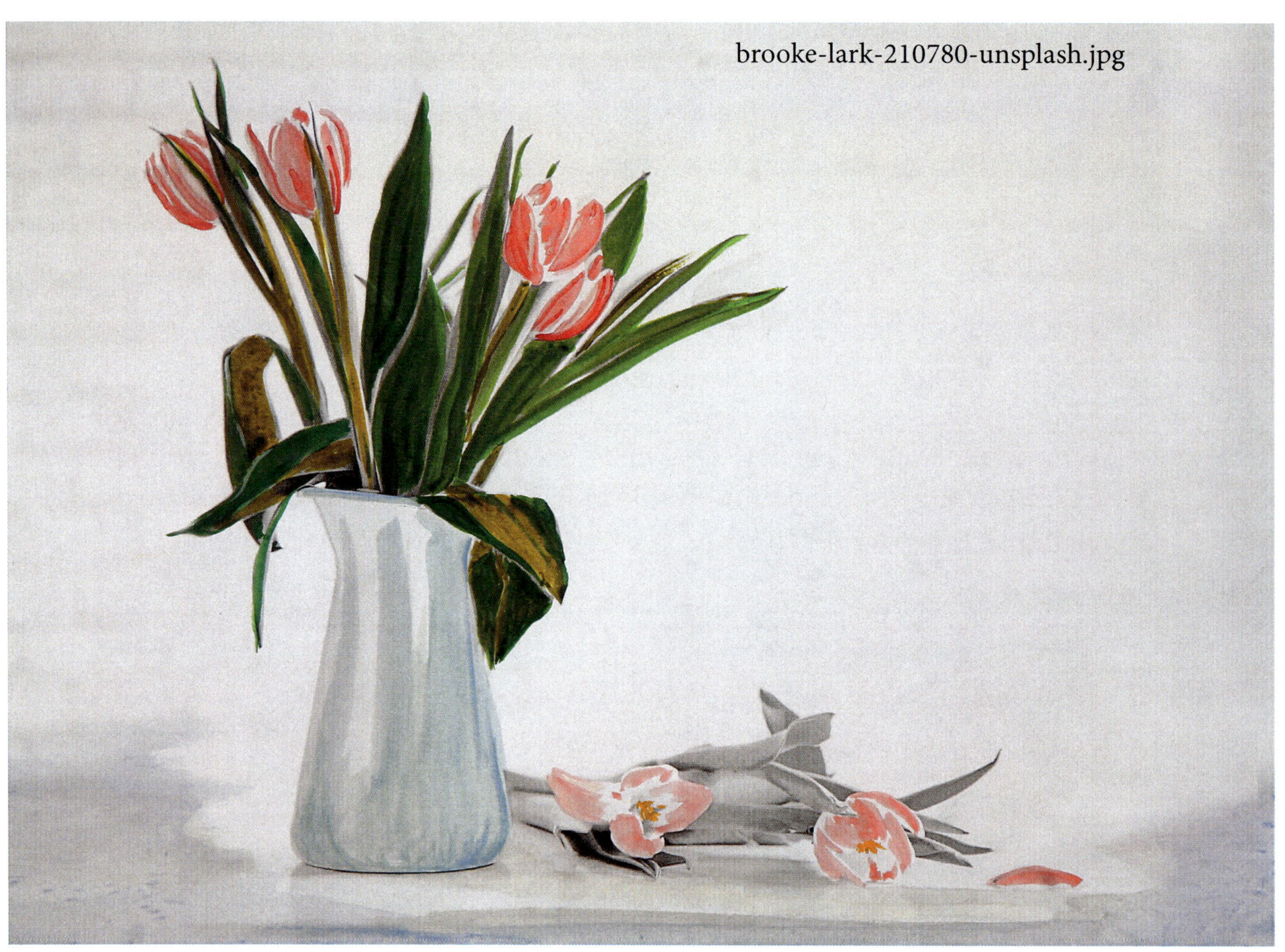

This photograph was printed onto watercolour paper. In order to create a soft colour wash on the jug, it was first brushed with clean water then a very diluted blue colour was painted on top of the dampened paper which further diluted the colour allowing it to bloom. The same tecnique was used on the flowers lying on the table and to create a soft colour wash to the bottom of the image.

A different technique was used on the flowers within the jug. Starting with the lightest colour as the base colour the petals were painted pink and allowed to dry. Then using the same colour but adding less water to it to increase the density of colour, details and shadows were added. The same process was repeated for the stems and leaves.

When layering with watercolours, it is important to start with the lightest colour first. This way, you can keep building upon those lighter colours until you get the results you want.

It's important to know that watercolours will become reactivated once dry if you paint over them with water again. This is really helpful to know, because if you are not careful you can easily muddy up the paints resulting in some not-so-fantastic results.

Tip: Use a palette
When mixing your own colours, a palette will be your playground. You can buy a watercolour palette with little wells for mixing different colours or you can use a flat, non-porous surface like an old plate.

Clean water and scrap paper are your most important tools along with two containers of clean water. Use one to help you thin paint colours and the other to wash the brush when switching colors. I cannot stress this enough - change the water out frequently to avoid colour contamination.

Use scrap of paper to test out colours and consistency before putting them to your actual painting. A small piece of watercolor paper is your best bet, or mixed media paper if that is what your photograph is printed on.

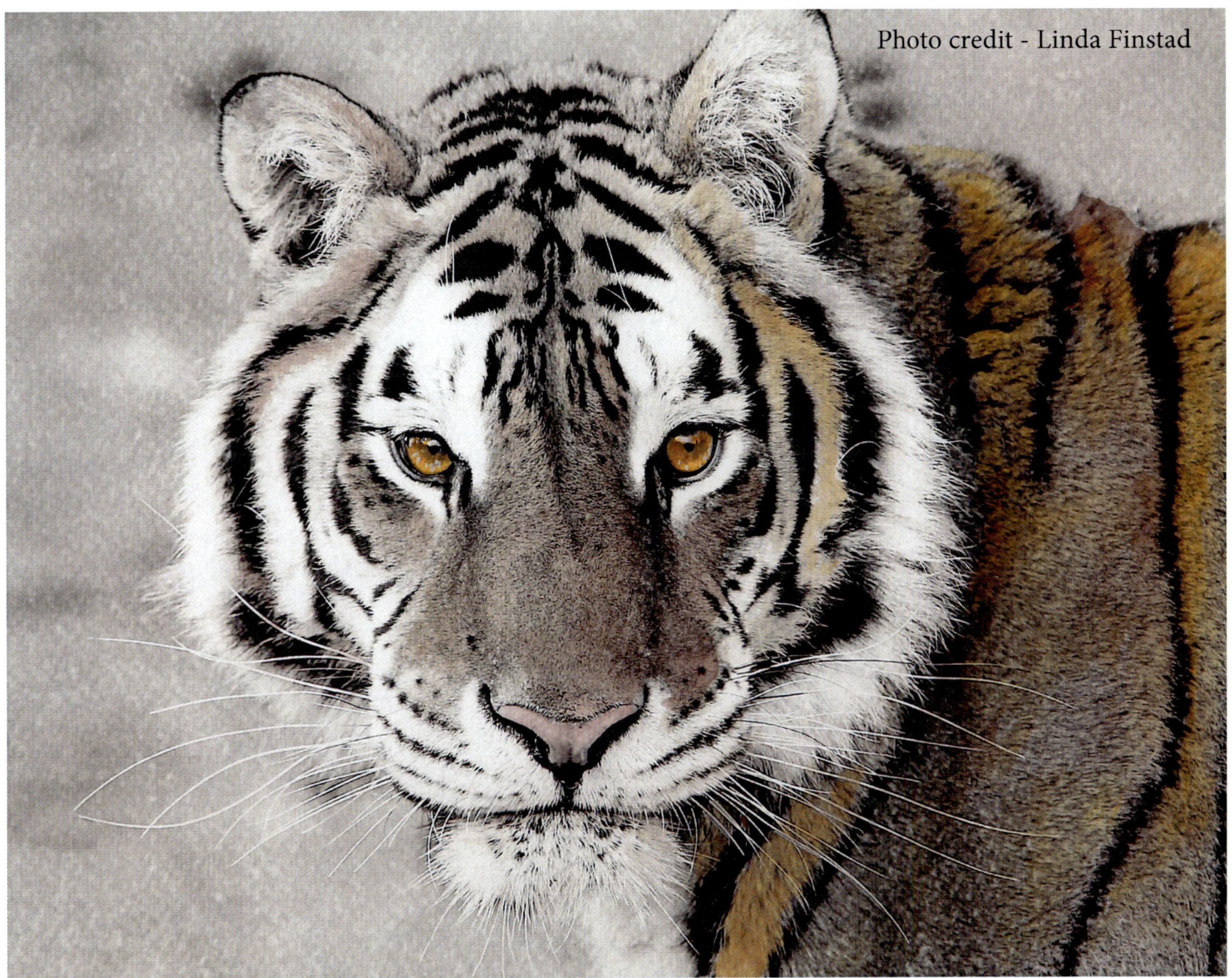

Dr. Ph. Martin's inks were used to colour the tiger. Inks offer more concentrated colour pigments than watercolour paints giving the tiger his intense stare (printed onto watercolour paper).

Watercolour inks are a fun and exciting medium, and can be combined with great success with watercolour paints. Because they are much brighter and denser in pigment than watercolours, when used together with your watercolours you can add areas of intensity to your paintings.

A word of caution, watercolour inks do not blend like watercolours and they are almost impossible to lift. They behave much like ink on an ink blotter, and once they are on your paper, that's it! Unlike watercolour paints - adding more water will NOT reactivate them.

Be sure to practice using the inks on scrap paper before you drop them into a painting.

Here is a fun twist. Due to their brightness, watercolour inks are often used by graphic designers and illustrators for work that's going to be photographed.

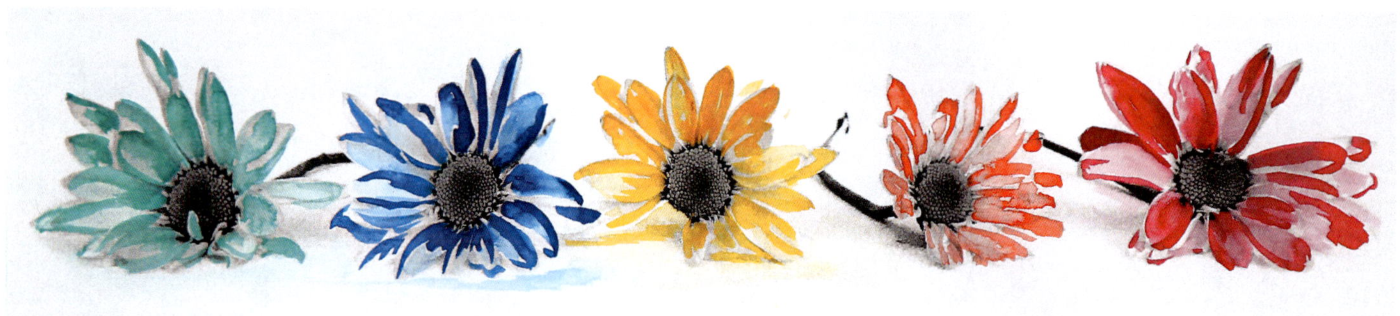

The row of multi-coloured daisies was printed on mixed media paper and hand painted using Dr. Ph. Martin's inks.

Pastels

There are five main types of pastels: hard, soft, oil, pan pastels, and pastel pencils, each with their own unique characteristics. Pastels are made by mixing dry pigment, some chalk, and a binder together to form a thick paste. The paste is fashioned into sticks and allowed to dry.

Soft pastels are the traditional form of pastels and also the most used. They have a very high concentration of pigment that is held together by the least amount of gum binder as possible. As a result, they crumble very easily, but their colours are wonderfully intense. Soft pastels come in a wide range of colours - more than other pastel types. Some manufactures offer up to 500 colours! Soft pastels come in cylindrical sticks and a range of sizes: whole sticks, half sticks, and thick sticks. You can buy them individually, but if you're buying your first pastels it may be easier to buy a starter set with a balanced colour palette that you can build on over time.

Pan pastels are a form of soft pastels, but instead of being moulded into sticks, they are set into pans or jars. This format allows for much less binder and probably the highest pigment concentration of any pastel product. The packaging protects the pigment, reduces waste, and allows for easy storage and transport. They are super easy to blend, they can be fully erased, and are compatible with other art mediums and surfaces. They're also cleaner to use and create much less dust than soft pastels.

This was the type of pastel I bought to experiment with when colouring photographs. The main appeal of pan pastels was they could be applied to the photograph using brushes, sponges, Q-tips and other tools.

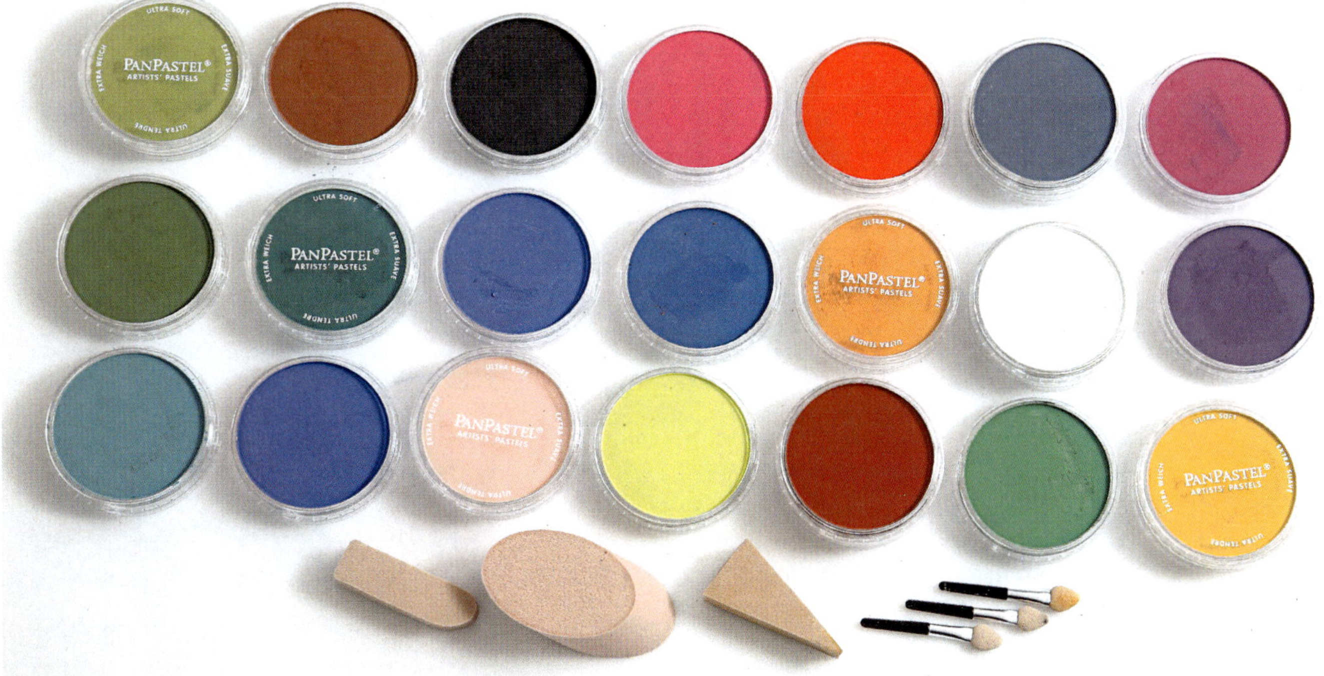

Hard pastels are made from the same ingredients as soft pastels, except they contain more binder and less pigment. This means their colours are not as intense but they don't crumble or break as easily. They come in cylindrical or square sticks which can be sharpened with a knife to create fine lines. They can be blended like soft pastels, and they're well suited to preliminary sketches, small details and finishing touches.

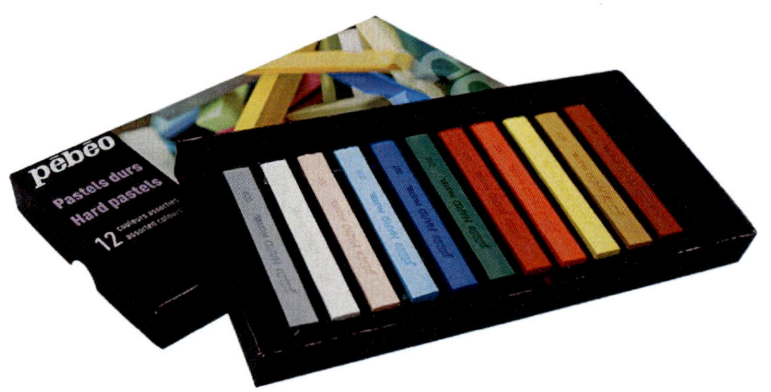

Pastel pencils are perfect if you're looking to create controlled, detailed works of art with pastel. They're just like conventional pencils, but encased within the wood is a thin stick of pastel that has a consistency in between hard and soft pastels. They can be used dry or wet and can be blended just like other pastels. You can sharpen them to a point to create precise details or use them bluntly for soft, hazy lines. Many artists also use them for preliminary sketches, which is especially handy given that graphite pencils aren't compatible with pastels. Pastel pencils are extremely useful for hand colouring photographs.

Pastels require a paper with some "tooth" and texture that allows the pastels to adhere to the page. This means glossy photographic prints are not suitable. Mixed media or watercolour paper do however work very well.

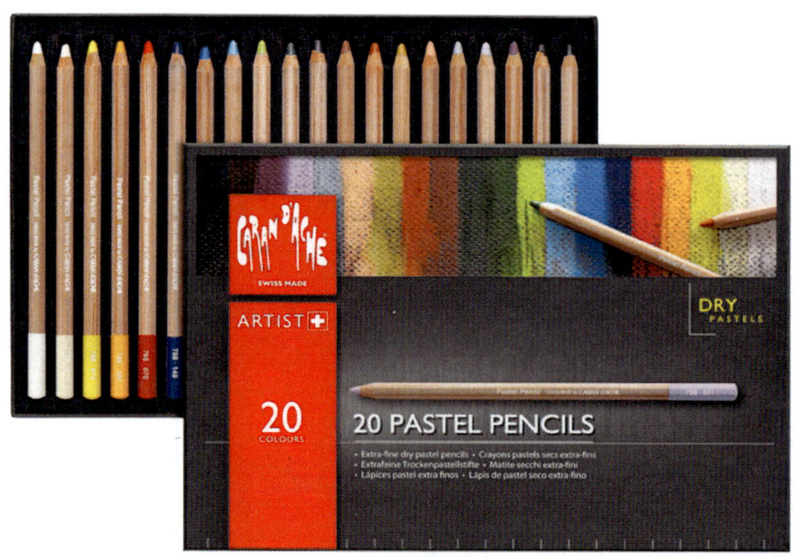

After carefully selecting your black and white photograph and printing it onto mixed media art paper, you are going to tape it down to a piece of foam core board, even though pastels are a dry medium, which means there is no moisture to warp and wrinkle the paper. It is a good habit to get into as it helps stabilize the image and prevents it from moving around as you work.

I had never used pan pastels before so I decided to pick an easy photograph to hand colour. This close up of a daisy was perfect. It has large clearly defined areas in which to place colour.

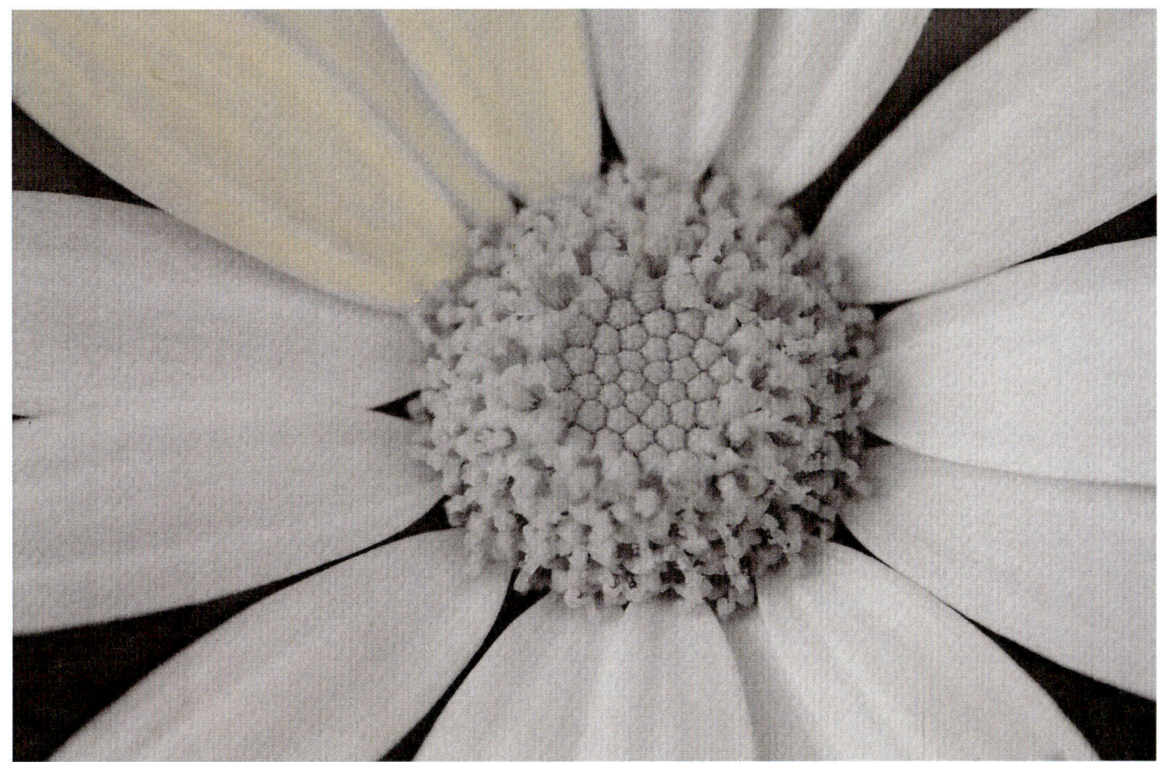

Using the foam tipped applicators included with the pan pastels I stroked a pale yellow colour onto the petals.

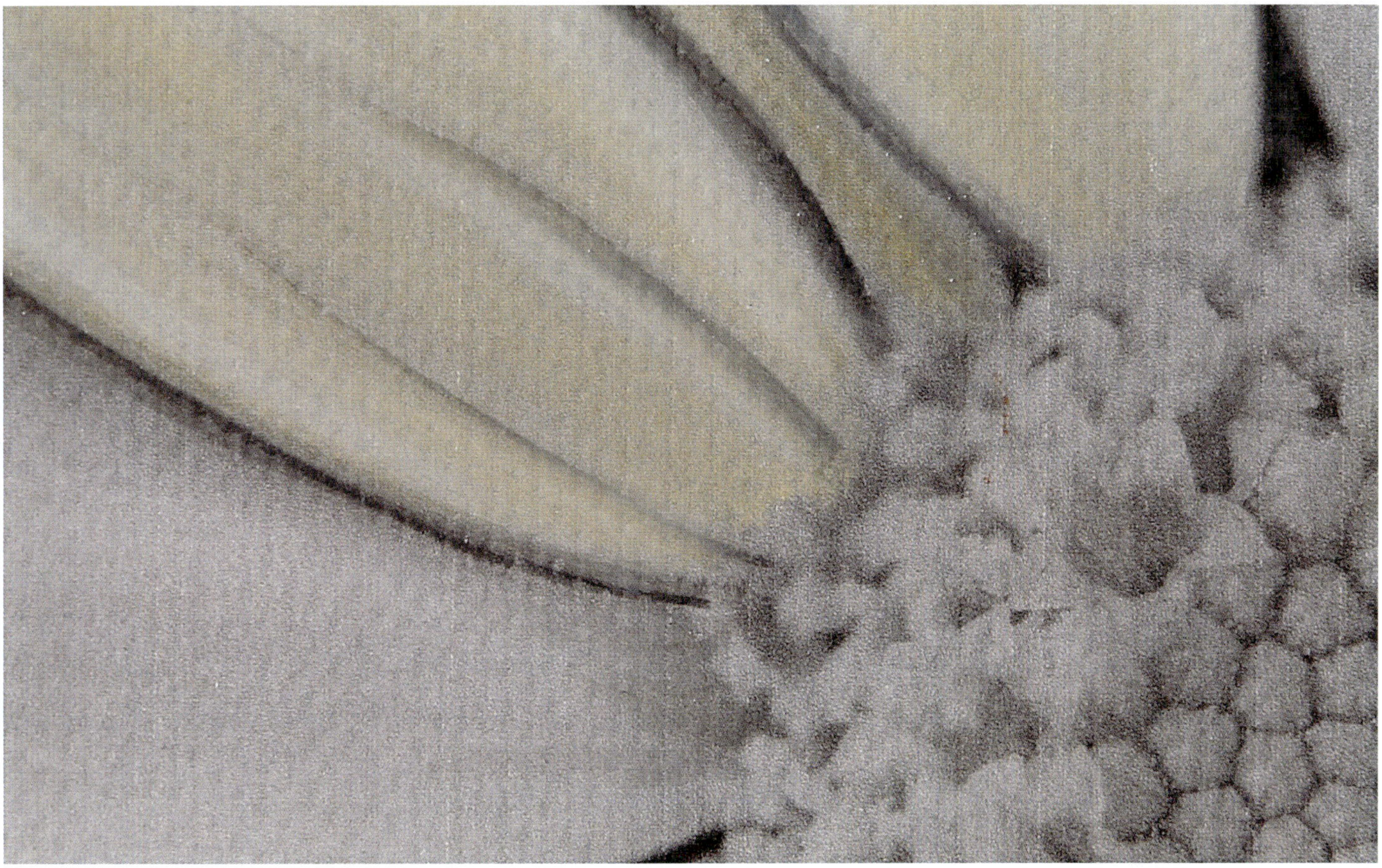

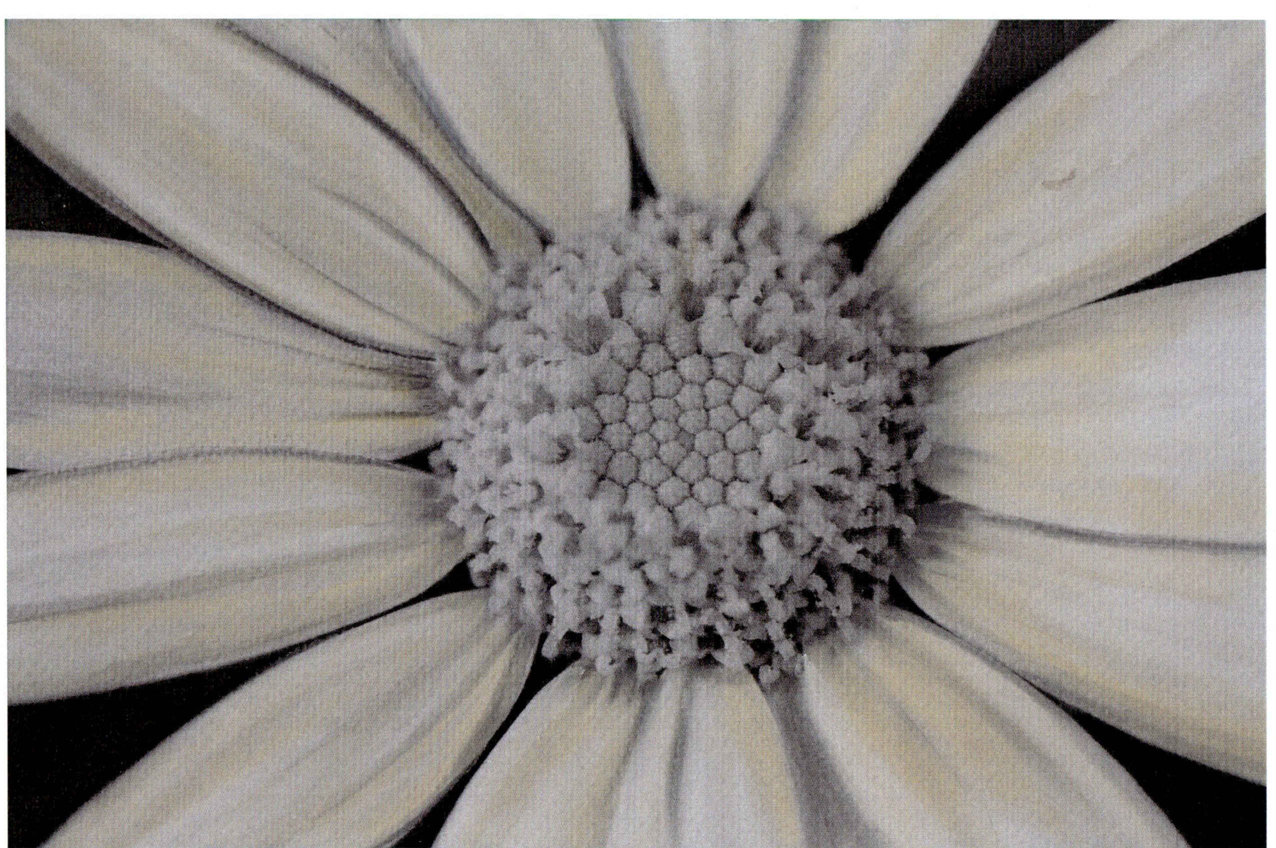

For the centre of the daisy I switched to a Q-tip to dab on the colours because I wanted to layer rather than blend a mixture of yellow, orange and brown pigments. The final touch was achieved by using white pastel on a foam applicator to add highlights to the petals.

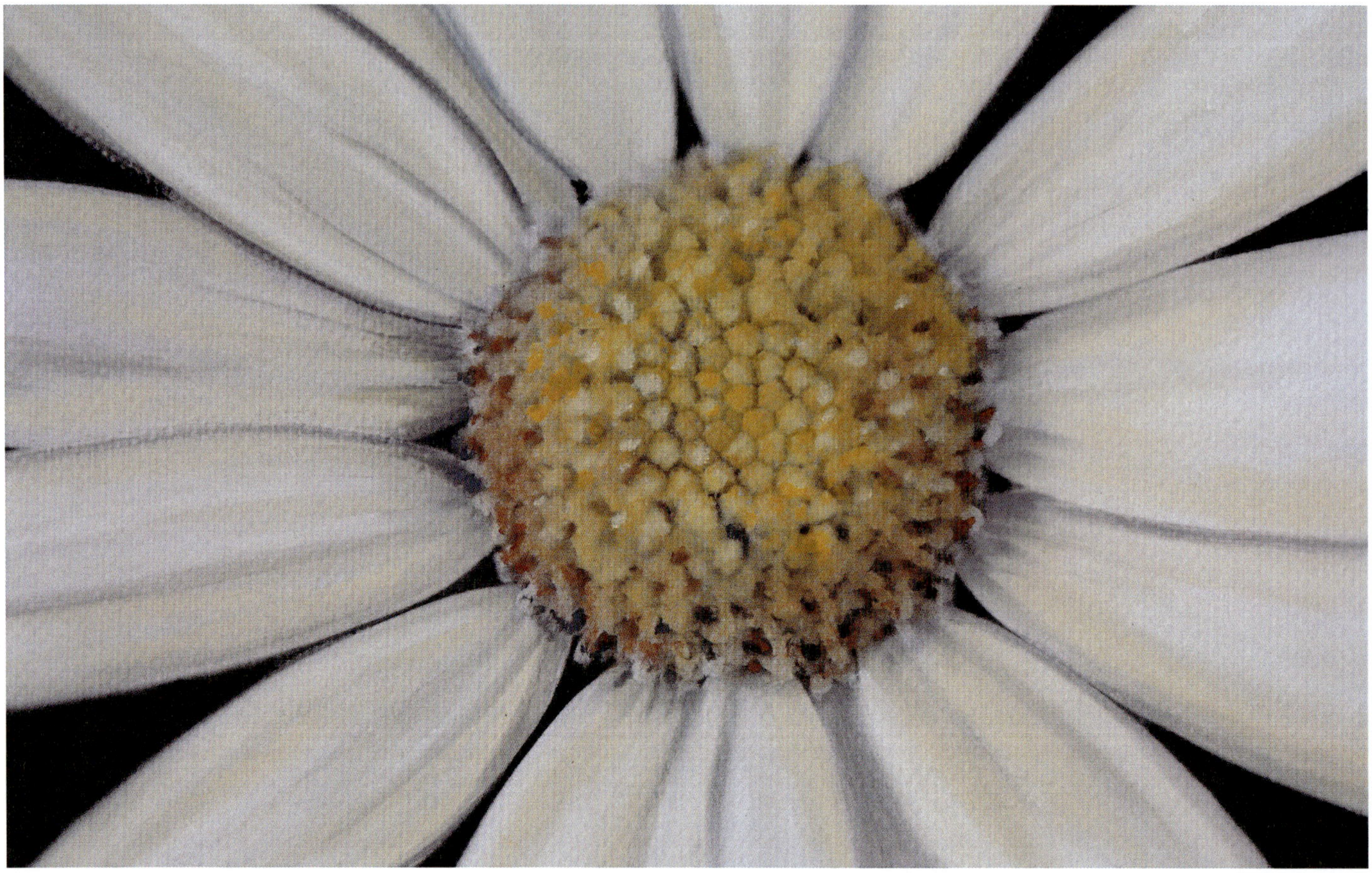

I found this delightful picture of a young boy fishing on www.unsplash.com and felt the soft buttery feel of pastels would be the perfect medium with which to hand colour it.

zhu-liang-749997-unsplash

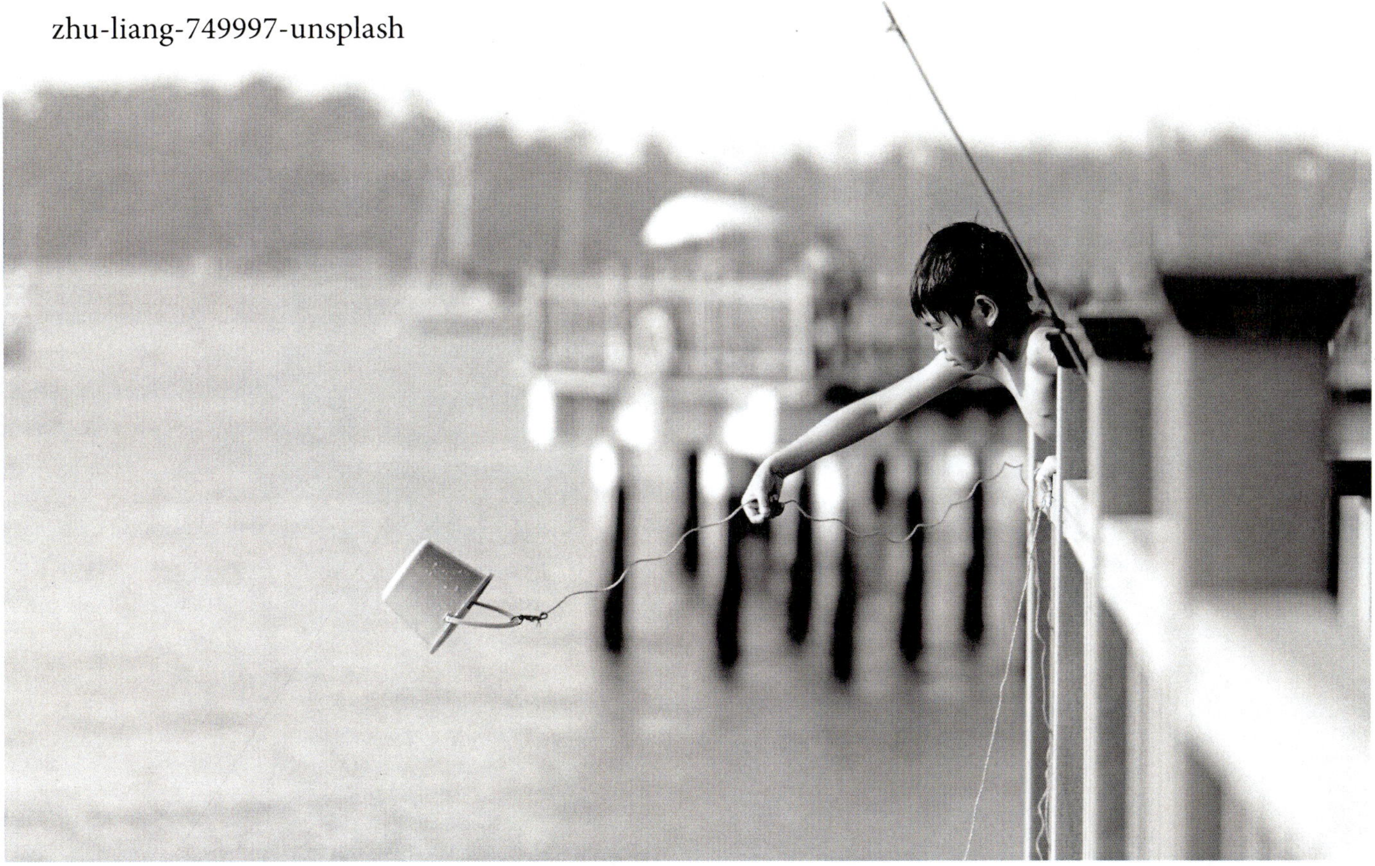

The pan pastels came with an assortment of foam tipped (washable) applicators. After loading one up with a bright red colour I carefully added pigment to the centre of the bucket. Then taking a Q-tip I blended the colour to the edges of the bucket and onto the handle.

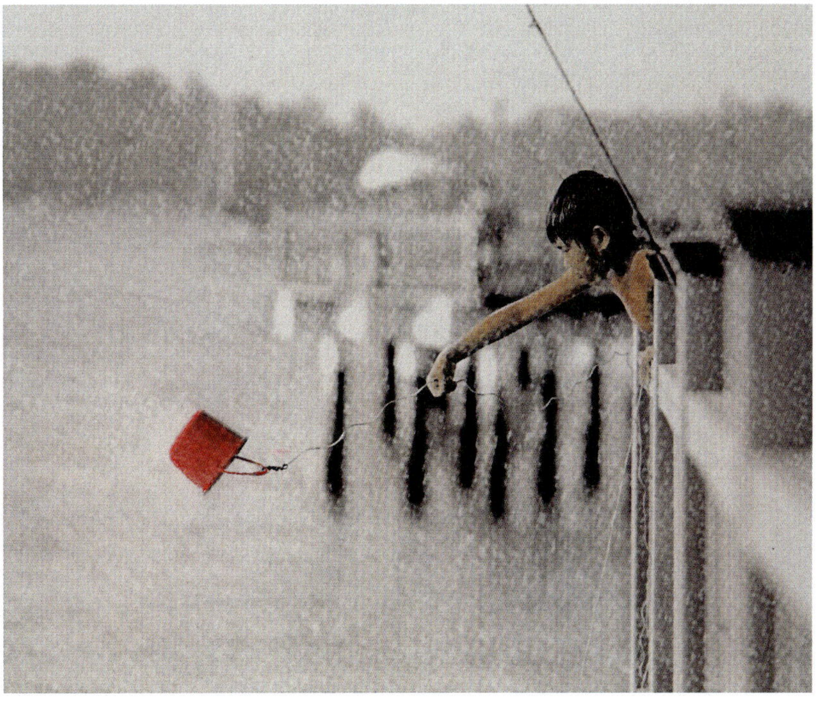

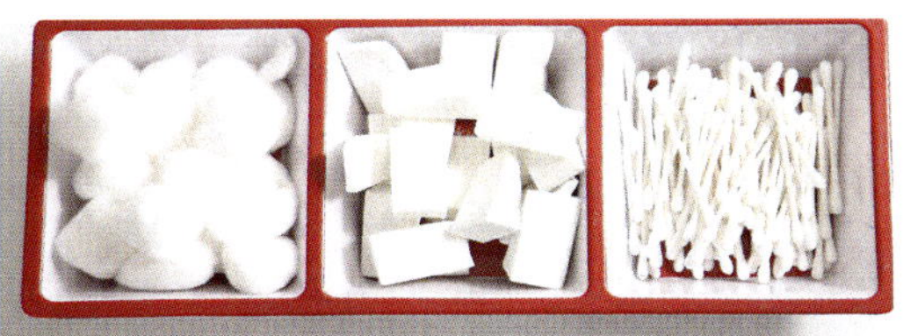

Cotton balls, make-up sponges and Q-tips are all fabulous tools for spreading and blending.

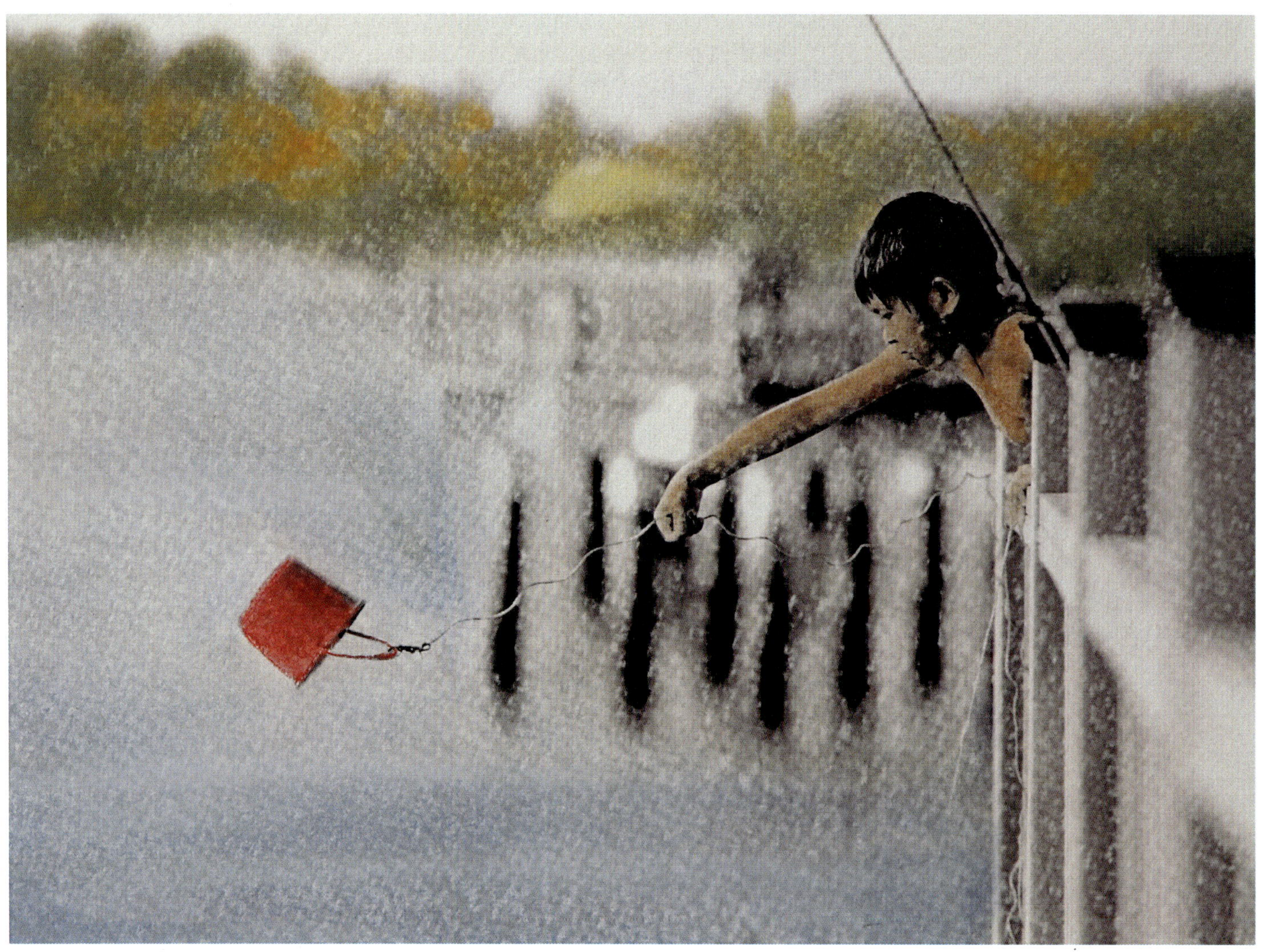

Next I worked on the boy's skin using a variety of skin toned colours and blending them together for a more natural look.

For the larger areas such as the water and distant shore I used make-up sponges to apply pigment and then blended with Q-tips. This process is very much trial and error to determine which applicators you prefer.

At this point the image had a nice soft hand painted feel to it. I could have stopped right here, and perhaps I should have, but I was having fun so kept going by adding some purple pigment into the shadows and on the water. I also thought the boy needed a little more colour in his cheeks and also on his shoulder.

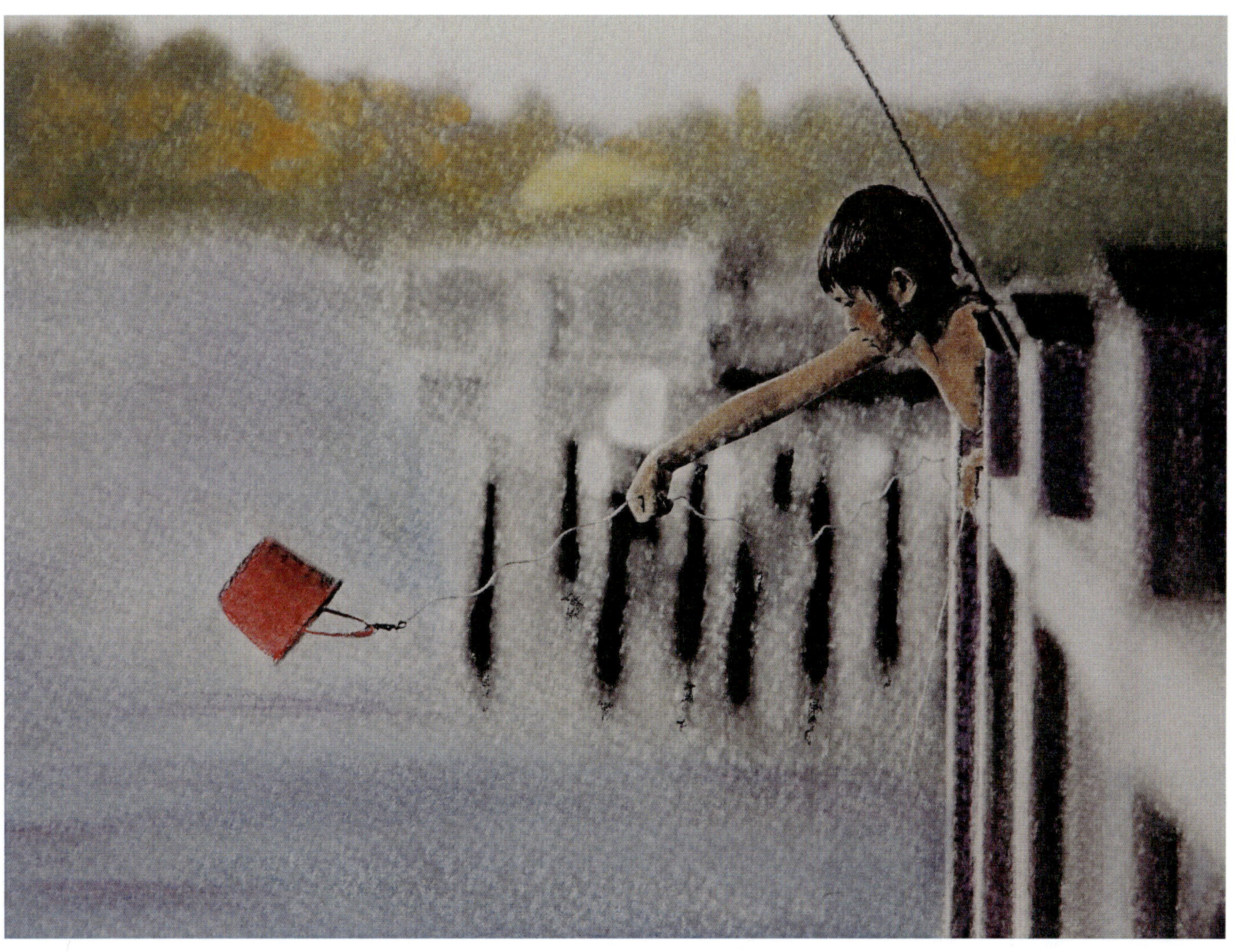

The reason I included both these pictures was to show you that sometimes less is more.

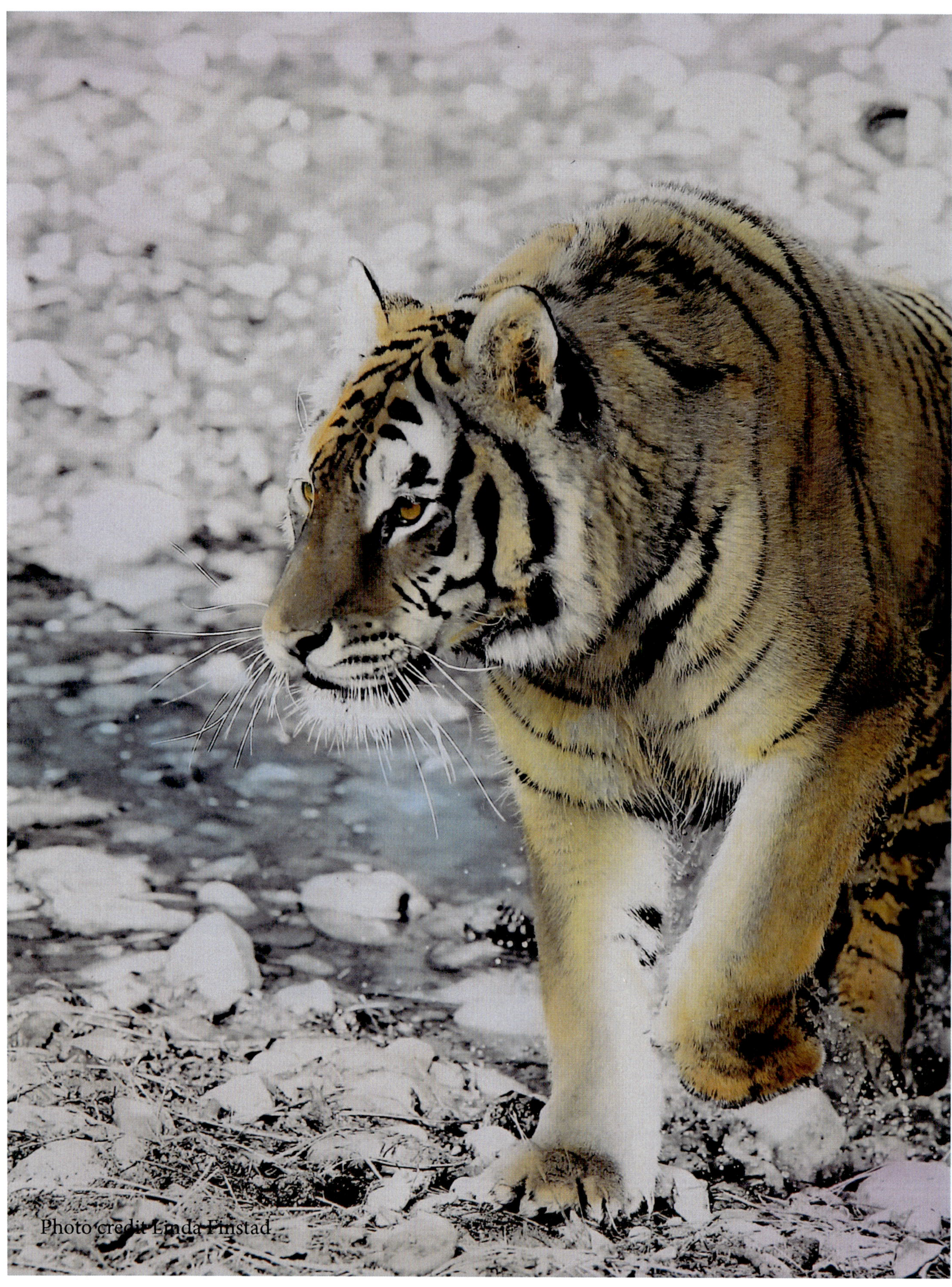

Photo credit Linda Finstad

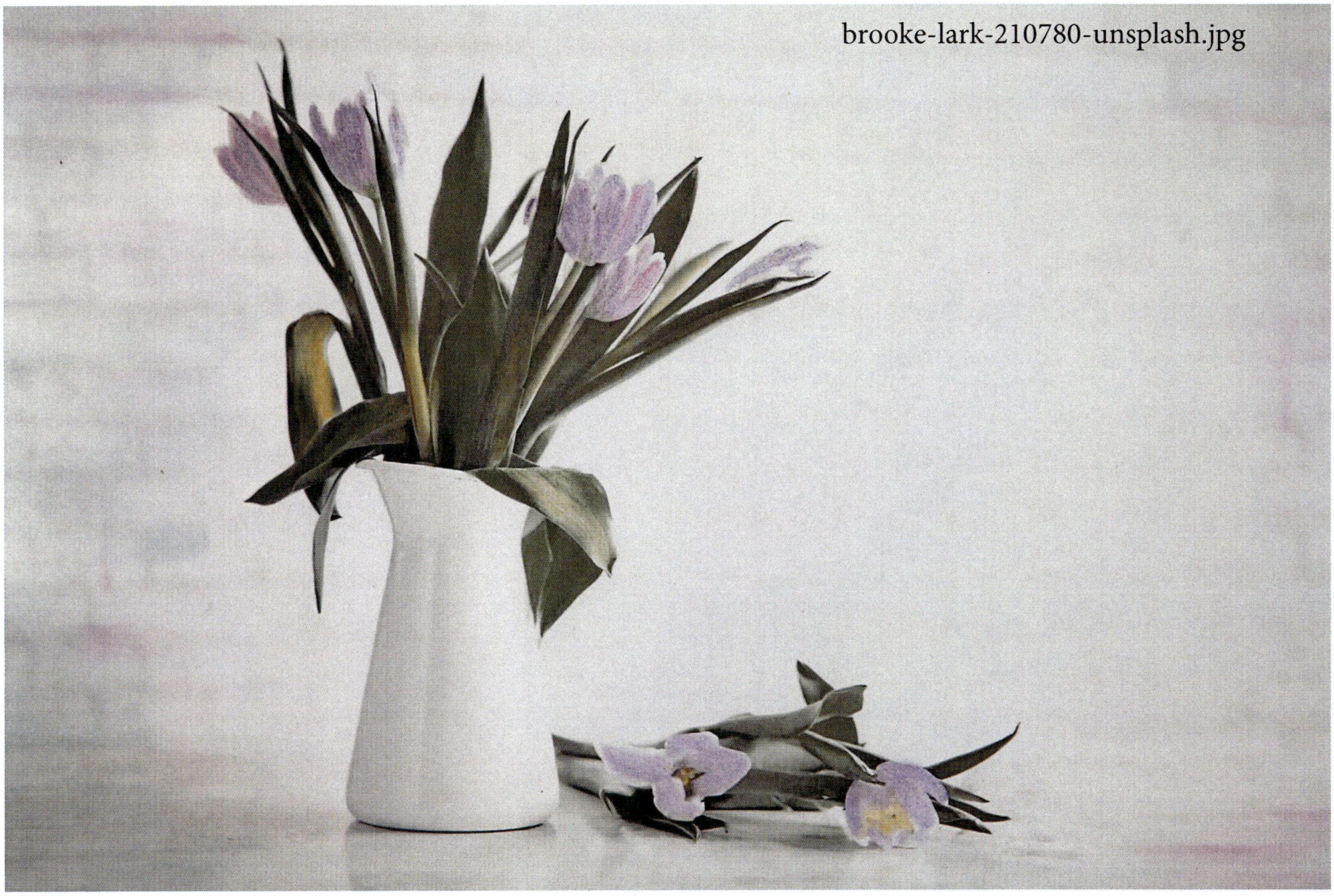

brooke-lark-210780-unsplash.jpg

If this vase of tulips looks familiar, that is because on page 44 where this image was hand painted with watercolours. When coloured with pan pastels the image takes on a completely differrent look.

Pastel is very easy to apply, but it also has a tendency to "move" on the paper, or rub off if the painting is touched. Spraying an occasional light layer of fixative over your painting as you work can help your pastels stay in place, so that you can build your painting in layers without feeling like you're wiping the pigment off as you go.

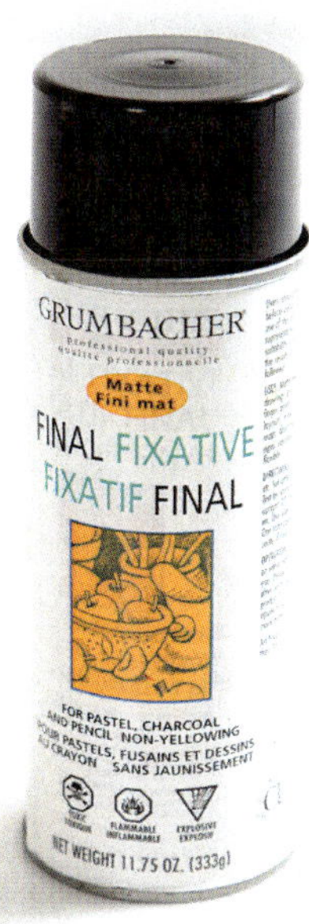

Maybe you don't like the idea of using fixative during the painting process—that's OK! However you will need to use a fixative spray before putting your finished work into a frame, so that the dust doesn't rub off onto the mat and glass.

The goal was to create a slightly surreal effect with this photograph of a majestic tiger. I did this by using a mixture of vibrant colours in the main areas of interest within the photograph, yet allowing less important areas of the black and white photograph to show through.

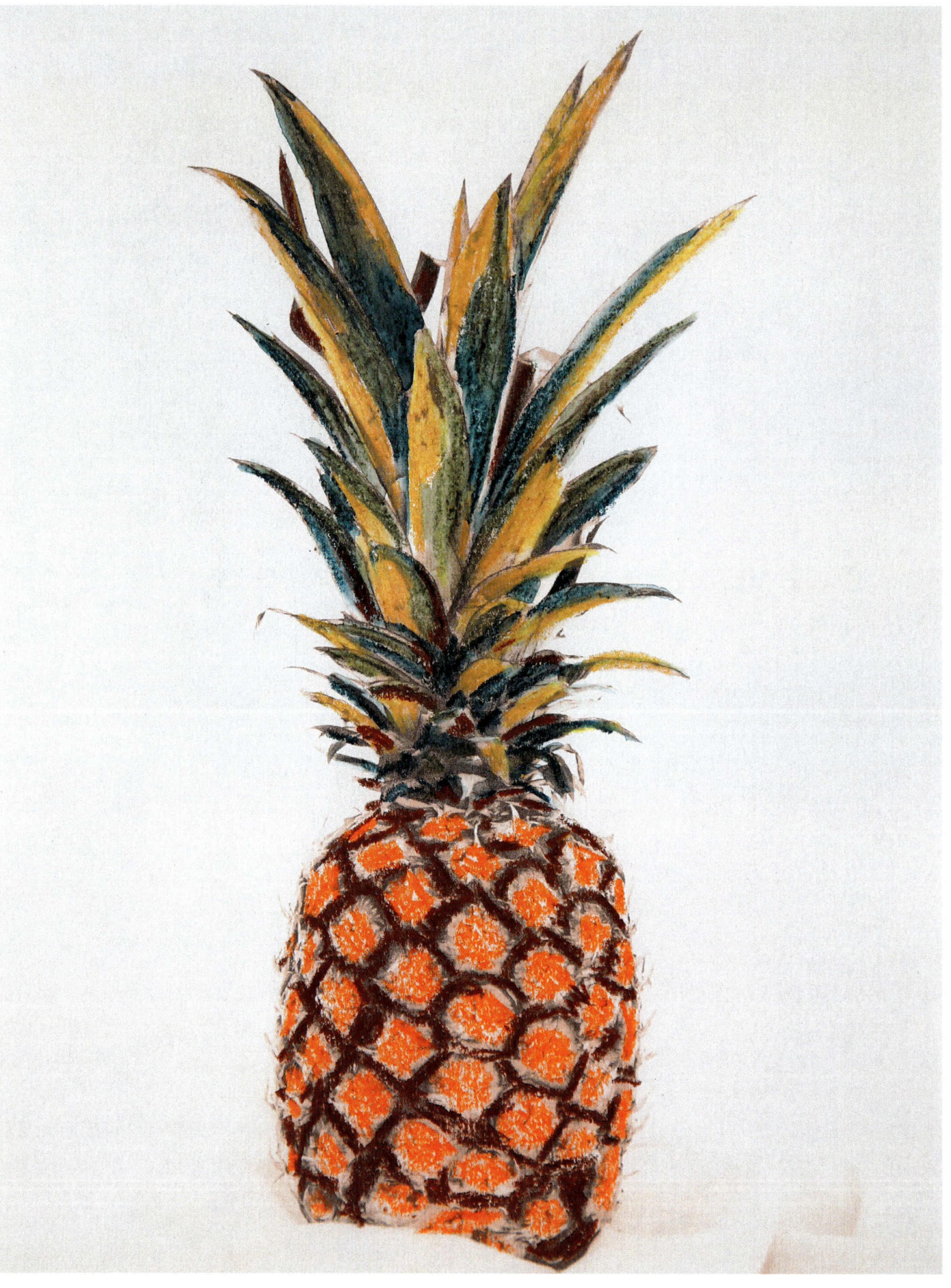

Watercolour pencils and crayons

For optimum results with watercolour pencils or crayons, print the black and white photograph you wish to hand colour onto either mixed media art paper or watercolour paper.

While exploring different possibilities with which to hand colour black and white photographs I became a frequent visitor to the local art store. For a creative person, browsing through the aisles at an art and craft store is probably one of life's most sublime pleasures. The old saying "like a kid in a candy store" springs to mind and I am certainly no exception to the allure of new paints and mediums. I am excited to share with you one of my greatest discoveries.

Allow me to introduce you to watercolour pencils and crayons.

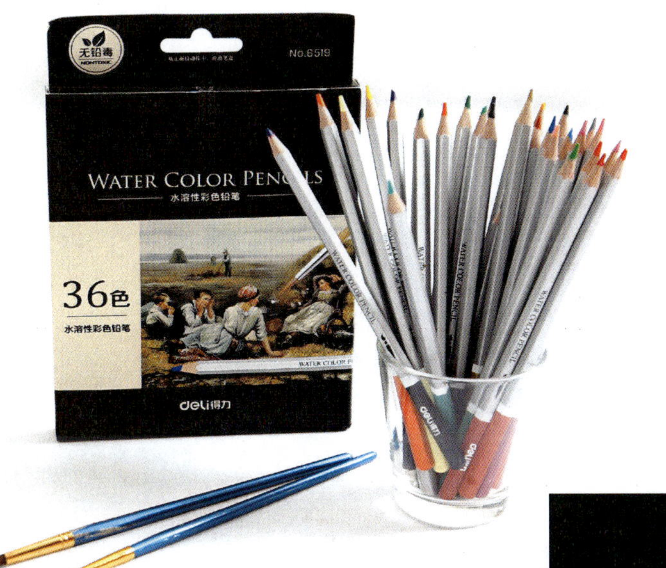

Watercolour pencils and crayons look like regular coloured pencils, and you use them the much same way.You hold them the same way, you sharpen the same way with one exception.

When you add water to your drawing, something incredible happens.
You've suddenly got watercolour art.

How does this happen?

The binder holding the coloured pigment in watercolour pencils is water-soluble.

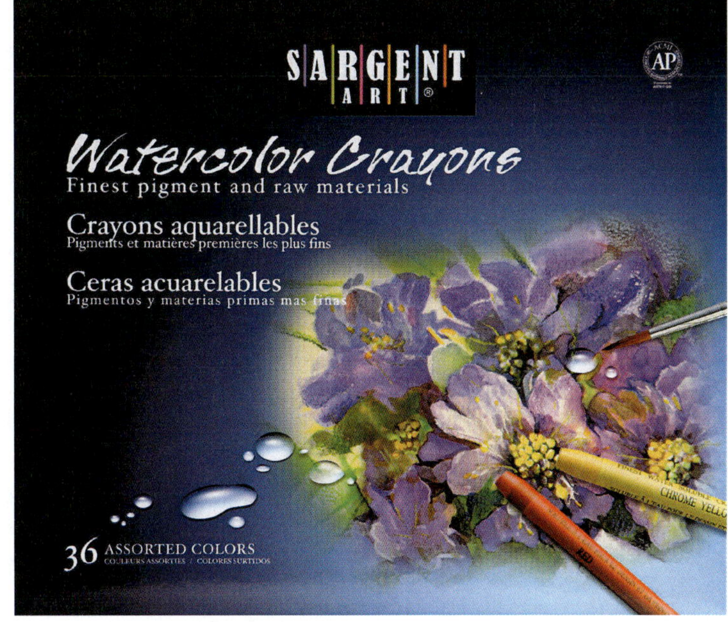

Until now I had only used watercolour pencils to sketch the outline of paintings on canvas and they were perfect for this purpose. The sketch lines easily dissolved and disappeared as I painted over them and any remaining unwanted lines could be wiped away with a damp cloth. The thought of using the watercolour pencils as my main pigment source had never occurred to me.

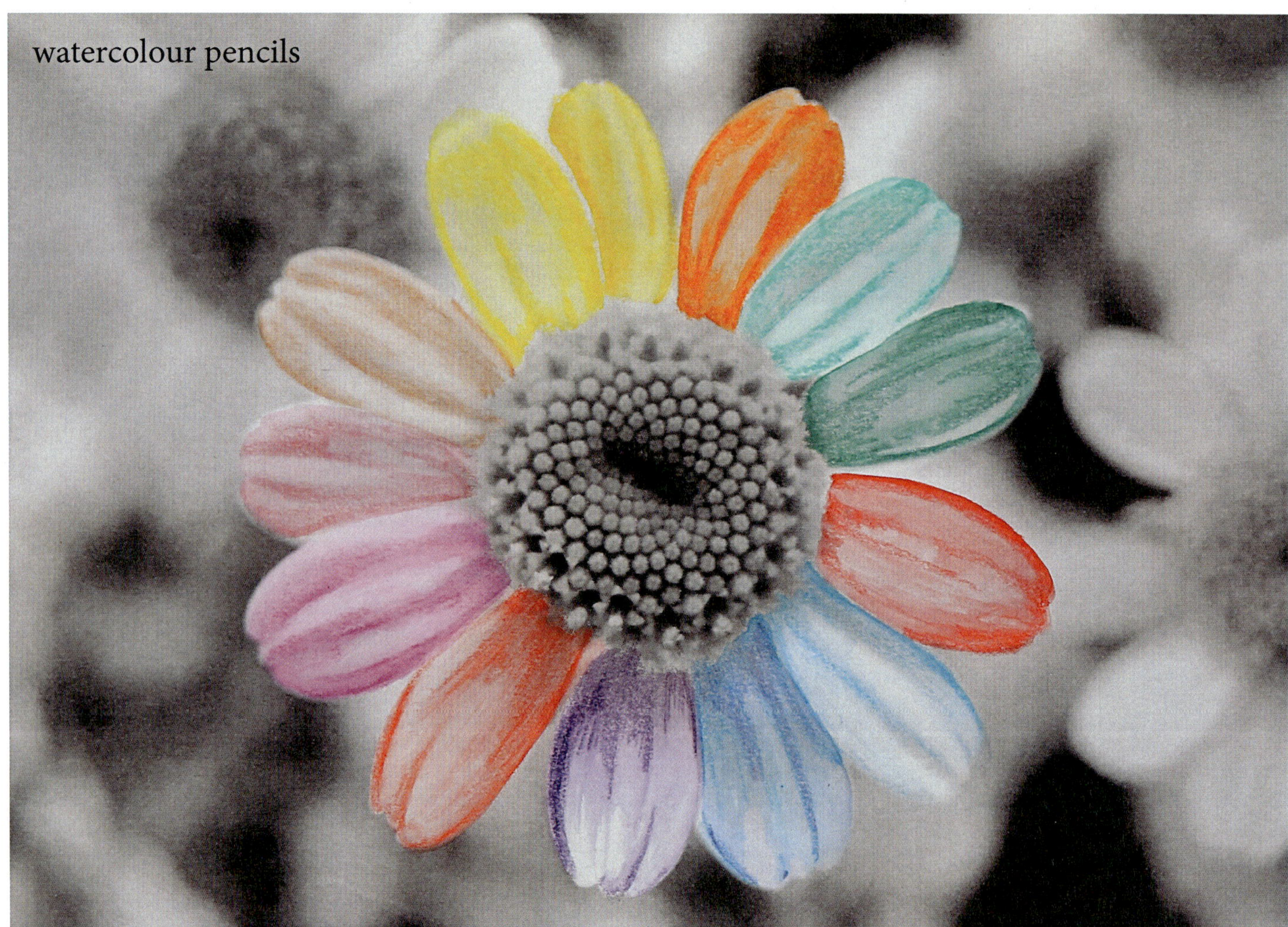

When you buy any new paints or mediums it is important to test the colours to see how they look when applied to paper which you will be applying them. Remember, their colour and the way they move will vary depending on the type of paper you will be applying them to. The colours look very different dry than wet. Typically they are darker and more vibrant when wet. This picture of a daisy provided the perfect pallette to test the watercolour pencils and create a pretty colour reference sheet.

When I saw the box of watercolour crayons (which look very similar to wax crayons a child would use) in the professional art supplies section at the store I was intrigued and popped the box of crayons into my basket. I must admit they are now my favorite medium.

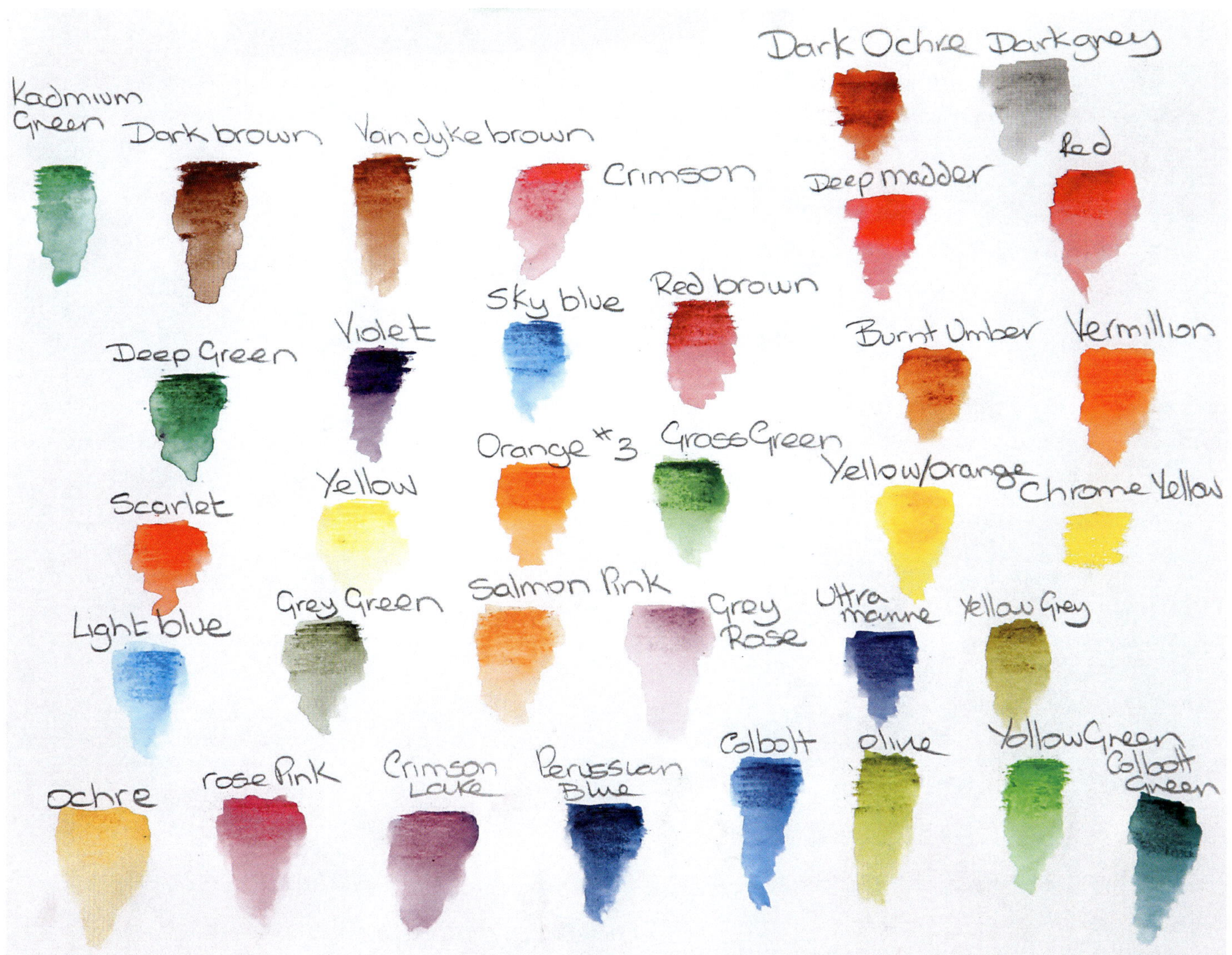

Watercolour crayon sampler

Creating a sampler will be invaluable when working on your actual photograph. Be sure to name the colours to correspond to the crayon or pencil

Both pencils and crayons are very easy to use - just draw, then brush with water.

The more pencil or crayon you add to your photograph, the more intense the colours will be when they're wet. For lighter colours, try to colour in a "loose" manner and use a very light pressure. You can even layer different pencil colours to blend a new hue !

There are a couple of ways to apply colour to your photograph. You can draw a spot of colour on an area of your photograph and brush it with water. This will create a pool of colour. Or you rub your wet paint brush directly against the tip of the pencil or crayon to pick up pigment. Then apply the paint the photograph using brush strokes.

Tip: When working with watercolour pencils or water-soluble crayons, make a point of keeping the tips clean to ensure your colours don't get muddied. Wipe the tip on a damp cloth or scribble with it on a scrap bit of paper.

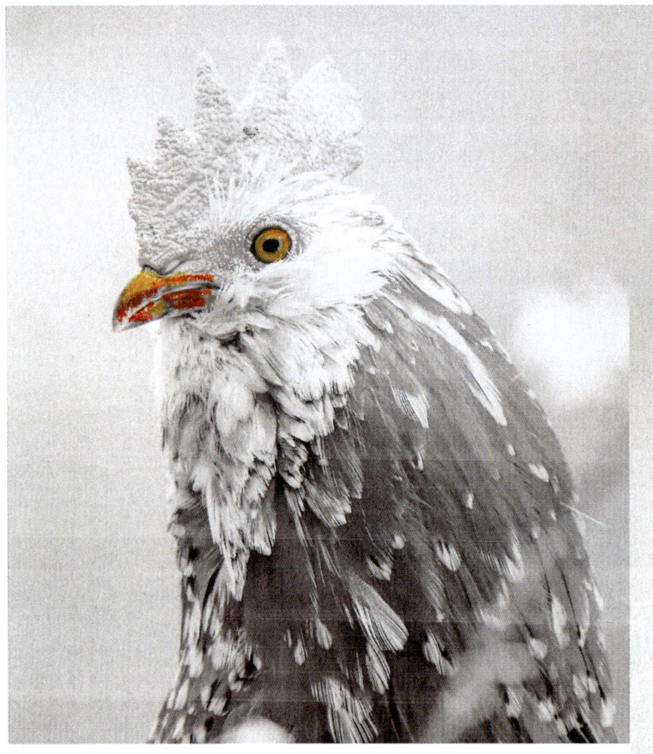

I started colouring this picture of a chicken with watercolour pencils on the beak and eye because these were small delicate areas. To be honest, if I messed up the eye and beak there would be no point continuing colouring the rest of the photograph.

Next, using a mixture of crayon and pencil I coloured the comb. Once the crayon was activated with water the colours became rich and vibrant.

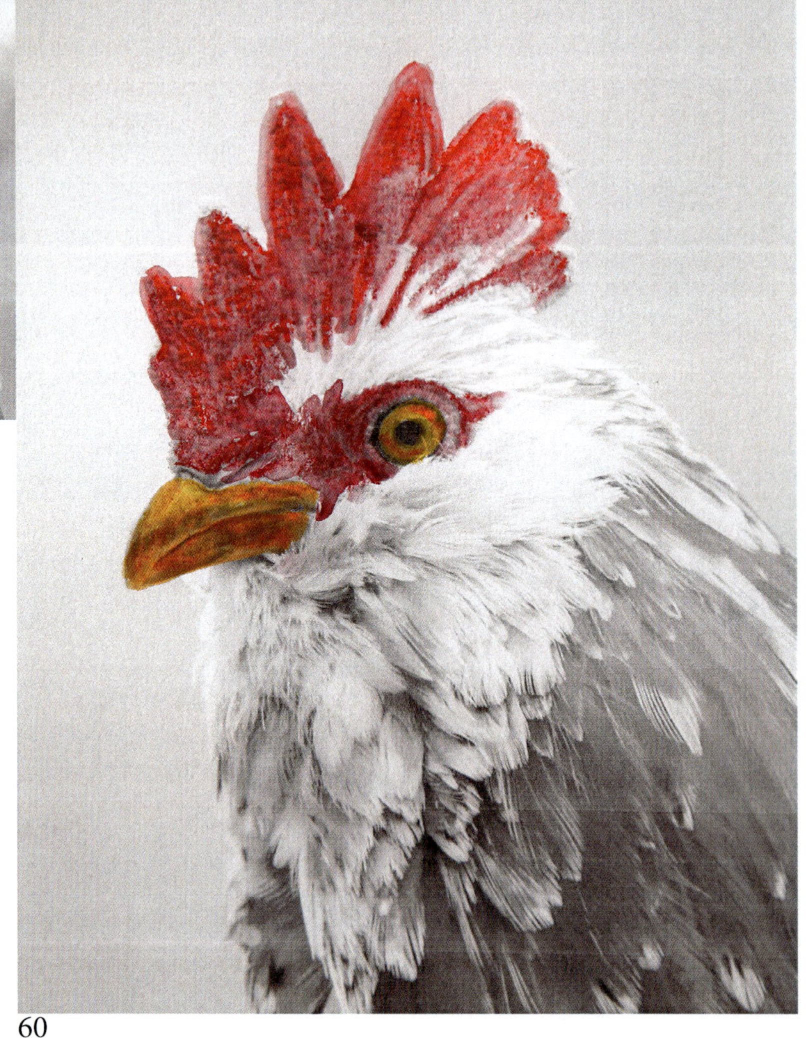

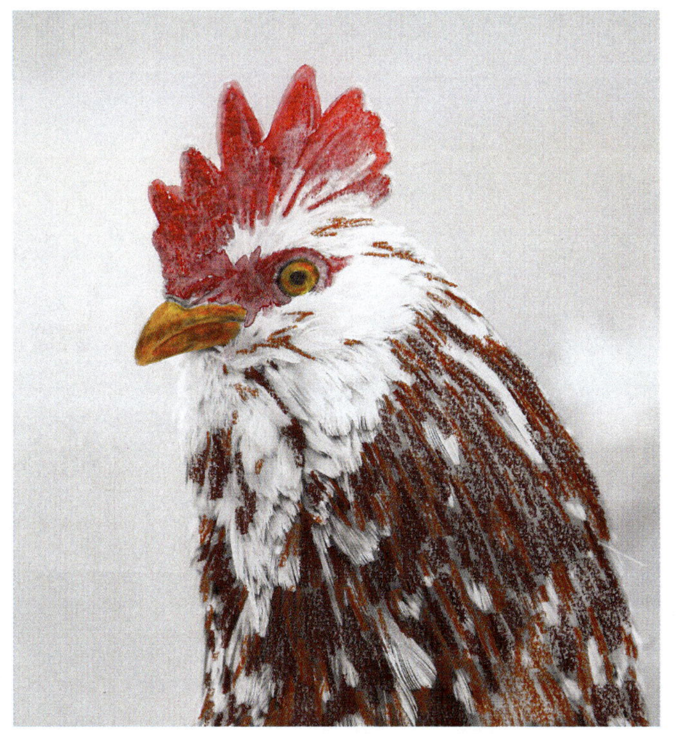

Dark brown crayon was loosely applied to the feathers.

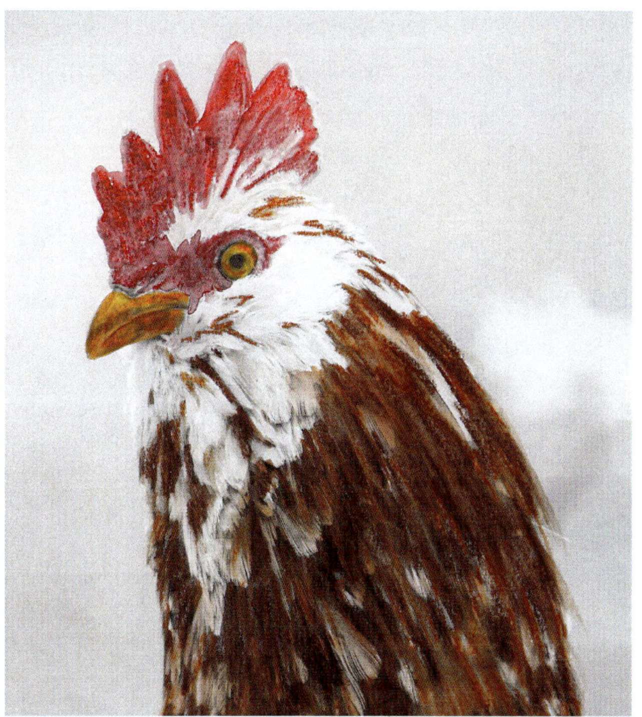

The pigment was then activated with water.

Allow the painting to dry before layering on more colours. If you attempt to crayon over wet paint and damp paper you will risk either creating a muddy mess or tearing the paper.

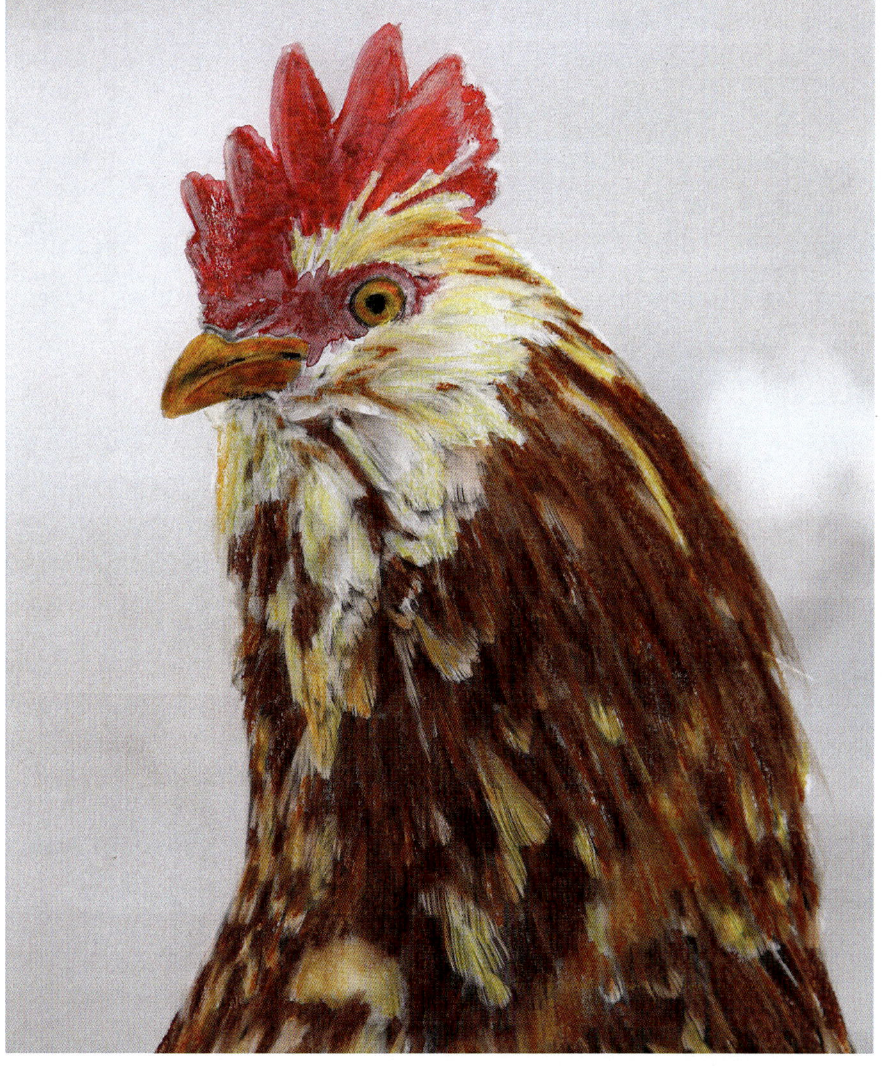

In the previous example the finished piece looked more like a water colour painting than a photograph. There is no right or wrong. This is your art and you decide how much or how little of the image you want to colour.

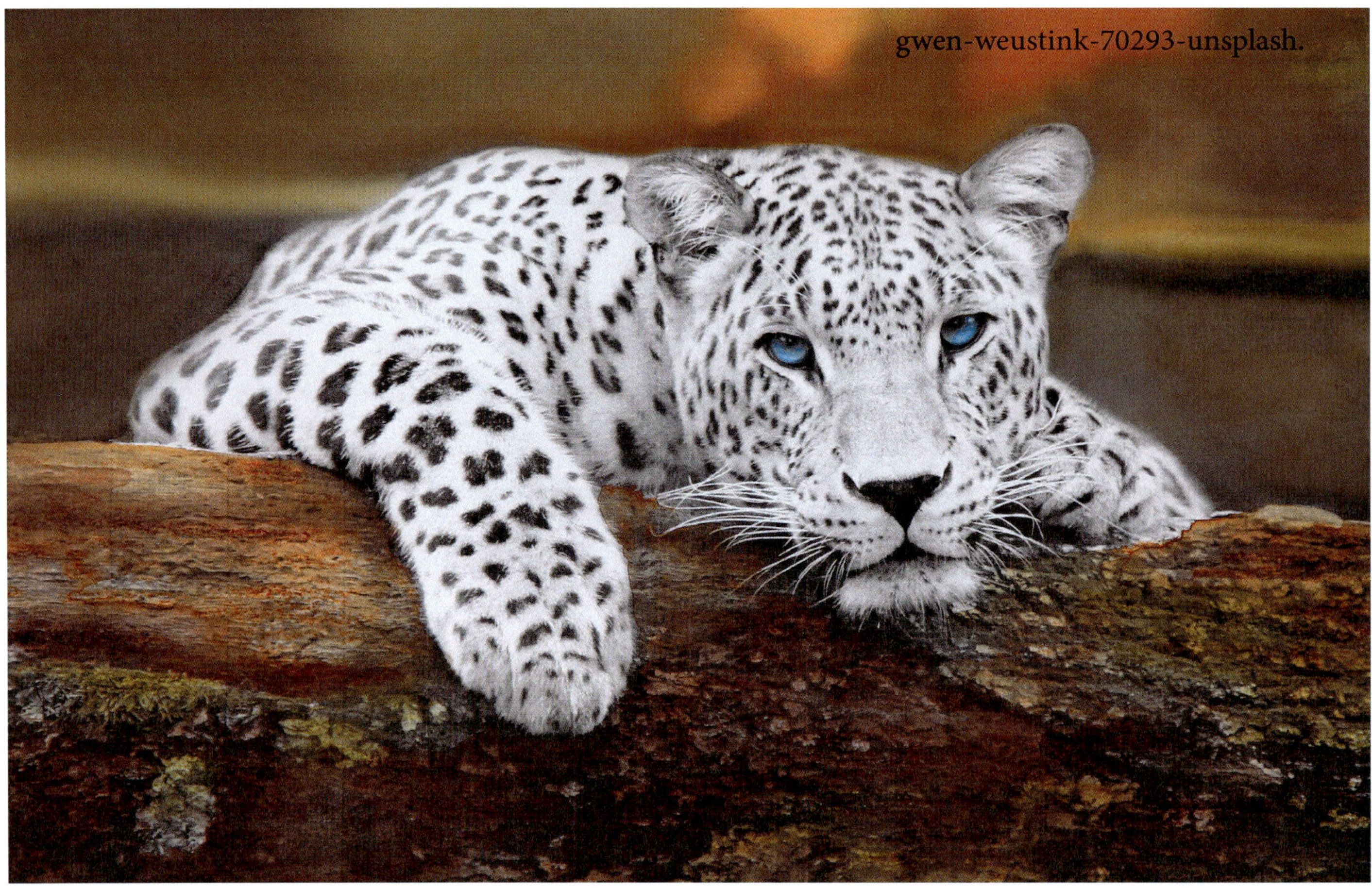

In this example only the background and the leopard's eyes were coloured leaving the black and white photograph as the main focus of the image.

Tip: The extent to which the colours mix depends on how hard you scrub with the brush at the pigment you've applied to the photograph. If you go back and forth, back and forth, you'll dissolve all the pigment. If you just go lightly over the top, you will only dissolve the very top layer.

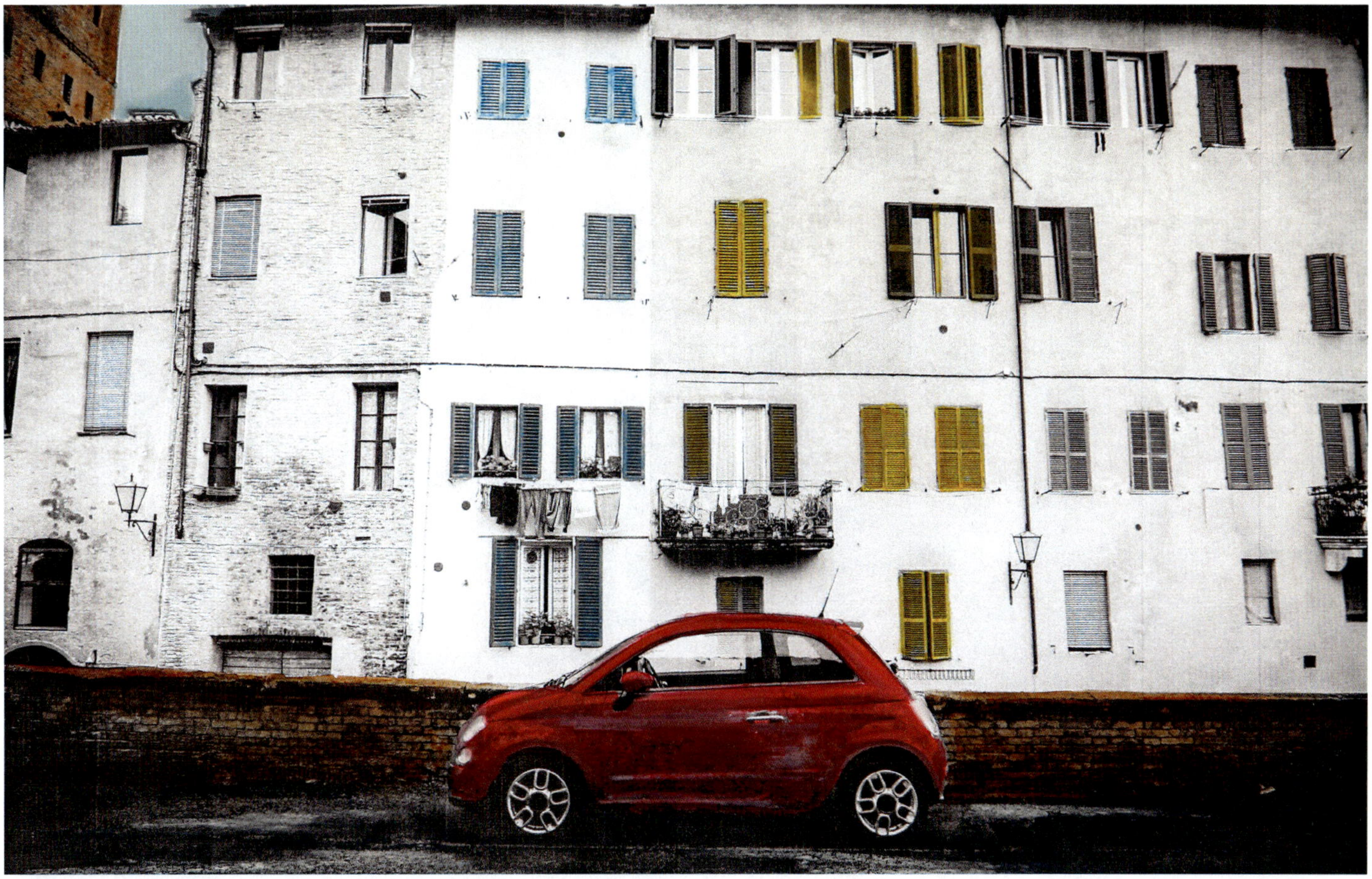

jace-afsoon-YfBlYeYnu_g-unsplash.jpg

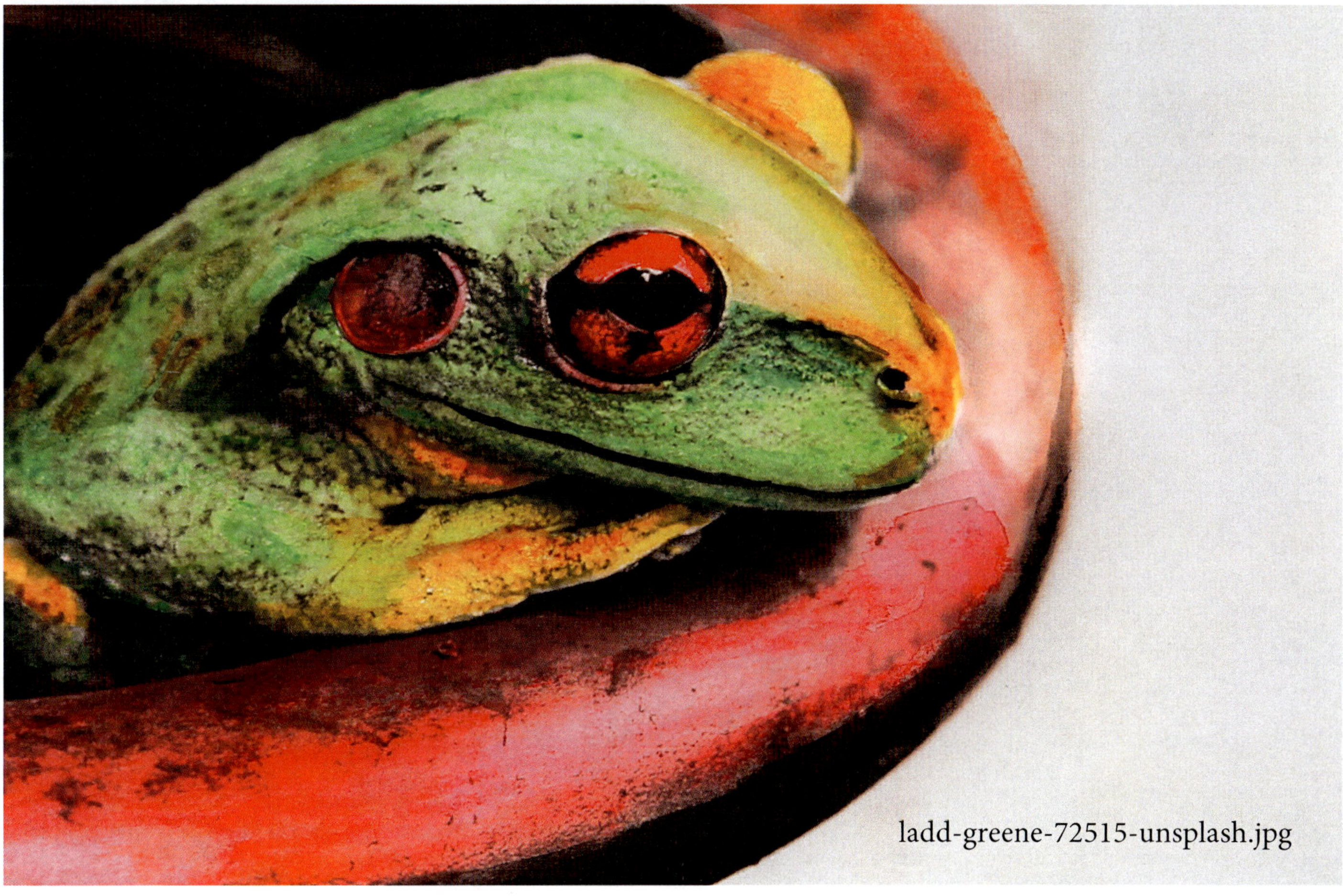

ladd-greene-72515-unsplash.jpg

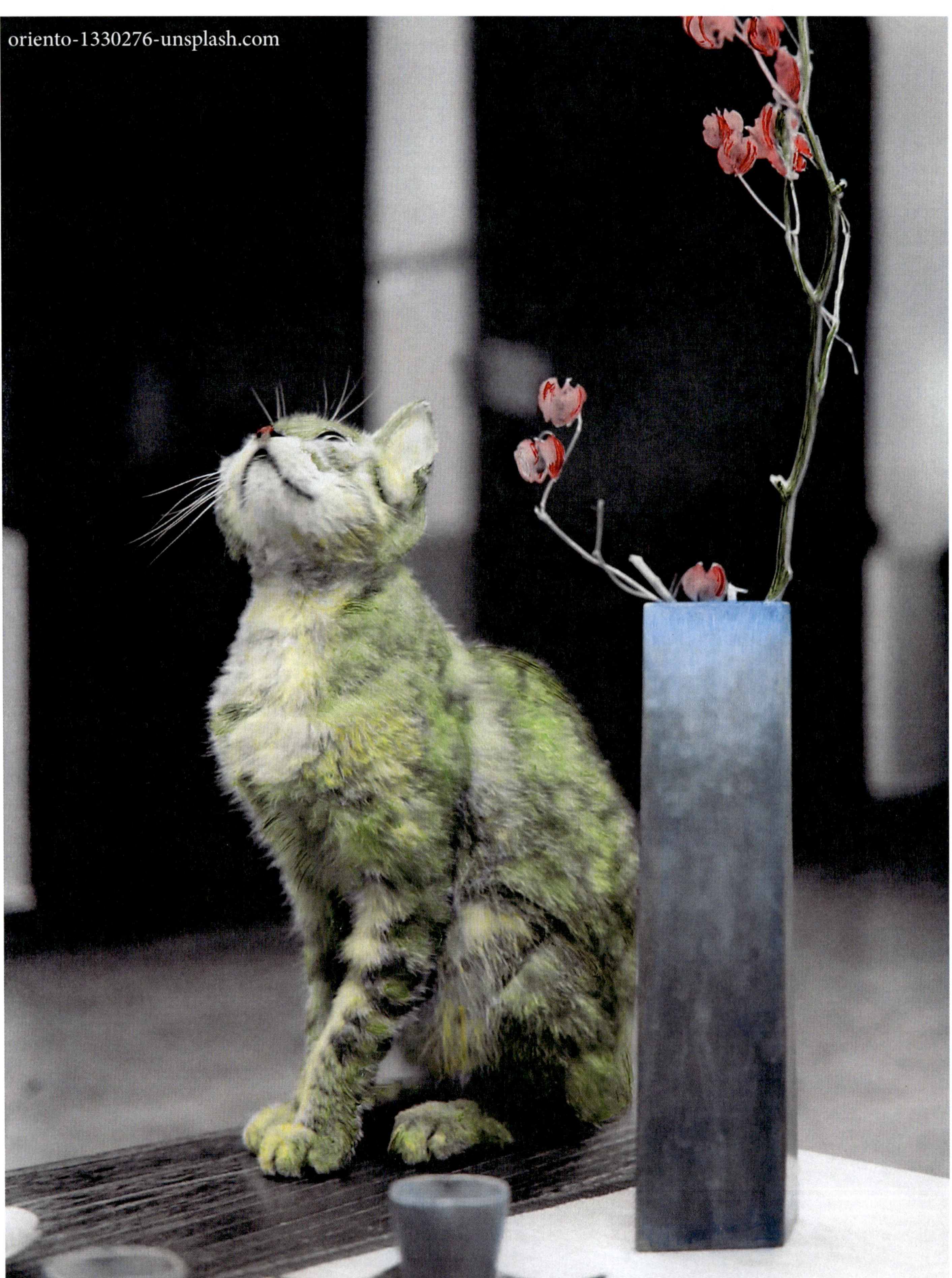
oriento-1330276-unsplash.com

Marshall's Photo Oils

Marshall's Photo Oil Paints are the classical way to hand tint and colour photographs. These specialty oil paints are transparent and specifically designed for tinting black-and-white photographs. They are highly concentrated which means they come in teeny tiny tubes and are very expensive. However they are acid-free and archival to ensure the long-term stability of your artwork. Marshall's oils are probably the only translucent paint that will adhere to glossy photo paper.

To learn how to use this medium I referenced traditional methods of hand tinting and was dismayed to find that most of the techniques required the artist to apply the paint in very small quantities and then proceed to rub most of it away. The original purpose of this technique was to give the illusion of a colour photograph by adding subtle colour.

Although subtlety is neither my personal style or strong suit I decided to give it a whirl.

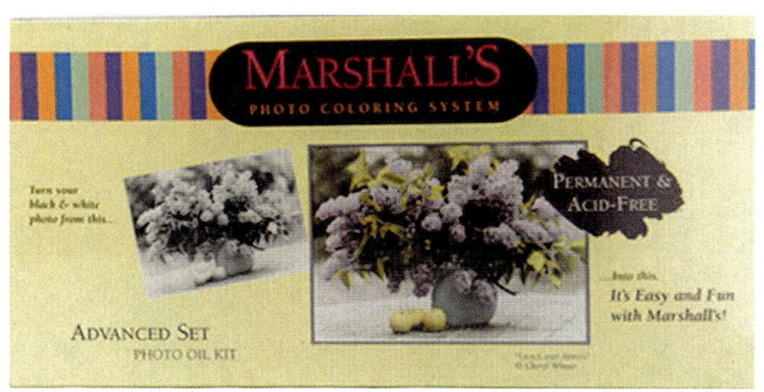

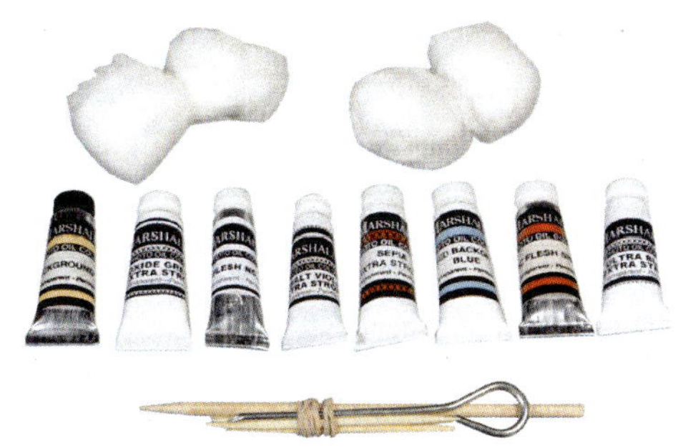

Here is a list of the basic supplies needed to get started with traditional hand colouring.
Photographic oils (oil tubes, oil pencils) Although there are a few brands available, by far the most widely used photo oils on the market are Marshall's Photo Oils and their oil pencil sets. The pencils can be useful when colouring smaller areas of detail and, since they are manufactured by Marshall's, the colours are meant to complement the photo oils.

Cotton balls - be sure to buy a brand that promises only 100% cotton is used. Synthetic fibres are strongly discouraged. Not only will synthetic cotton not hold the oils as well as 100% cotton, but they also tend to lose fibres which can end up on your painting.

Q-tips, both rounded and pointed tips, as an aid to applying small amounts of oil.

Toothpicks, wooden skewers for use as hand made cotton skewers to apply or blend oils in small areas.

Kneaded erasers to clean out areas of your print where you don't want colour.

Preparing your photo

When you open a box of Marshall's Photo Oils, you will see you have been provided with a few "extras", the number of which will vary depending upon the size of the set. However, all sets will come with a small bottle of a prepared medium called PM Solution. This is an archival medium used to moisten the top emulsion of your print. You can make your own solution by mixing equal parts of odourless turpentine with vegetable oil. PM Solution is fundamentally the same but is more stable.

The Solution helps with the flow of the oils, and makes blending and rubbing down colours easier.

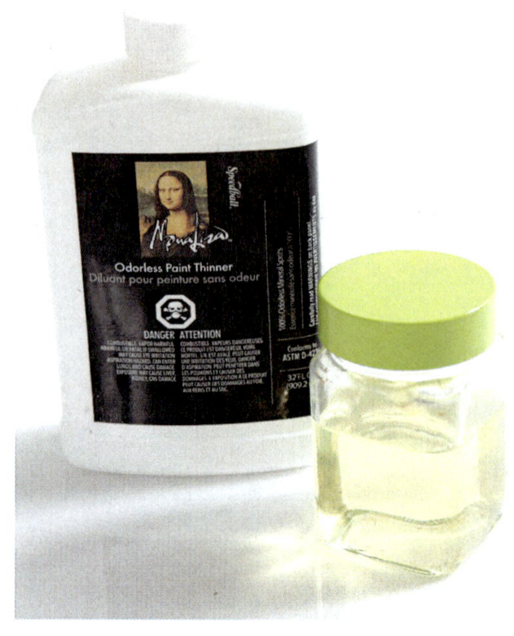

Getting started

Tape down your photograph to a foam core board and assemble all your supplies. Before starting work on your photograph prepare the surface by dampening a cotton swab – not soaked to where it's dripping – and apply the PM Solution in an even, circular motion until the entire print is lightly coated.

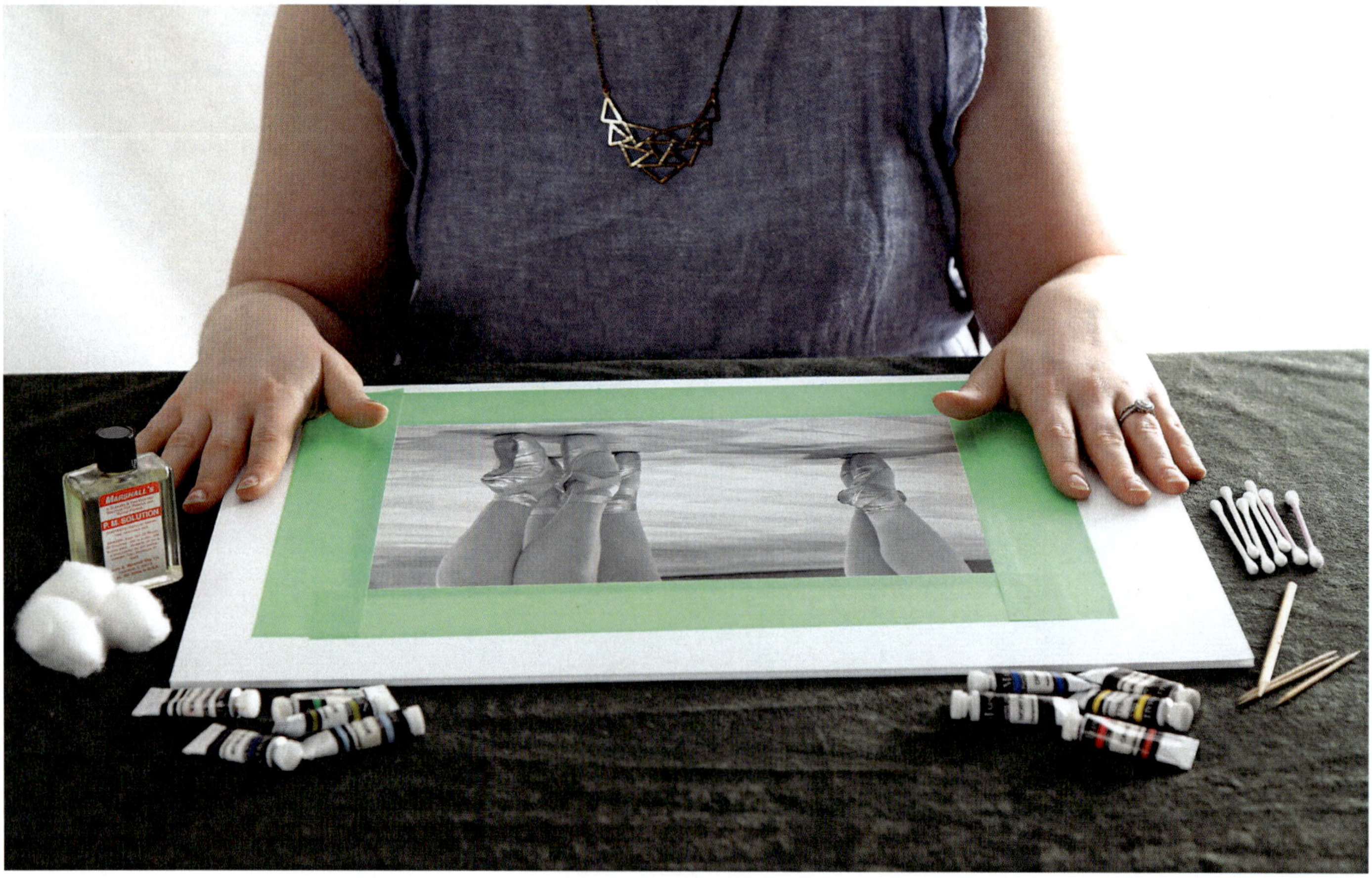

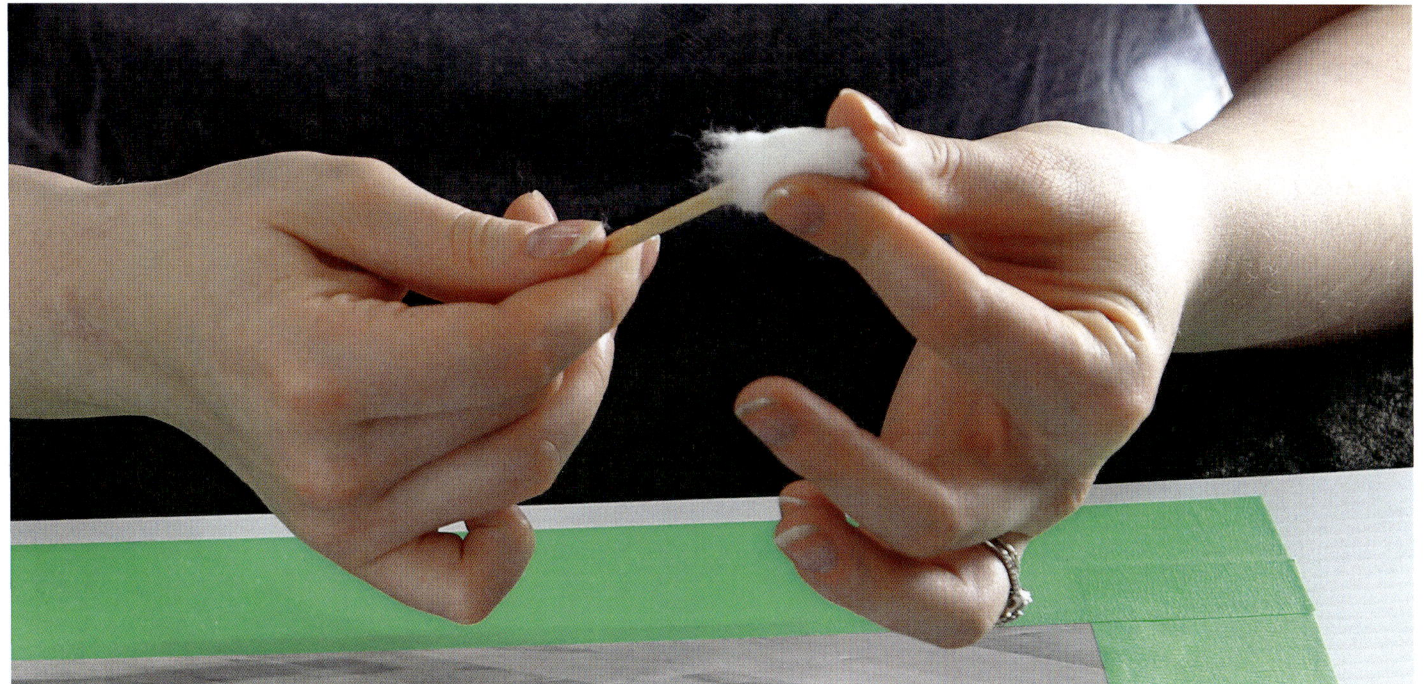

While you let your print dry, make yourself some skewers. Using a toothpick and a tiny amount of cotton, slightly moisten the tip of the toothpick (I dip mine in a small glass of water) and twirl the cotton around it to form a tiny, rounded cotton-tipped end, covering the point. It takes a little practice, but is easy.

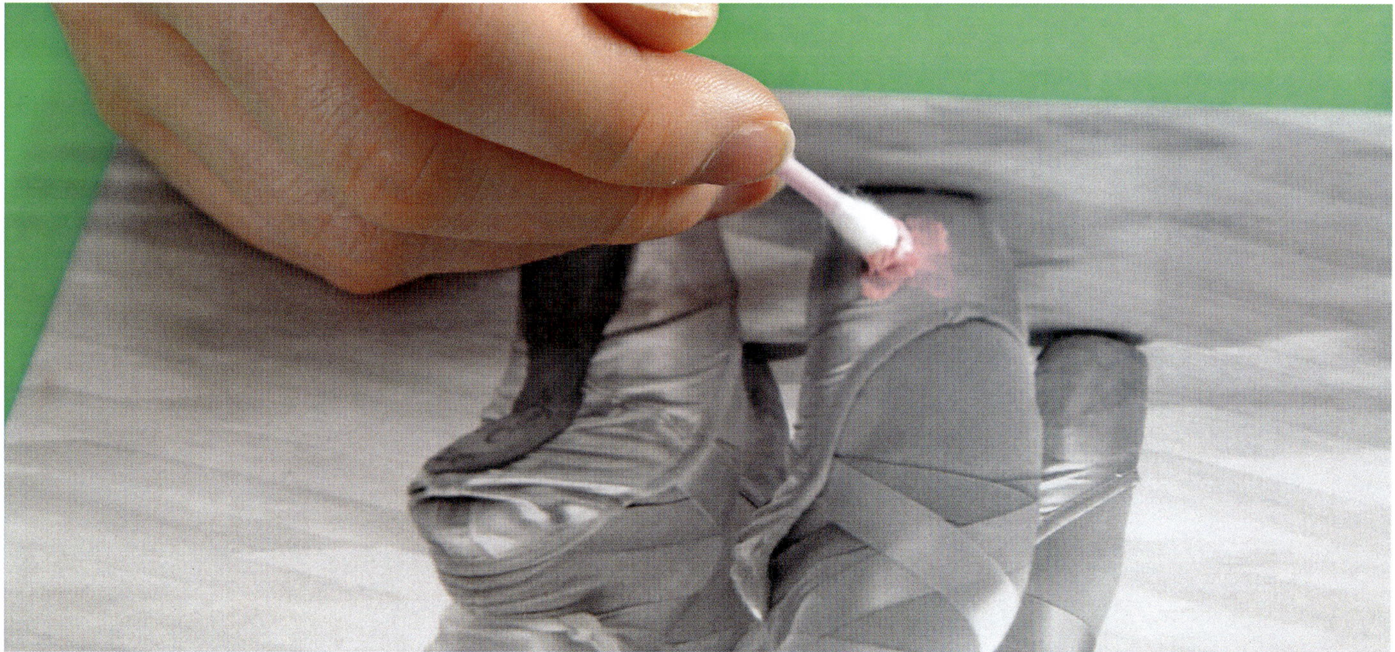

After wiping down the surface of the photograph, pick up a small amount of paint on a Q-tip and dab it onto the photograph. The photo oils go a long way so use very sparingly. You are going to "rough in" the colour in the general area you want to paint first. Using a new Q-tip gently spread the paint into the area you wish to colour.

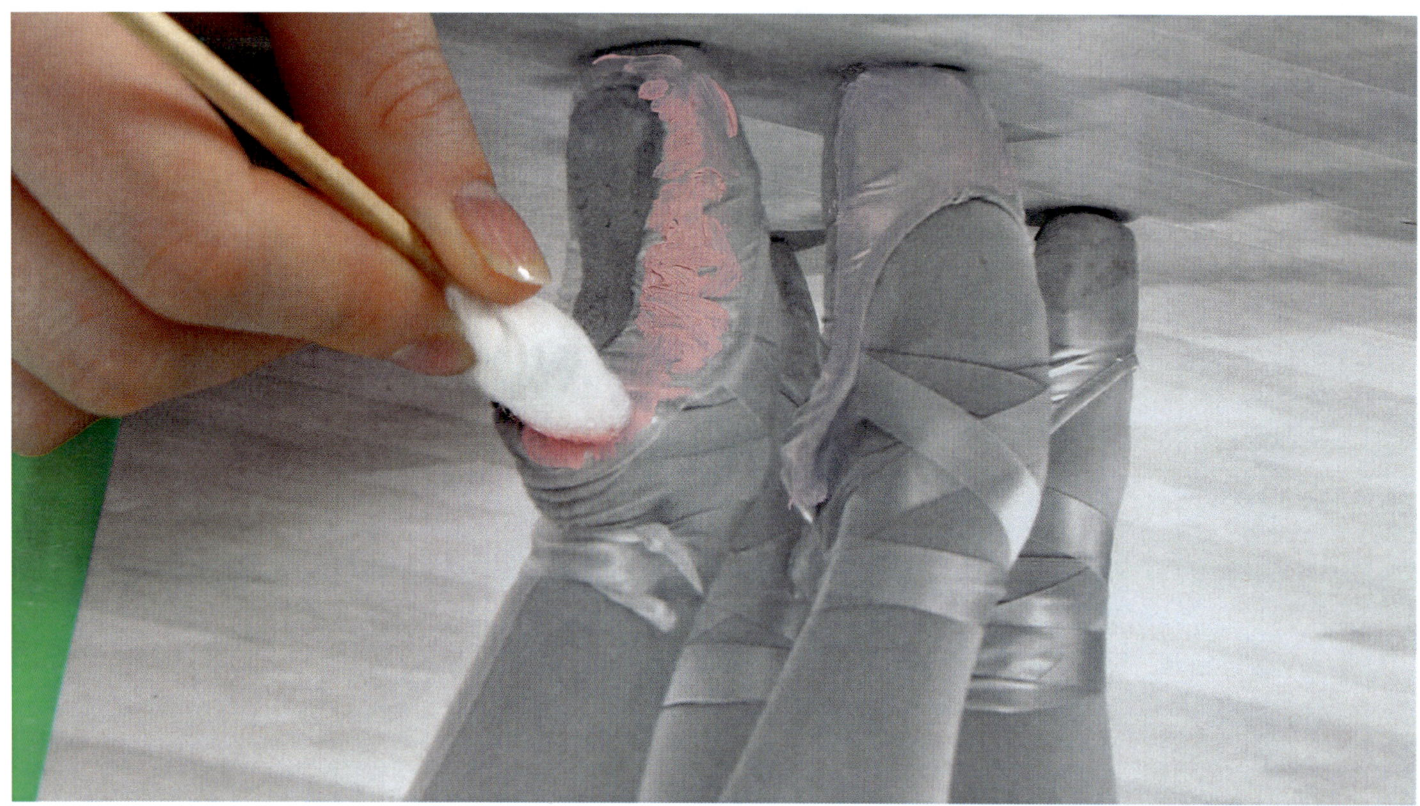

It can be a little intimidating to look at a perfectly good B&W print and think that you're going to improve it by hand colouring! The best way to get past those doubts is to dive right in. Go ahead – make your mistakes, hate what you've done and start all over – just keep plugging away until you suddenly see that you got it right, and it's exactly as you envisioned. Bear in mind that some prints will simply be easier to colour than others. So when starting out aim for photographs that contain large areas where you want to add colour rather than highly detailed images.

Repeat for each colour you want to apply. Take your time; this is not something you can rush or be sloppy with.

When it comes to fixing mistakes
a kneaded eraser will become your best friend.

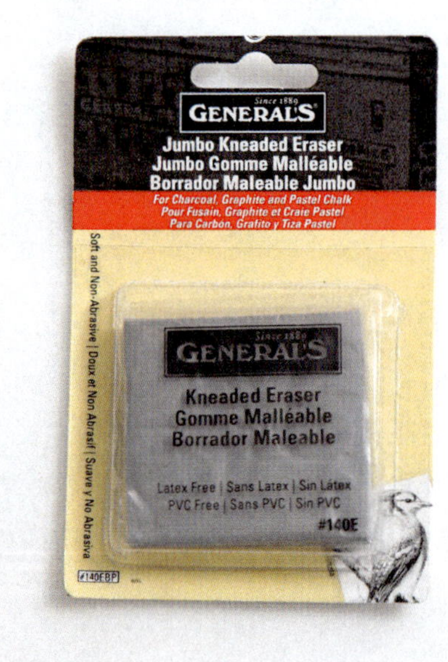

If you have over painted an area where you did not mean to, don't worry as it is easy to correct with the kneaded eraser. Simply knead the eraser to a point and touch the surface of the photograph to lift the paint. Wipe the tip of the eraser on a clean piece of paper and repeat as necessary.

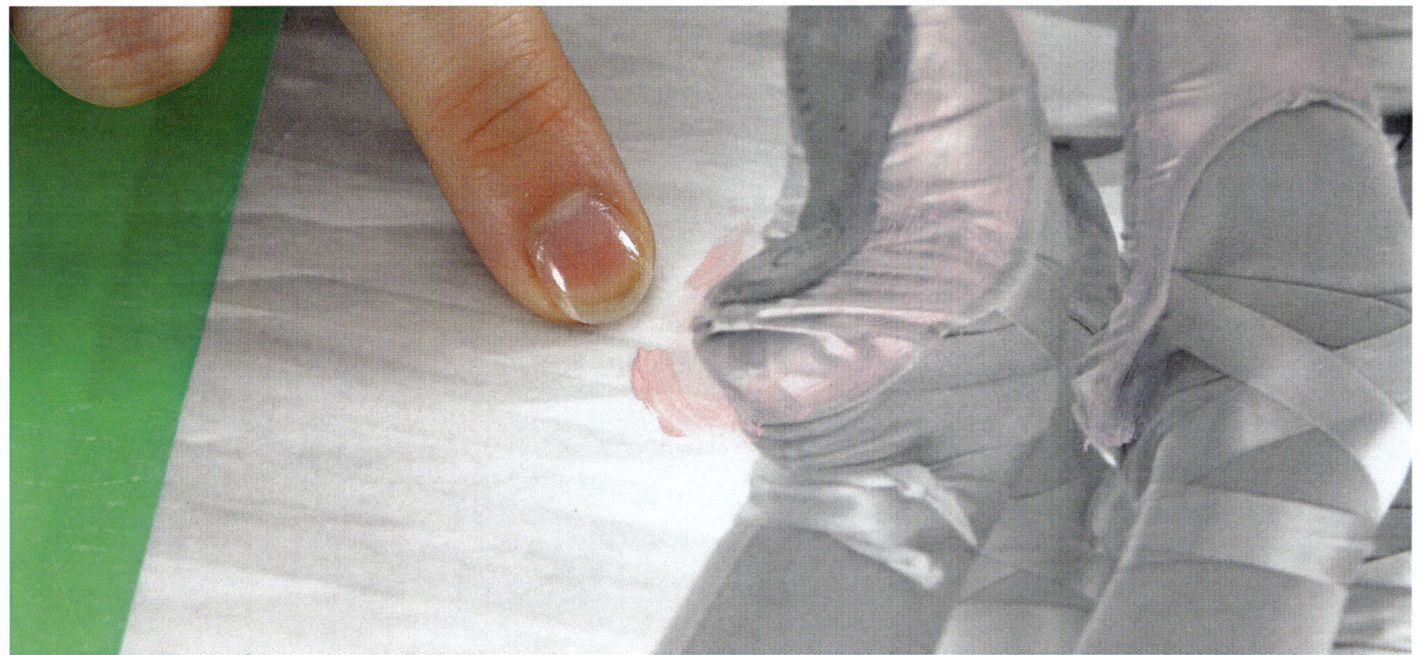

If the area is large you can add a little PM Solution to a Q-tip and completely wipe away the paint.

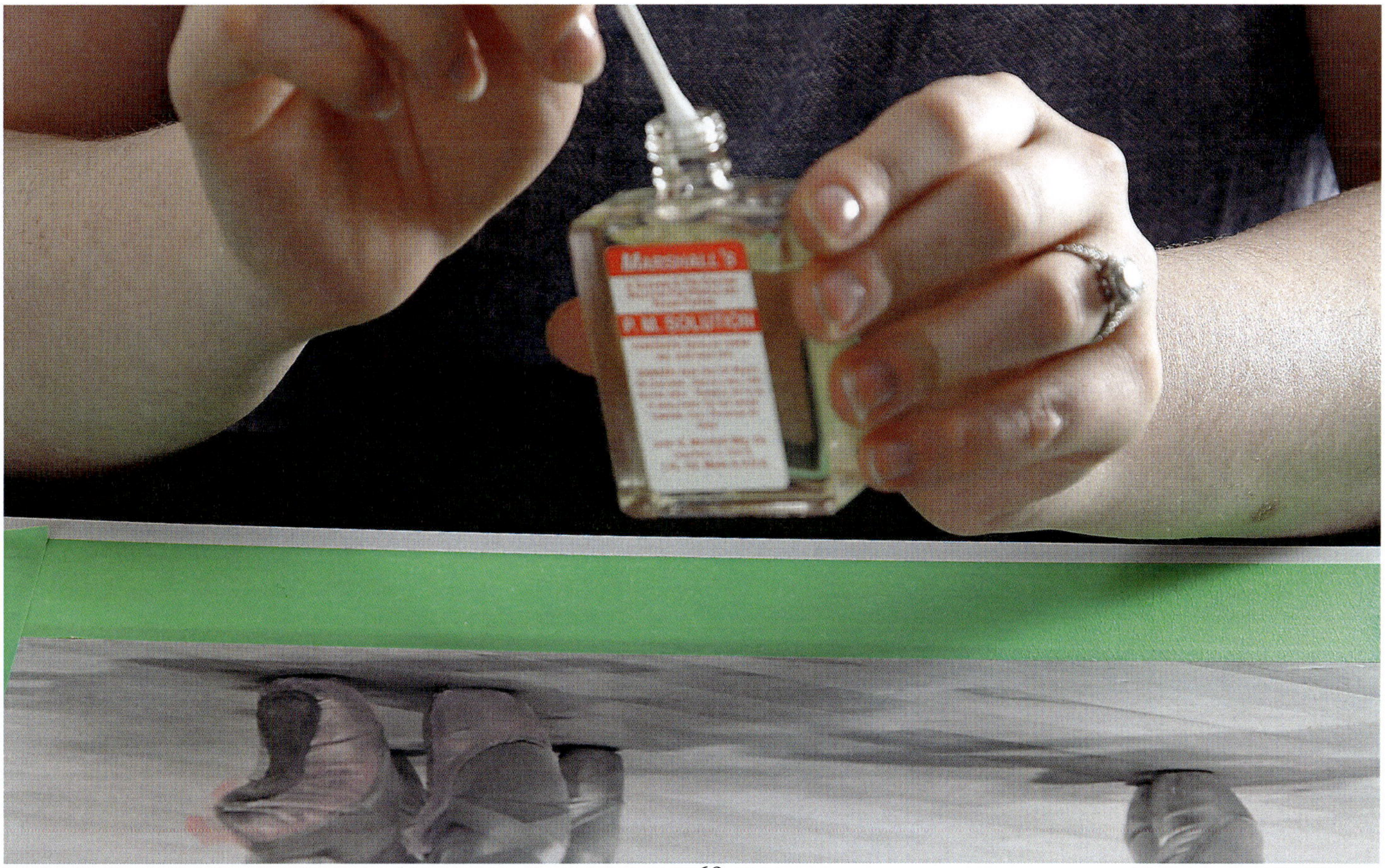

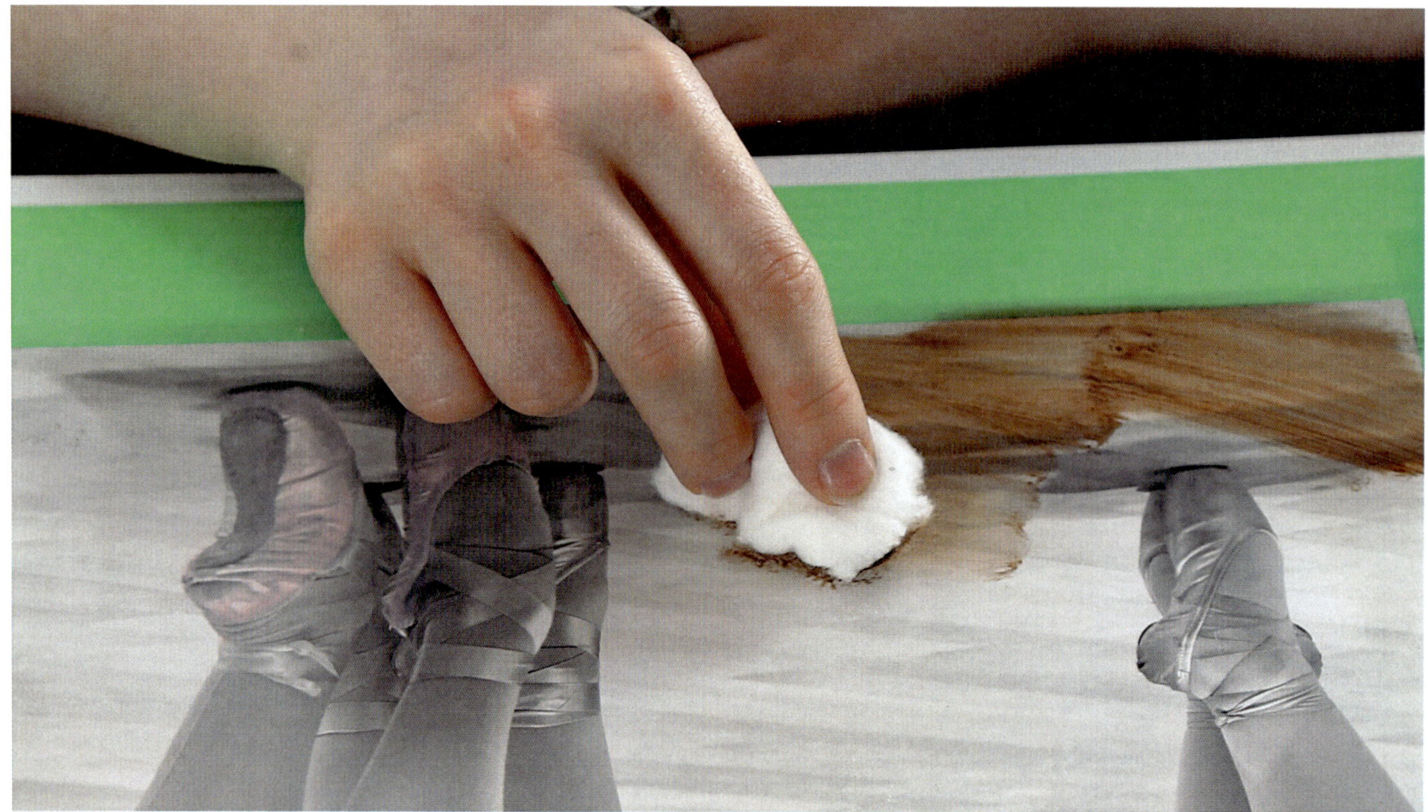

For larger areas on your photo that you wish to colour apply the oil paint with a cotton ball and gently spread the colour. Then take a Q-tip to refine the area you are colouring. Remember a little goes a long way.

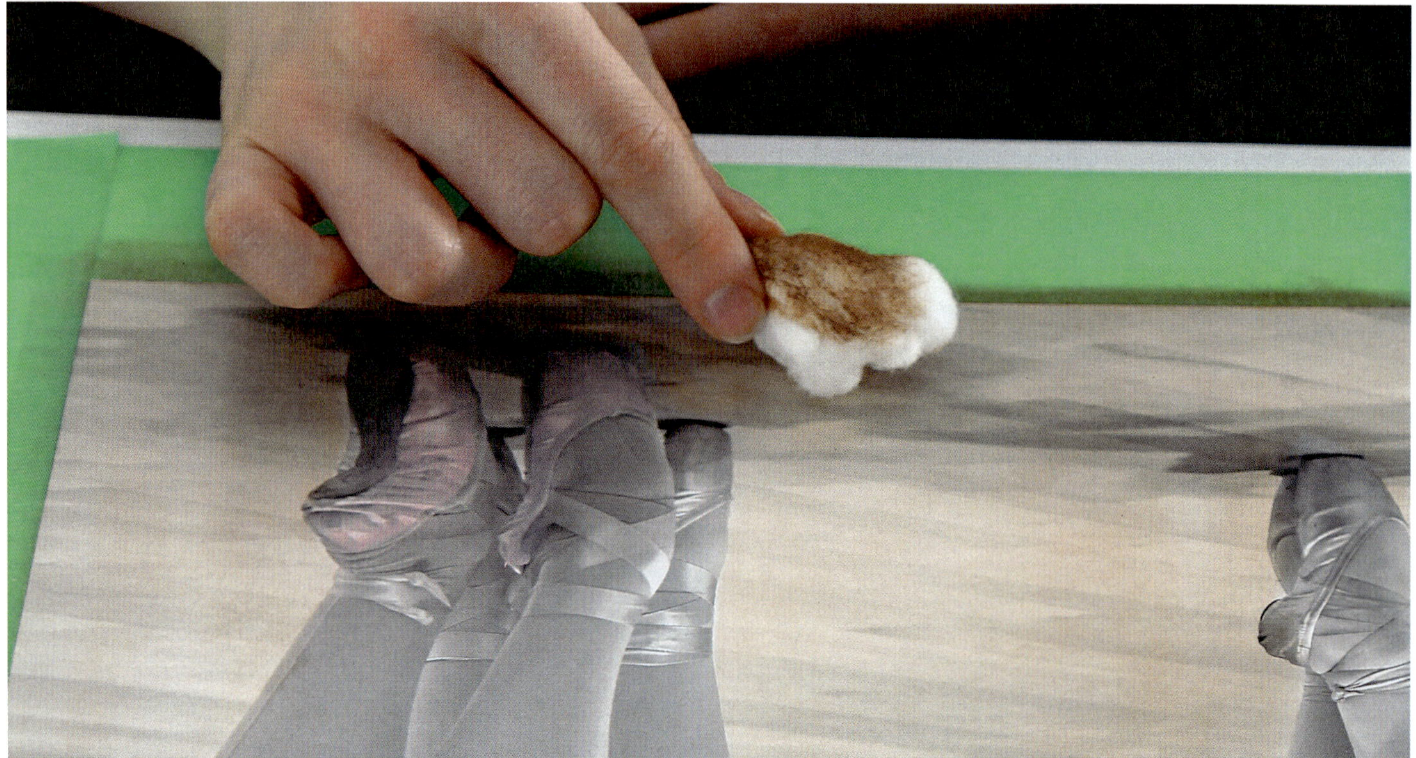

With this method your goal is to tint the photograph rather than paint it. So you will continue rubbing and blending with both cotton balls and Q-tips until you have a nice even colour. The translucent paint will allow the underlying photograph to show through.

Marshall's Oil Paints take a very long time to dry which allows you the luxury of time to blend and correct your work. It also means you need a safe place to store the painting while it dries to prevent it from getting damaged.

Your finished painting can take 3 - 5 days to dry depending on how much paint was applied.

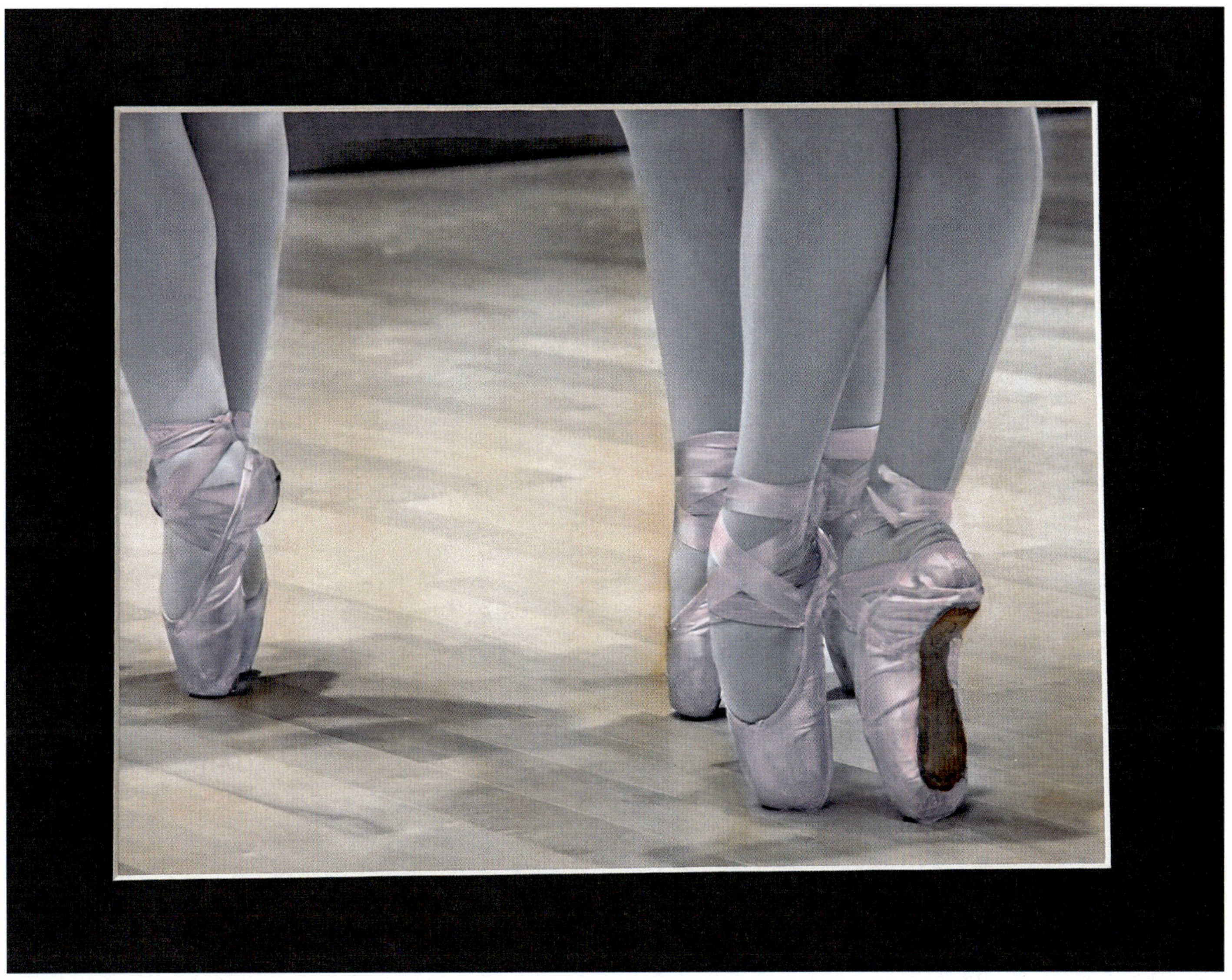

I do not pretend to be an expert in this area, and the ballerina photo was my first attempt at hand tinting a photograph using Marshall's Oil Paints and I am sure that you will render much better results.

Blending and removing the majority of paint applied to the photograph was a difficult concept to come to terms with. In all honesty, this method although it is the traditionally recognized method of hand tinting was my least favorite.

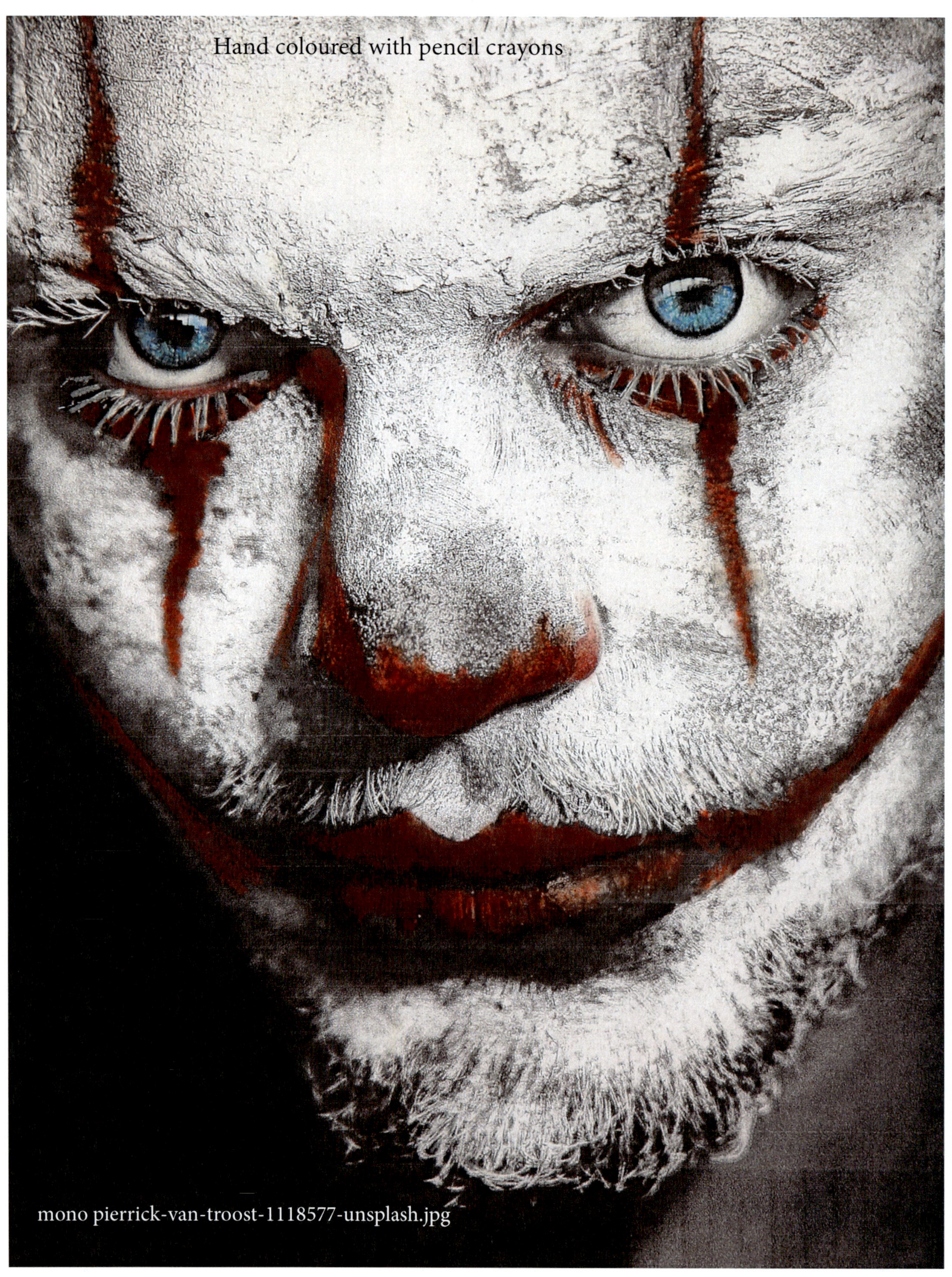

Hand coloured with pencil crayons

mono pierrick-van-troost-1118577-unsplash.jpg

Pencil crayons and coloured markers

What once was an activity designed to both entertain and encourage creativity in children, has re-surfaced as a growing trend in adult entertainment. Once adult colouring books were an obscure novelty, now they are everywhere. This adult trend also touts therapeutic elements. According to the American Art Therapy Association, the process of making and creating artwork is used to "explore feelings, reconcile emotional conflicts, foster self-awareness, manage behavior and addictions, develop social skills, improve reality orientation, reduce anxiety and increase self-esteem." So basically, it's similar to good old therapy.

Coloring also allows us to switch off our brains from other thoughts and focus only on the moment, helping to alleviate free-floating anxiety. It can be particularly effective for people who aren't comfortable with more creatively expressive forms of art such as dance or drama.

This medium is perfect for hand colouring photographs. I would like to suggest that hand colouring vacation photos would allow you to re-live that relaxing holiday experience. I am certainly no therapist, but holiday snaps would make a fabulous subject to colour.

Choosing the best pencils and markers

With this exploding trend there was also an explosion of choice at the art store. Whole aisles are devoted to coloured pencils and markers which makes selecting the right brand extremely difficult.

For this particular application it is important to select a pencil crayon that has a soft lead and will not scratch the surface of the photograph. The crayons used in this book are Prismacolor Premier. They are artist quality coloured pencils with a rich colour saturation.

But more importantly they have soft thick cores which make them ideal for blending and perfect for our purpose.

They were not the cheapest coloured pencils on the shelf but certainly not the most expensive and they are packaged in nice metal tins which helps to protect them when not in use.

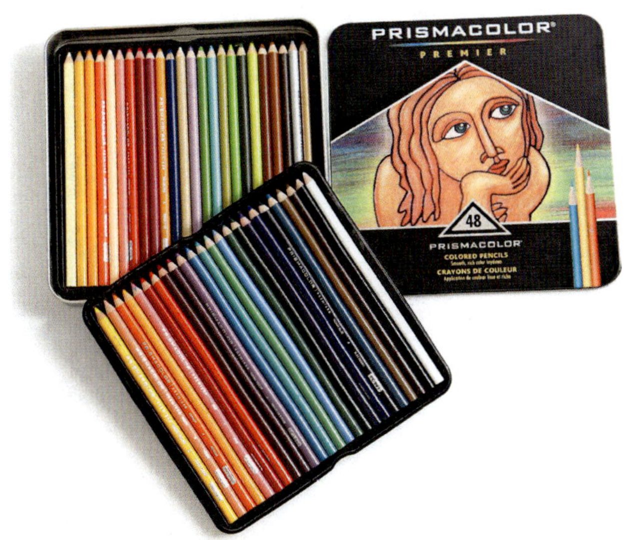

Choosing coloured markers can be just as overwhelming so let's break it down into two main types of markers, alcohol markers or water-based markers.

Alcohol markers are typically permanent. These markers are made of ink as the main solvent, a resin, glyceride, pyrrolidone and a colourant that actually makes it resistant to water. They are fast drying and smudge proof but their most redeeming quality is, they will adhere to pretty much any surface but once laid down are almost impossible to remove.

Water-based markers, unlike alcohol markers, use water or a combination of water and glycerine to carry the pigments. They take longer to dry than the alcohol versions which means they can be blended. They do not produce permanent ink which can also be seen as a plus especially if you accidentally get it on items where it is not wanted.

The real benefit to watercolour markers for our particular purpose is that you can treat them in much the same way as watercolour pencils and using a paintbrush and water dilute and spread the pigment to create a translucent colour wash.

A word of caution when blending colours, if you apply layers of colour one after another this can result in the paper piling up and tearing as water saturates it.

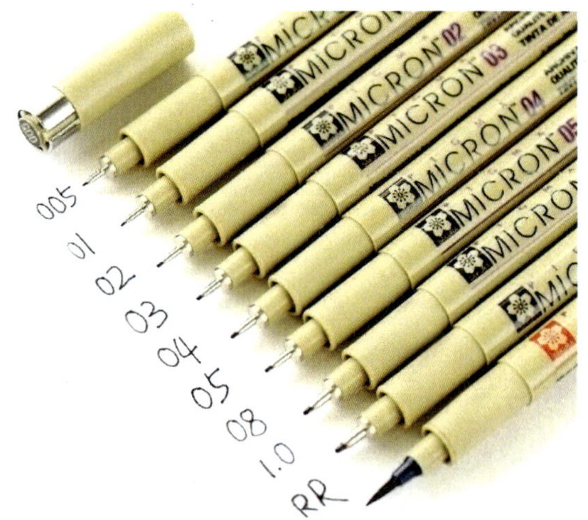

As for which brand or tip size is best for you - I am really sorry to say that I have not tried and tested them all. To be perfectly honest I bought an inexpensive selection of each type of marker from the craft store to experiment with and combined those markers with what I already had on hand.

I did invest in a set of Sakuro Pigma Micron fine tipped markers, with archival ink which were fabulous for enhancing fine black lines. I would highly recommend these markers as a valuable addition to your art supplies.

Perhaps this method of hand colouring photographs should have been at the very front of the book because of the relaxing non-threatening qualities of using coloured pencils. Or perhaps we saved the best for last?

This brings us to the question of what types of paper are suitable for use with coloured pencils and markers. The good news is that pretty much all of them, including traditional photographic prints for the photo lab (matte not glossy) are suitable.

Not all papers will react the same way especially if you want to blend the colours with either water or the PM Solution mentioned in the previous chapter. So we will take a look at the pros and cons for each paper choice when using coloured pencils and markers.

This image of a vintage car was printed on matte paper at the photo lab which means it has a non-porous surface with just a slight amount of tooth for crayon adherance.

The image has large areas to colour making it a good image with which to learn this technique.

However to achieve a realistic effect it will be necessary to blend and smooth the colours.

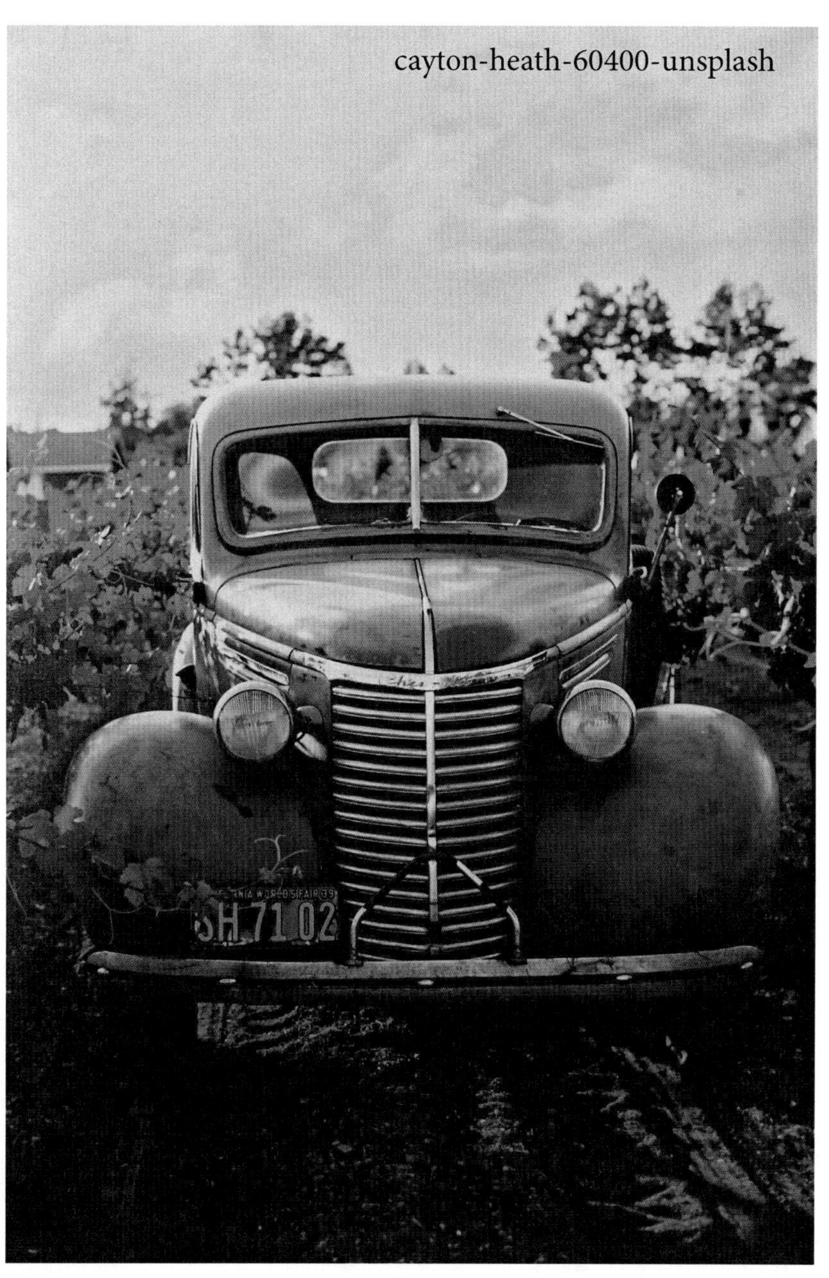

cayton-heath-60400-unsplash

As always the print was taped to a foam core board to prevent it from slipping.

Using a “light cerulean blue” pencil and light storkes I added some colour to the sky.

Next I took a “pink” pencil, again using light strokes, added a touch of warmth to the sky area.

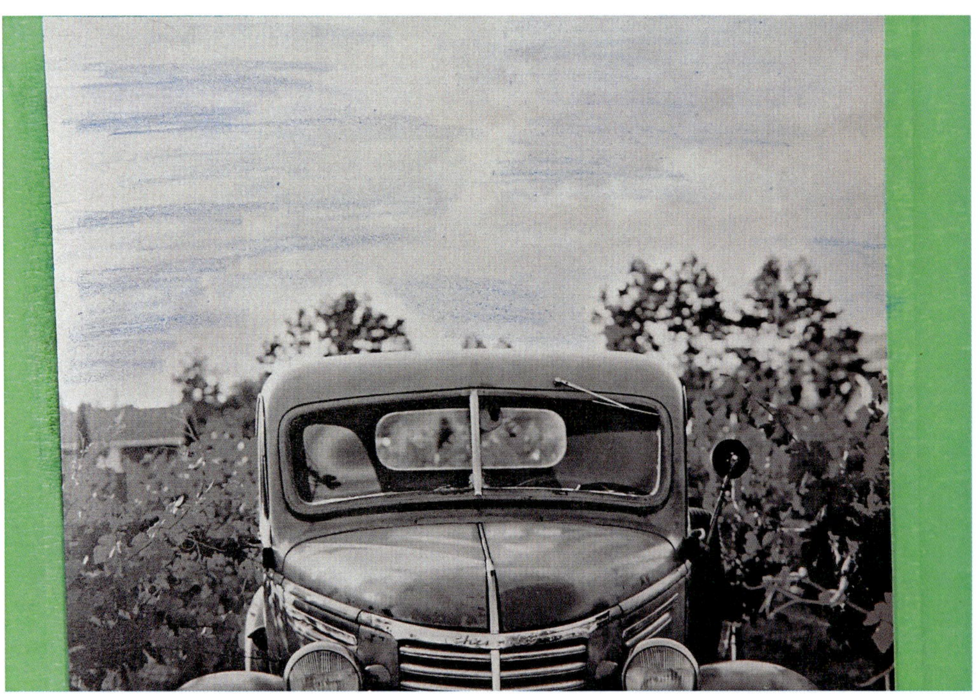

At this stage it looks terrible but the magic happens when you smooth and blend the colours. To achieve this, take a cotton ball and add a small amount of the PM Solution. If you don’t have any don’t worry as baby oil will also soften the pigment and allow you to gently blend your colours.

Note: The PM Solution and baby oil will also remove any unwanted pigment so go lightly or you will have to start over. A little goes a long way.

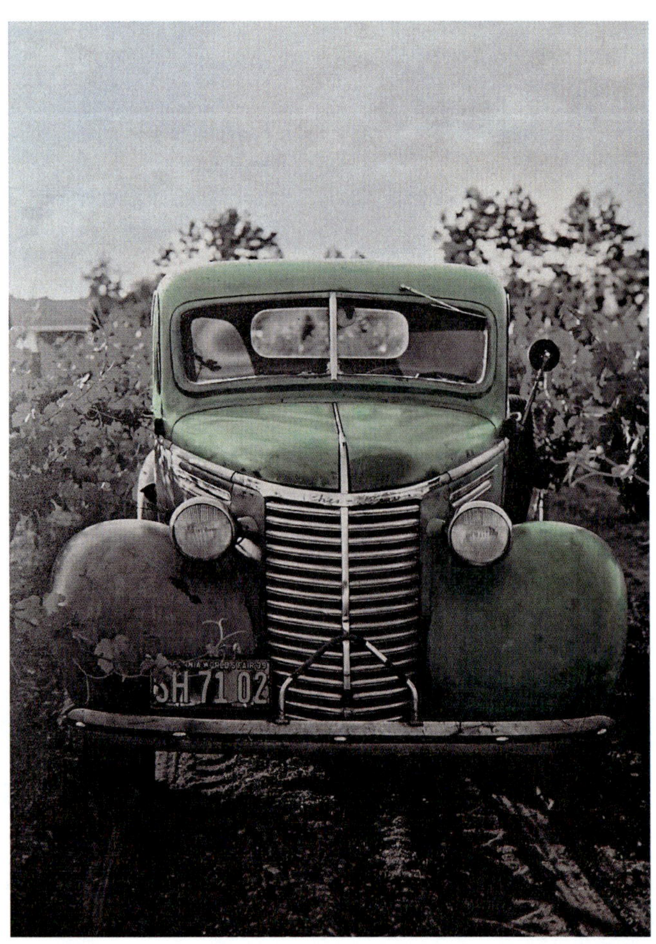

The body of the car was coloured with “grass green” and using the same technique the pencil marks were smoothed and blended away with the PM Solution.

Note: Be sure to use a clean cotton ball for each colour you are blending to avoid transfer and colour contamination.

This was obviously an old car and not in perfect condition and so I felt a little rust colour may be appropriate and for that I used the “yellow orange” pencil.

The touch of red in the bottom right tire track was to balance and reflect the pink in the sky.

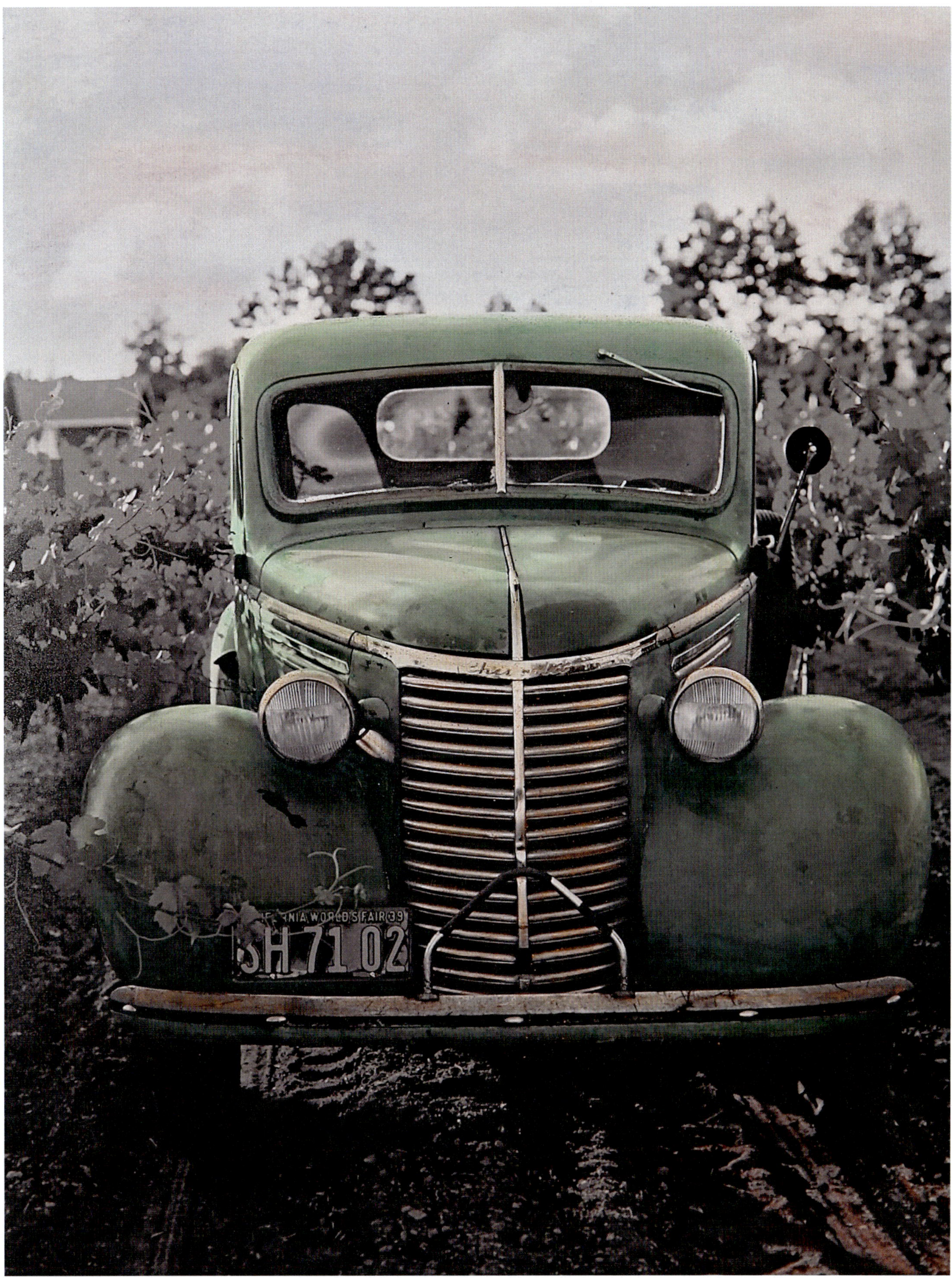
WORLD'S FAIR 39
3H 71 02

Note: When blending smaller areas within your picture add a little PM Solution to a Q-tip or for even finer more delicate areas make your own blending tool by wrapping some cotton around a skewer. Details of how to do that were in the previous chapter.

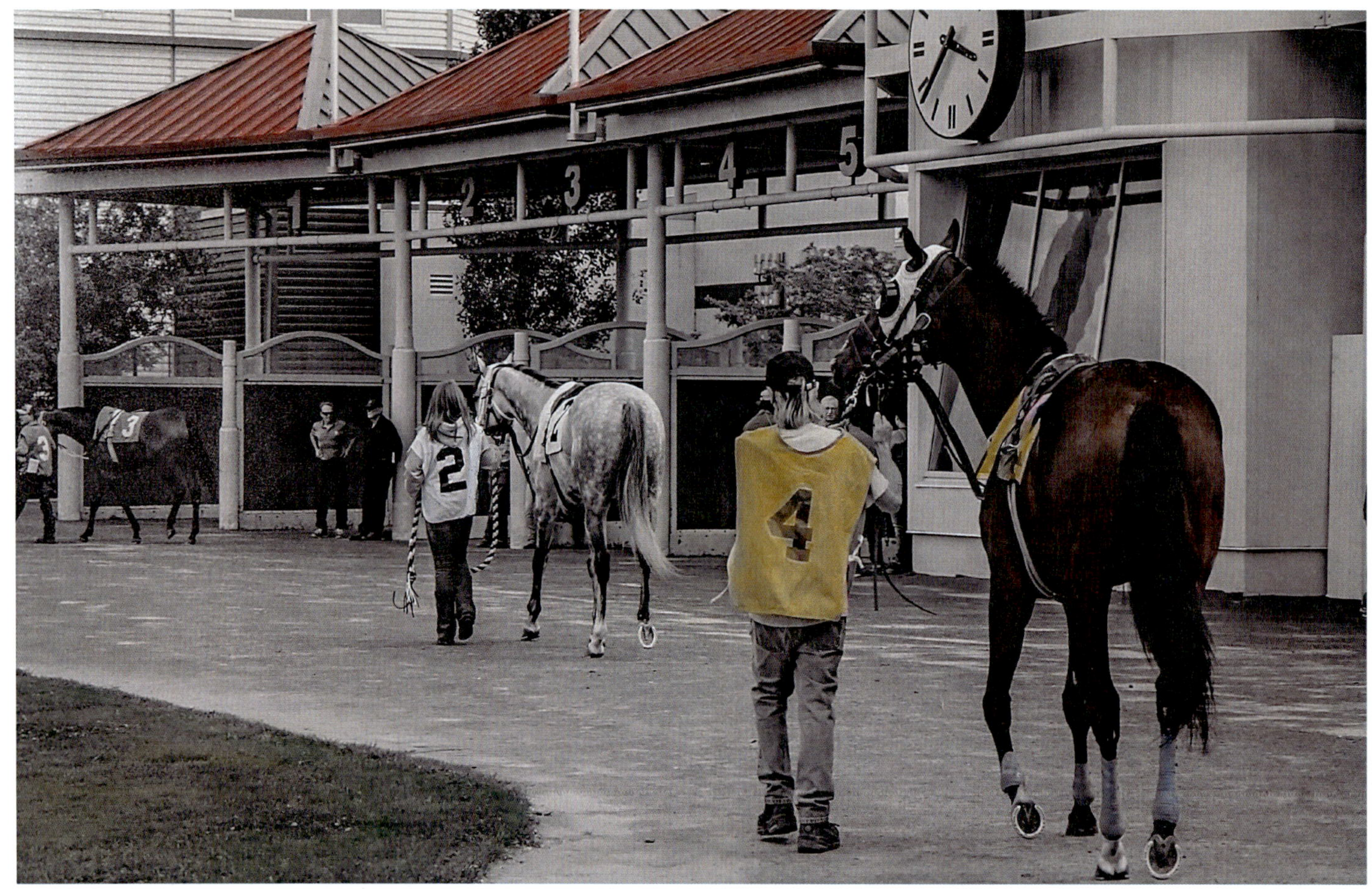

Racehorses in the paddock printed on matte photo paper.

You will notice I chose not colour the entire photograph. This is just my personal preference. I find the combination of both colour and black and white visually stimulating, but there is no right or wrong way. Feel free to enhance your photographs in any way that pleases you.

Just for fun I printed off some photographs and took them to my friend's day care centre. We invited the children to colour and blend the photographs. They had a blast with this little art project and I think they did a pretty nice job of the seagulls and wagons on the opposite page.

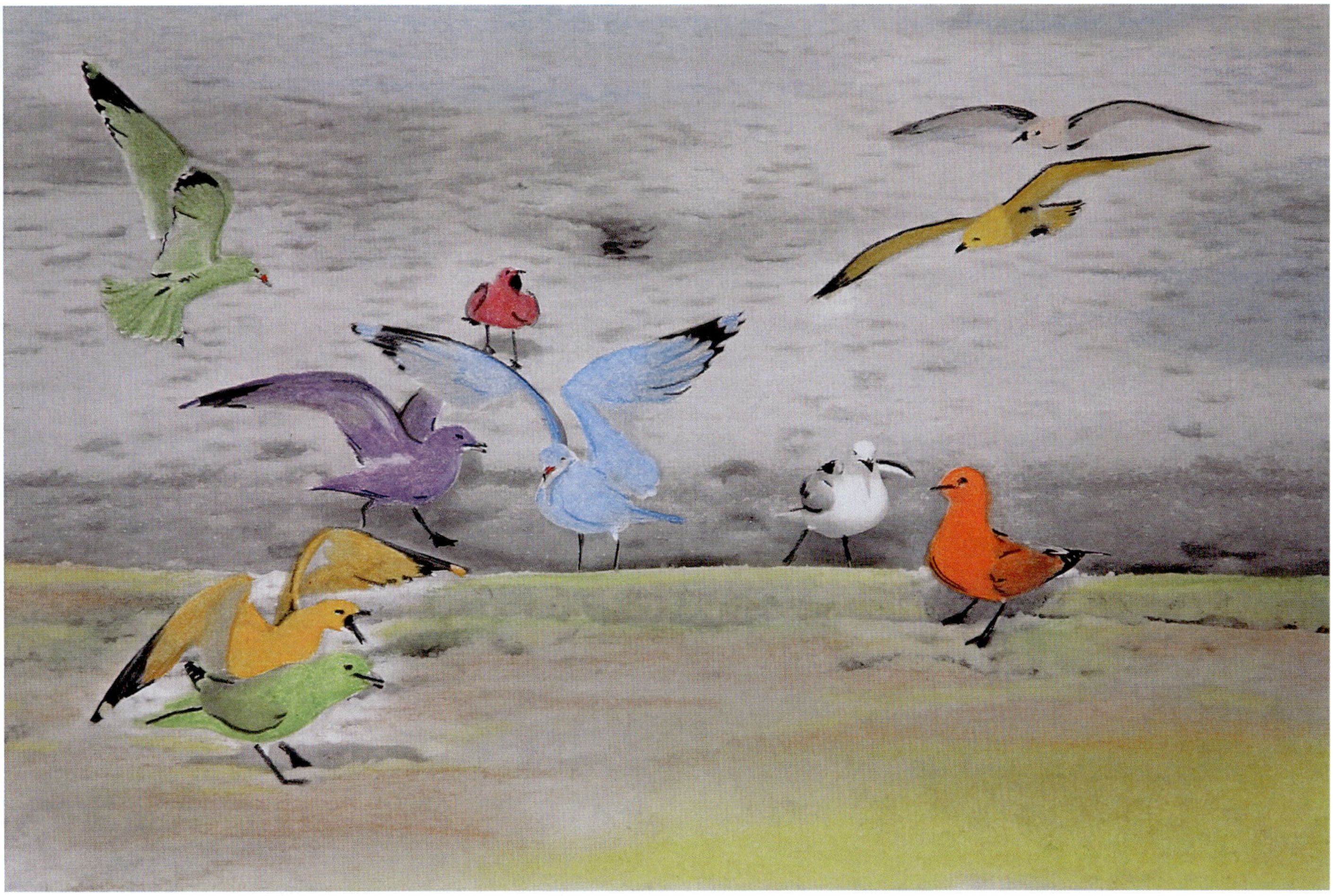

This photograph of seagulls was printed on regular card stock.
Wagons printed on mixed media paper.

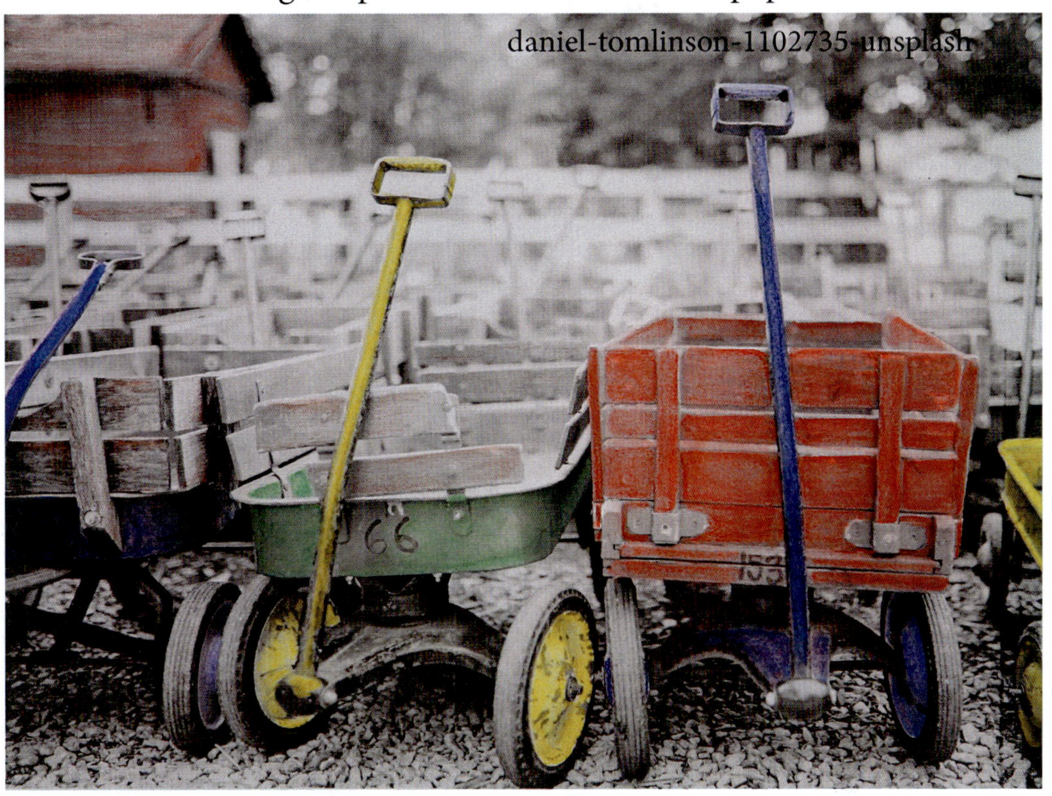

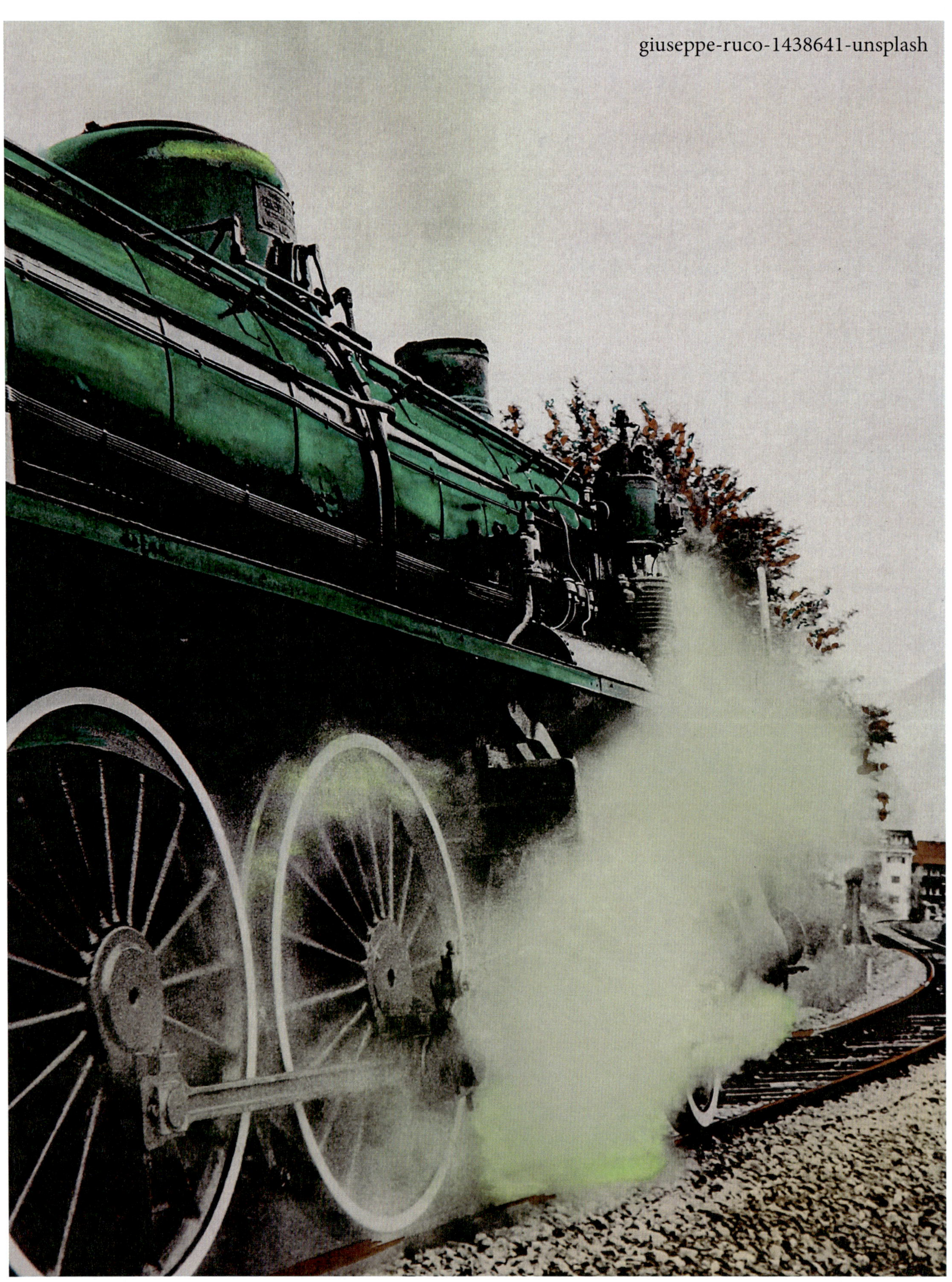

giuseppe-ruco-1438641-unsplash

Now let's look at how we can incorporate felt pens into the hand colouring process.

The vibrant, opaque quality of felt pens are especially useful when colouring dark objects like the train on opposite page. Most of the other mediums we have explored so far would not have covered this dark image and certainly not have appeared so vibrant.

This image was coloured with a mixture of alcohol based pens and also water soluable pens. I am sure you can figure out which pens created which effect.

That's right! The body of the train was coloured with the alcohol pens and the pale green steam was created by using water-soluable pens.

With this technique it is very important to work fast.

As always tape down your print - this is doubly important when you are going to be adding water to prevent the paper from warping and buckling.

Next, assemble everything you will need:
marker pens, clean water, paint brush, paper towel and a cup of tea (tea is optional).

Start by colouring the darker area of the image with permanent alcohol-based markers.

Next lightly dampen the area you want to colour with water-based markers. Starting at the bottom of the image (where you want the colour to most intense) lighly colour with a pale green marker. You will notice the pigment reacting very much like watercolour paint as it touches the damp paper and blooms outwards. Continue by alternating between adding more water to the paper and adding colour from the marker until you have the effect you like. **Warning:** If you wet the paper too much you may damage the page when using the marker on it. This is a fine balancing act - so I suggest you print several copies of the image to allow

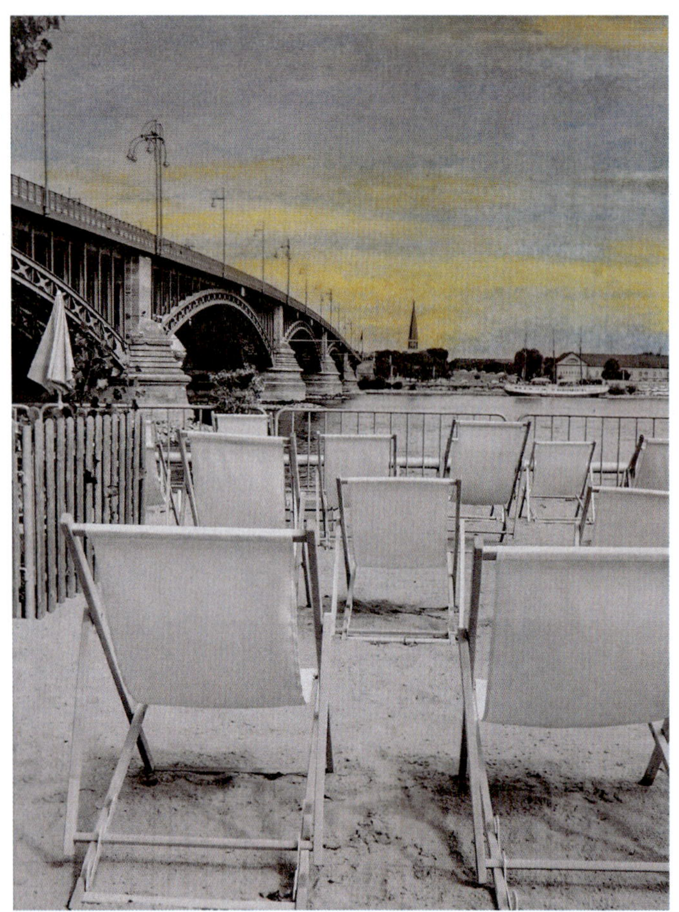

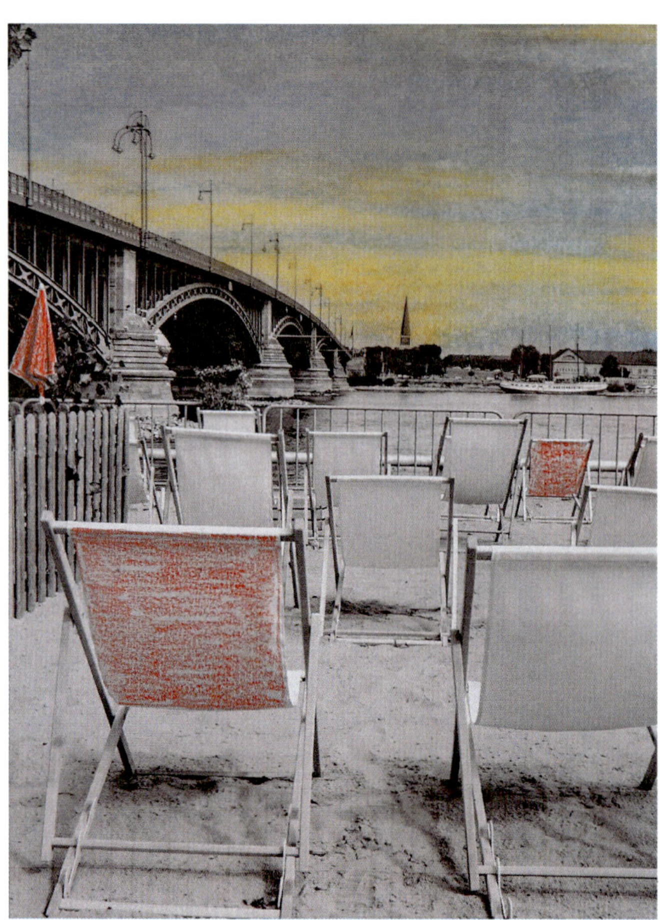

Some images call for a mixture of both coloured pencil and markers.

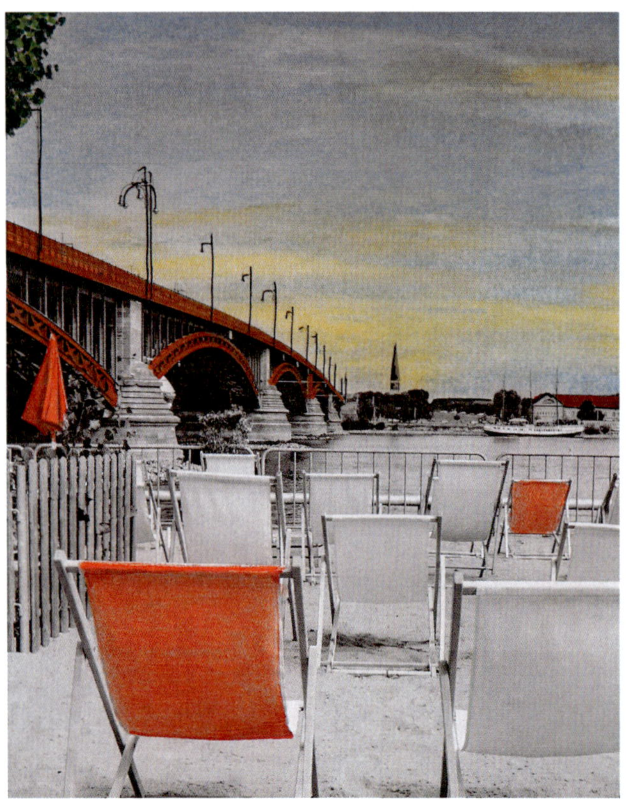

Details, such as the lamp posts and distant ship were enhanced using fine tipped alcohol-based markers.

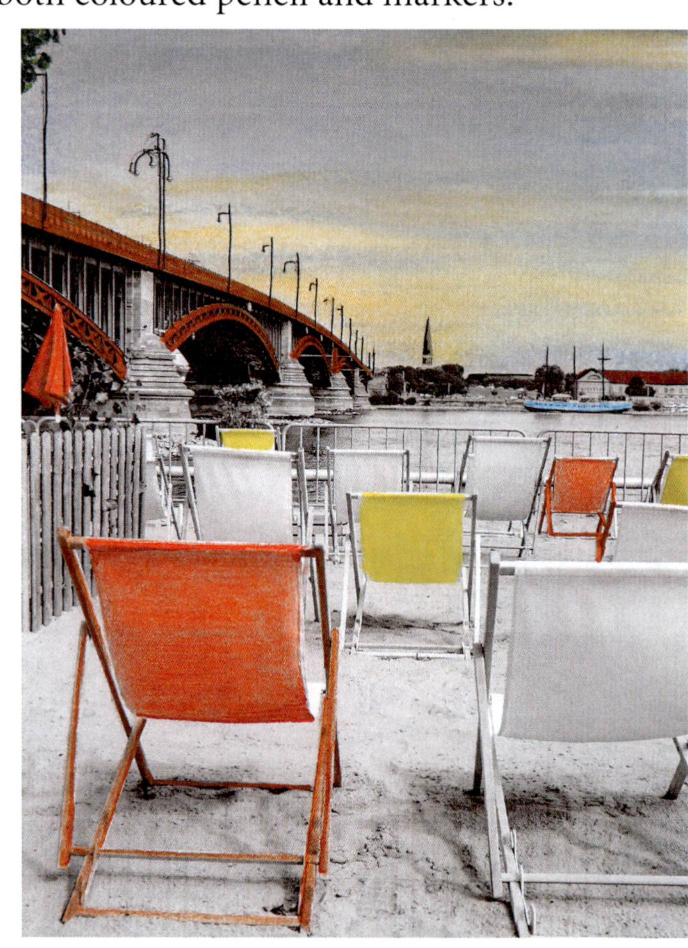

Congratulations

You made it this far - I hope you have enjoyed exploring different ways to hand colour, tint and paint potographs. Before we move onto the guest artist chapter, I wanted to share **five ways creating art is good for you even if you are bad at it.**

1. Making art may reduce stress and anxiety.
In one recent study in the journal, Art Therapy, researchers found that after just 45 minutes of art-making, levels of the hormone cortisol — which is associated with stress were reduced regardless of the person's artistic ability.

2. Creating visual art improves connections in the brain.
Art's benefits have been observed at a neural level, too. One 2014 study published in the journal, Plos One, found that making visual art can improve connections throughout the brain known as the default mode network.
This system is associated with the brain's state during wakeful rest, like daydreaming, but it's also active when we're focusing on internal thoughts or future plans.

3. Mindless doodling and sketching can help us focus.
Cognitive benefits don't come only from purposeful, serious art. Oddly enough, doodling can help us pay better attention when we're listening to something boring and remember it later. It helps us focus and keeps our minds from wandering.
One study published in Applied Cognitive Psychology found that, when aided by doodling, participants were able to recall 29% more information on a surprise memory test than those armed only with their determination.

4. Making art can help you achieve "flow".
The psychologist Mihaly Csikszentmihalyi defined "flow" as being "in the zone," totally absorbed by and enjoying the task at hand. "A good life," he has argued, is one in which this state is not so elusive. While flow can come from all kinds of activities, art is one of the classic flow experiences, where the art-maker is not motivated by some end goal, but is fully engaged in the process itself.

5. Making art can help us get over sadness.
There are many health benefits of creativity including: inspires self-expression, promotes relaxation, improves social functioning, increases focus and concentration, enhances self-worth, acts as a type of meditation, helps people focus on positive life experiences, decreases physical and emotional distress, and most importantly, in this case, lowers feelings of depression.
Researchers found that distracting yourself by making unrelated art was far more effective than either venting your feelings through art or just sitting in your sadness.

Guest artist gallery

Trixi Fredrick

Robyn Kern

Marjorie Shannon-Graham

Bev Schakel

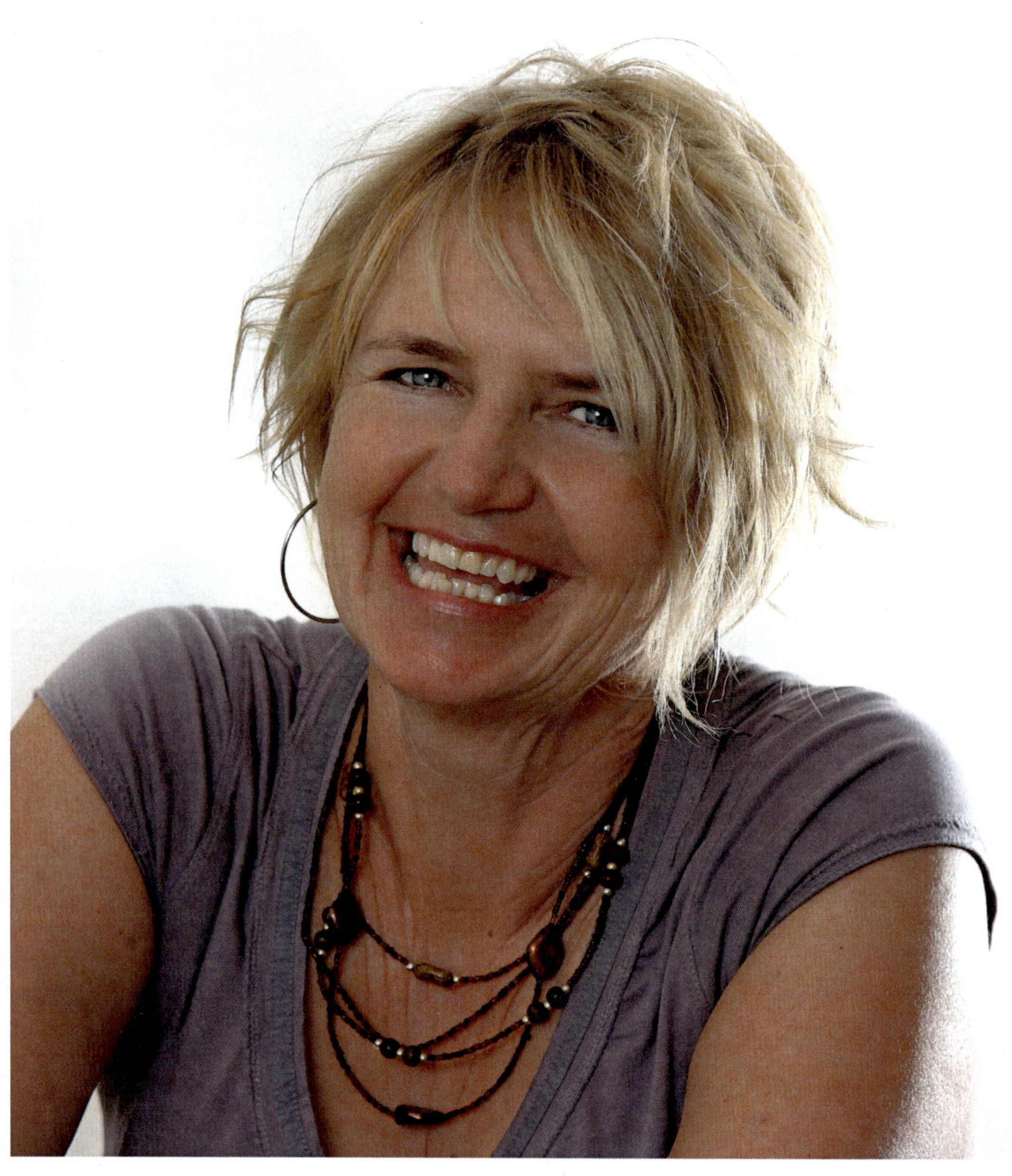

Trixi Fredrick

I came by my love of art honestly as my father designed and built with bricks and mortar, and my mother allowed her creativity to shine through as a hair stylist. As a child growing up I loved to draw, sketch, and build things. My teachers would tell me that architecture was my future. However life took me in many different directions.

It wasn't until I left a job in finance that art came back into my life. I started creating for myself and others using acrylic paints and any medium I had on hand, from coffee grounds to drywall compound and my subject would vary depending on my mood. Lots of different things inspire me so I like to mix it up and not just paint the same theme all the time.

Painted with Marshall's Photo Oils - applied with a brush and not rubbed down.

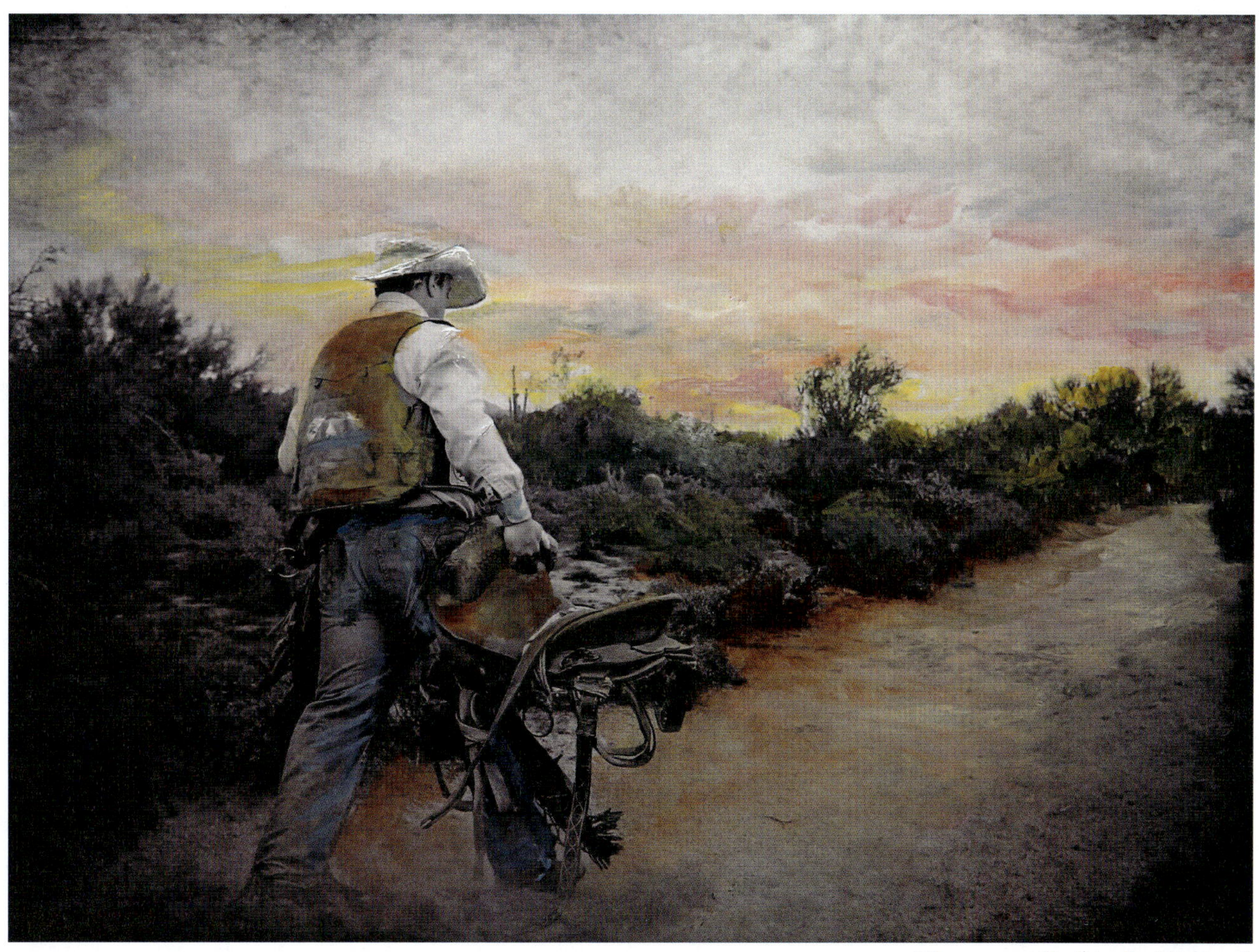

Photo credit Linda Finstad

Unlike most artists who enjoy the peace and quite of a studio I prefer to create with others, so I started an art business called JustaBrush Creations. I offer small private paint night events which allow me to help people along with their paintings. I find enjoyment in watching people create the outcome doesn't have to be great, just enjoyable.
Not only do I have a wonderful husband and three equally wonderful daughters, all who have amazing artistic abilities. I feel truly blessed that I am able to spend my time making art and inspiring others.

My business e-mail is trixi.create@gmail.com
You can also find JustaBrush Creations on Facebook

Tinted using pan pastels.

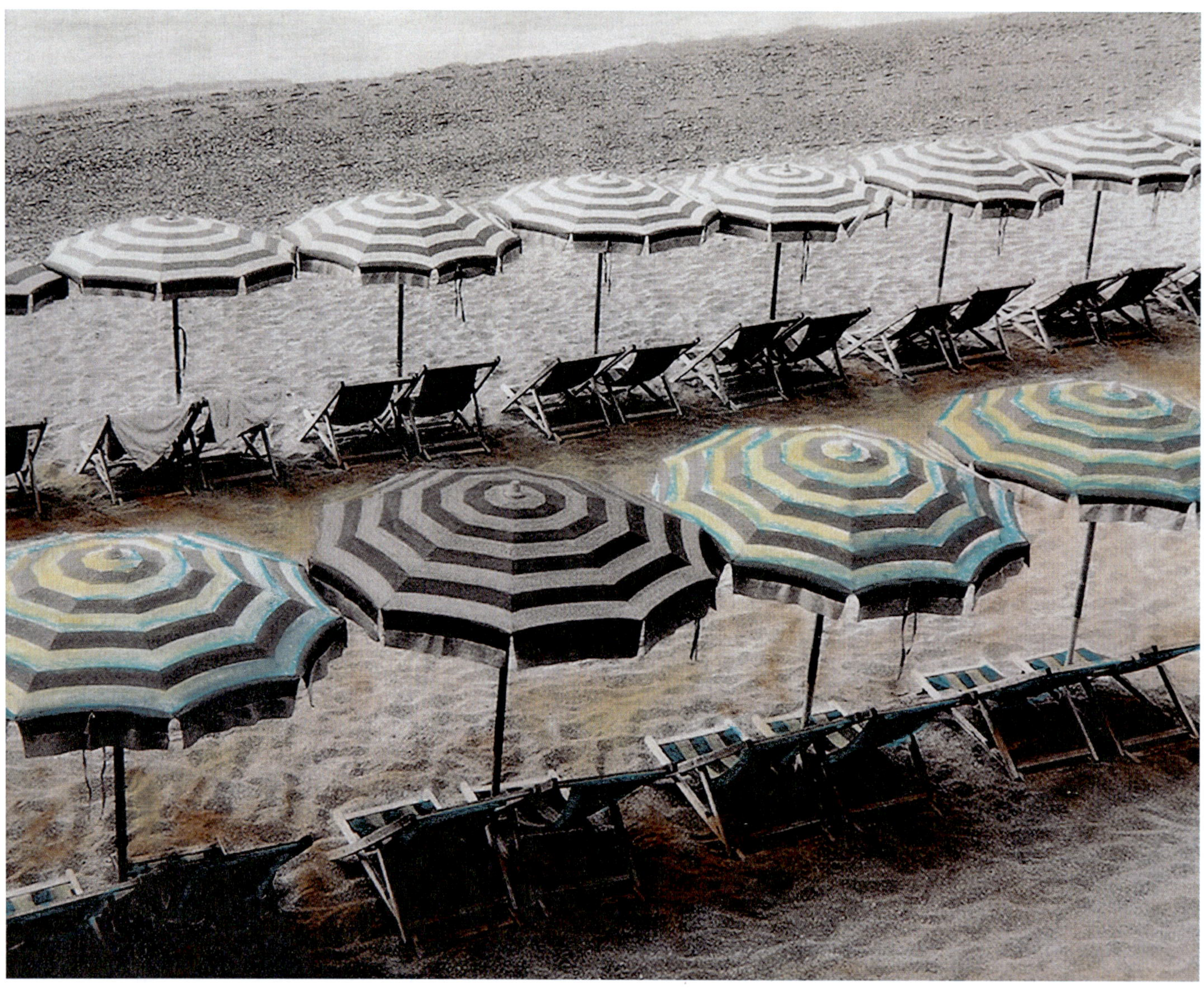

Is painting on photographs art?
Many artists sketch out their work first, so is it much different to use your own photograph as the base image. With new technologies comes new forms of art. I think it's a good thing, we all have a variety of tastes. Some might say "You just coloured a photo, anybody could do that, how is this any different from colouring books?"

People who don't know art don't see beyond what's right in front of them.
Notice the choice in colours, the shading, the story I'm trying to tell, especially with the cowboy on the previous page going from black and white to colour and back again, how the work boots and chicken feel like they're coming off the page.

But as always art is subjective and in the eye of the beholder.

Enhanced using pan pastels and pencil crayons.

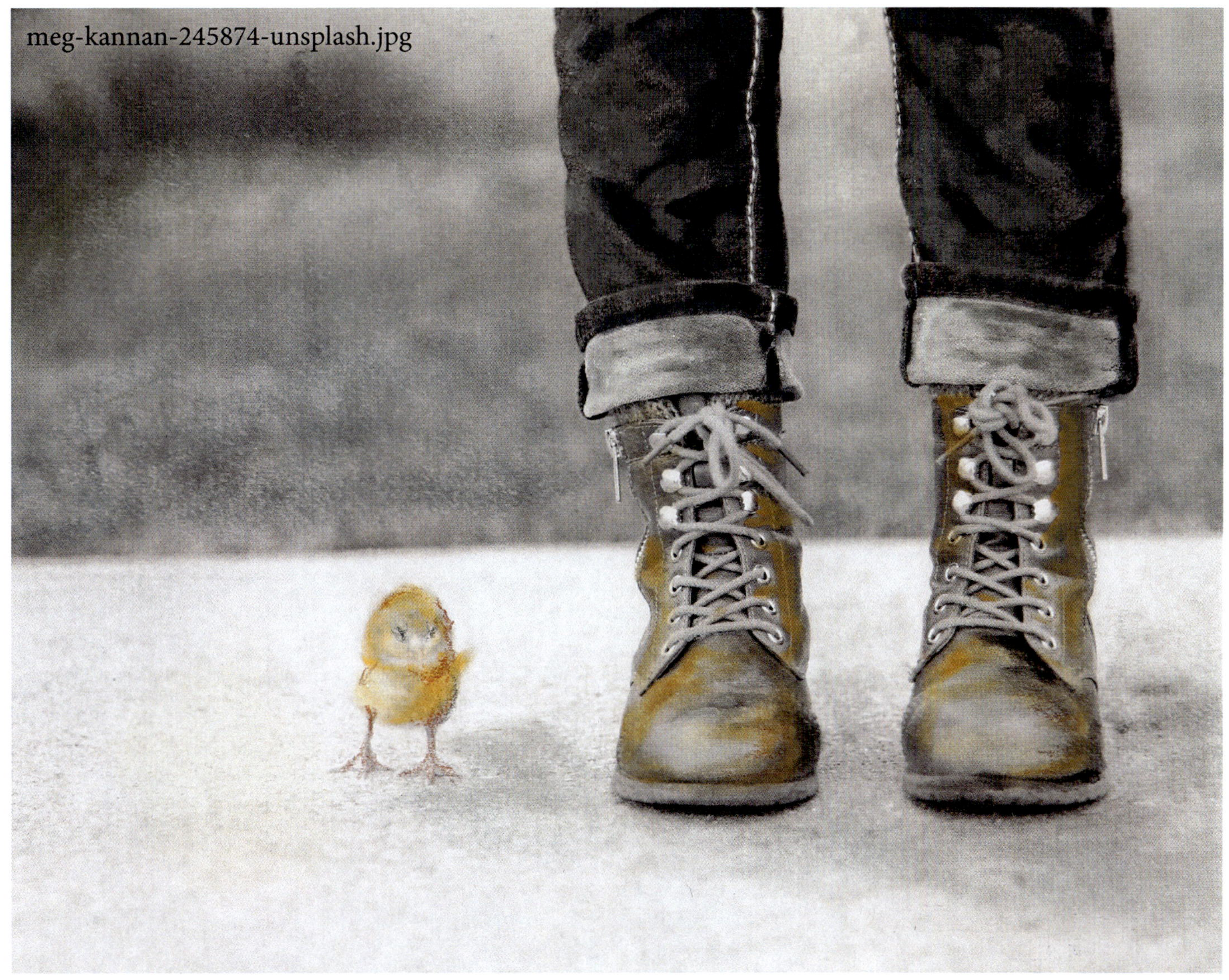
meg-kannan-245874-unsplash.jpg

Was the process relaxing or stressful?
I really enjoyed the process it made a pleasant change from how I typically work.

What medium did you enjoy the most?
I tried a few different medium and mixed them up using both coloured pencils , pastels and oil paints in the same image.

Who do you think this type of art would be suitable for?
Colouring photographs would be suitable for anyone - the complexity of the finished result is only limited to the person's ability and imagination.

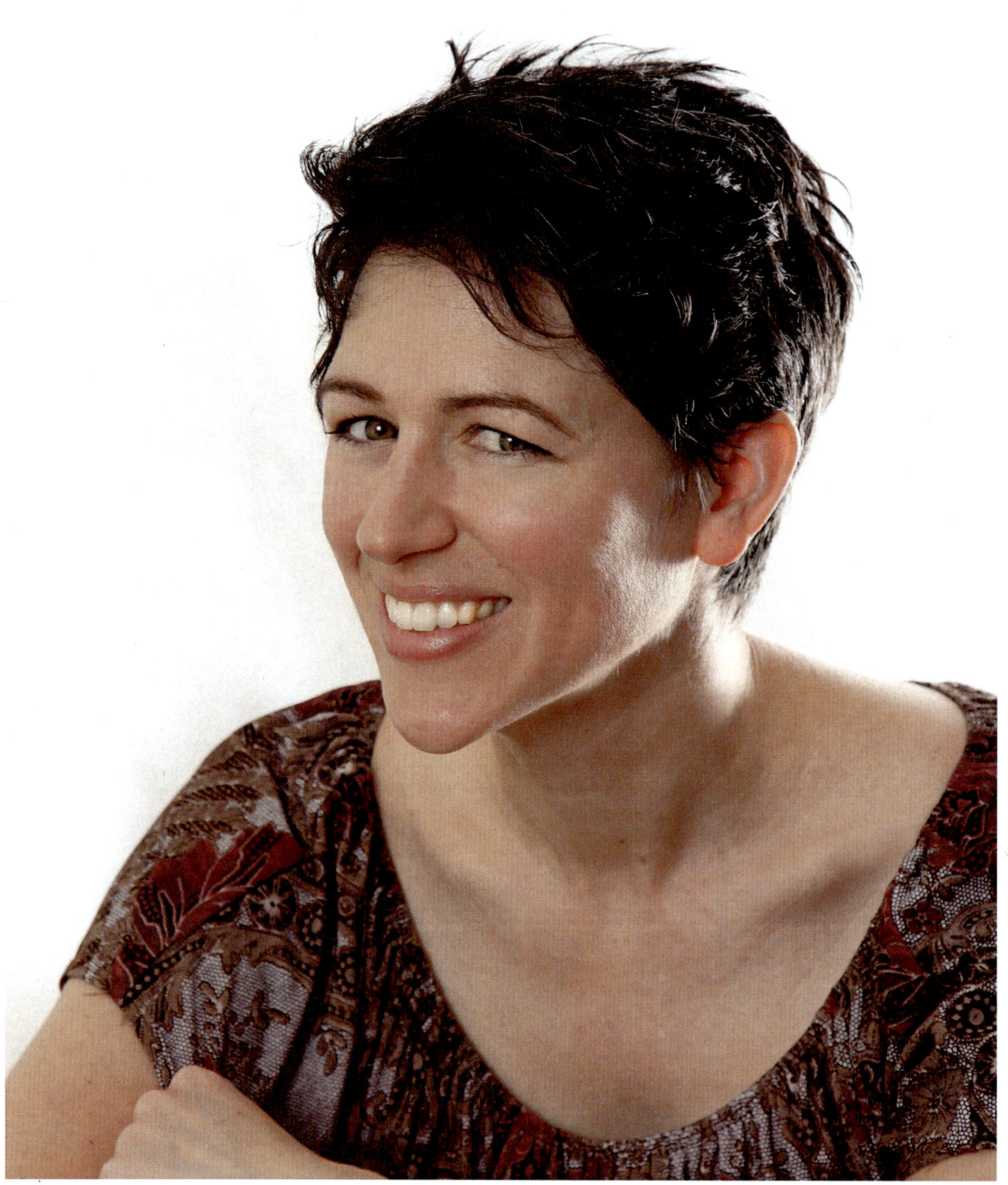

Robyn Kern

The creative process helps to anchor me and deal with the stress life can bring. I like using variations of the colours I see to help me think outside the box and add new dimensions to my subject. It's an ongoing journey to capture in paint that which inspires me. Horses are a big part of my life. Their beauty, honesty and presence inspires me. Painted them was a natural leap. I endeavour to capture their power, grace and personality in each painting. It is my hope that others see the beauty I see in these amazing animals.

http://www.thekerncreative.com

justin-aikin-655510-unsplash.jpg

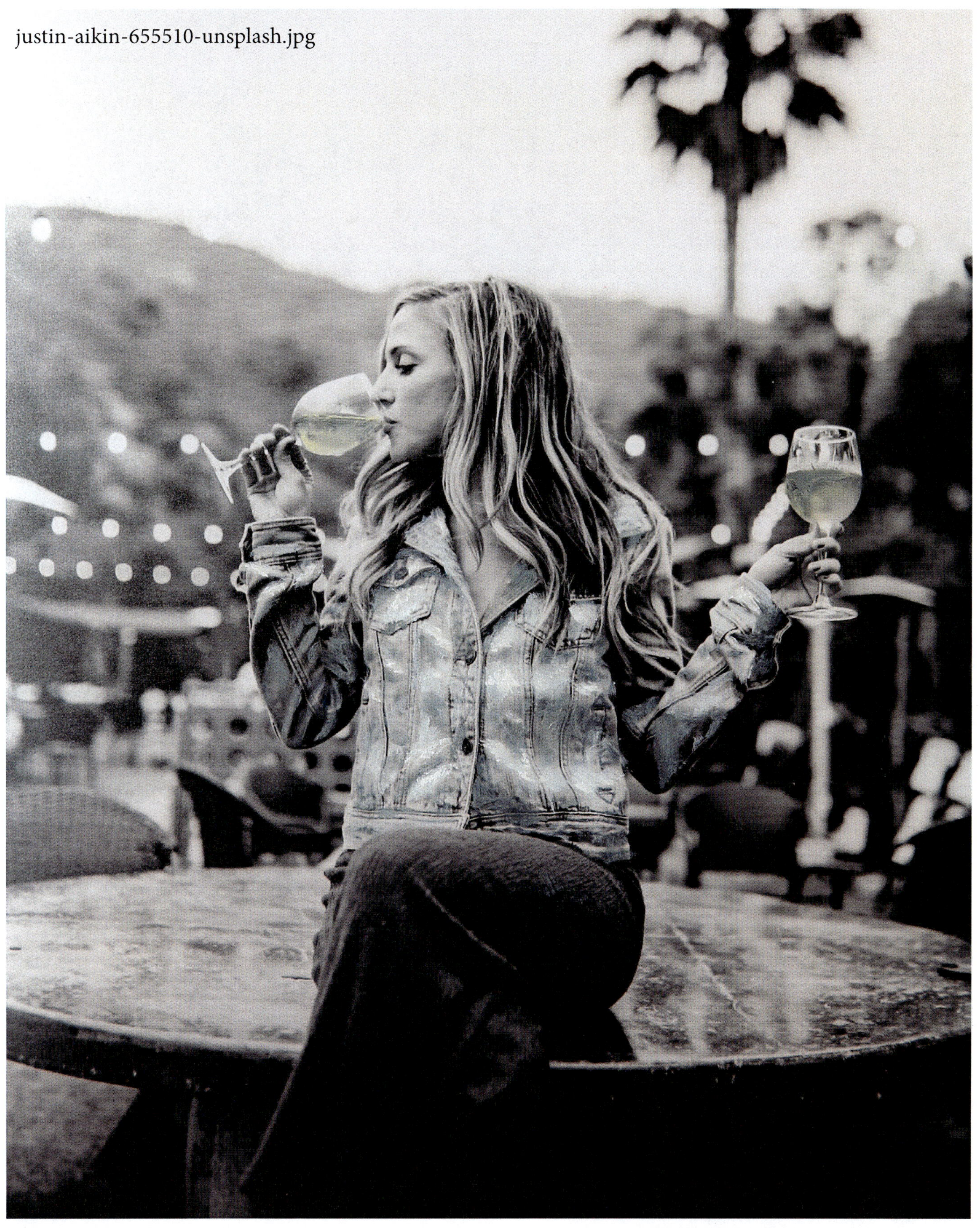

Tinted using Marshall's Photo Oils.

Enhanced with coloured pencils.

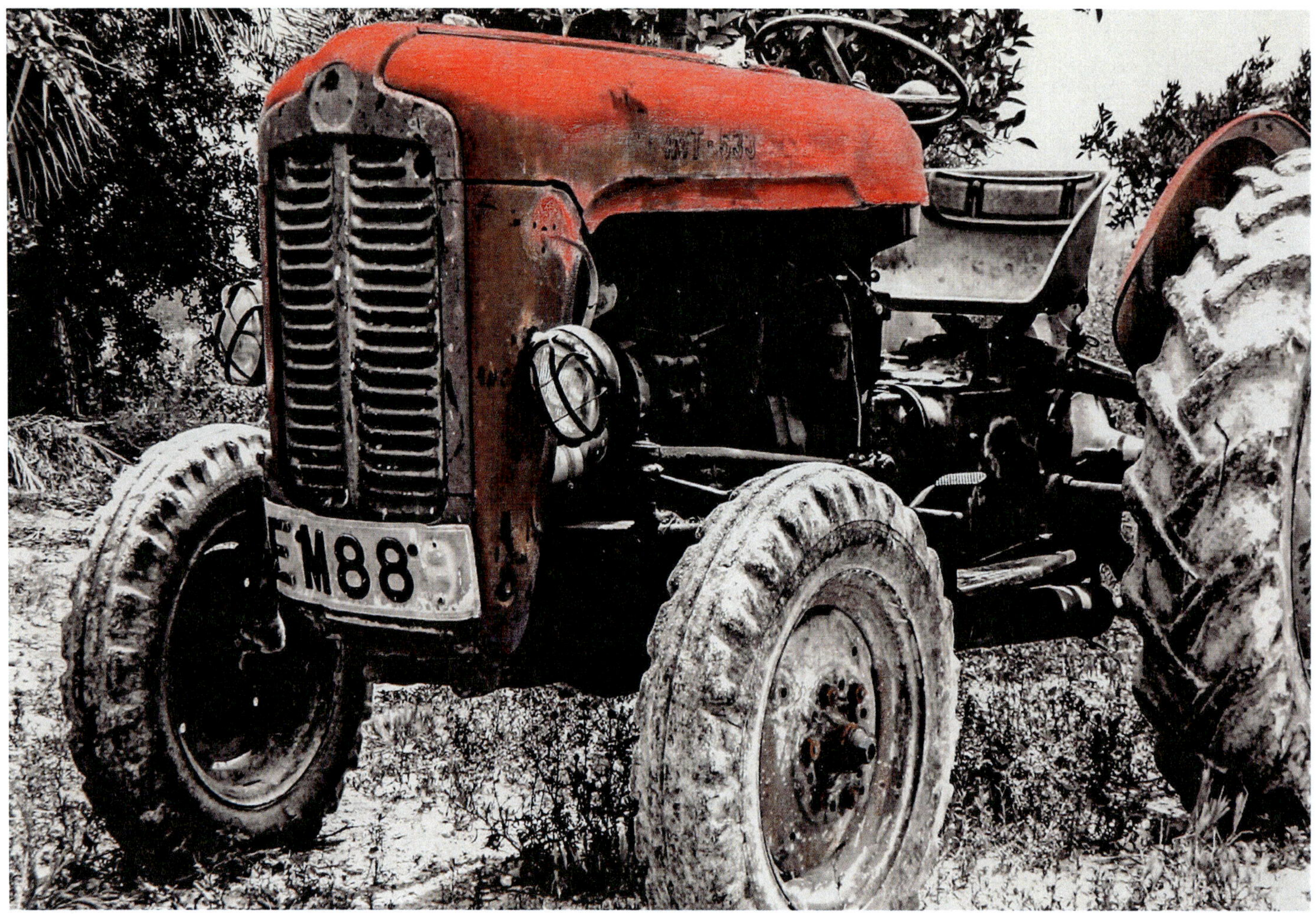

My favorite photograph to work on was the old tractor. It was fun to boldly layer and blend with the coloured pencils. I loved the contrast with the red vs the black and white photo.

I think I had the most fun working on these images because I didn't change the whole photograph. I just played where I wanted to and let the rest be.

I was interested to discover what the guest artists thought of this style of art, so posed the following questions.

What do you think of the overall idea of hand coloring or painting photographs?
I think it's awesome! Photographs can speak to us in a way images from a coloring book can't. You can take a picture that means something to you and enhance it in a way that makes it more meaningful to you.

Do you think this should be considered an art form?
"What is art?" Is very subjective. Art is using creativity and imagination so, yes.

What medium did you enjoy the most?
The coloured pencils. Probably strange for an oil painter, but I had more fun with that.

Was the process relaxing or stressful?
I found it very relaxing and the process was fun!

Who do you think this type of art would be suitable for?
Everyone. As a seasoned artist it was something different. As an artist coming back from a head injury it took some of the decision making out of the equation and allowed me to just have fun. It is also great for those starting out because the black and white photos help teach them about tonal values.

Did you experiment?
I tried a couple mediums which made a change from oil paints which I am most familiar and comfortable with. I enjoyed working with the coloured pencils on a heavier mixed media paper. However the photo oils on photographic paper were challenging. I guess it would take a little practice to get comfortable with that medium.

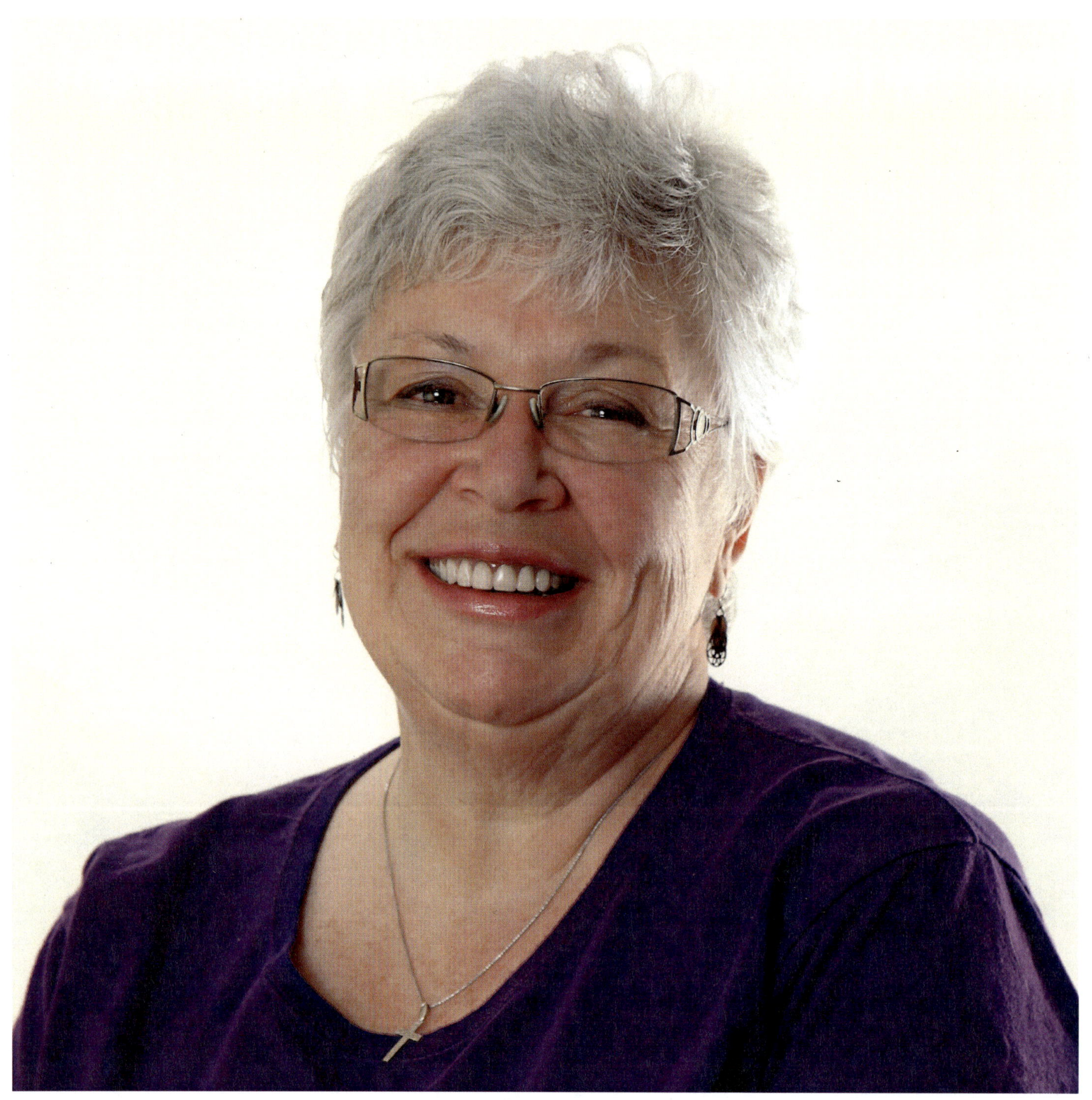

Marjorie Shannon-Graham

Marjorie spent an idyllic childhood growing up by the ocean in Nova Scotia. She re-located to Edmonton, Alberta and now spends her time surrounded by children and grandchildren, creating beautiful paintings. Her favoured medium is acrylic, and the majority of her work is influenced by nature in the form of flowers and animals.
Check out her work on Facebook "Thankful art by Marj"

https://www.facebook.com/Thankful-Art-by-Marj-310173216597526/

Marjorie's fabulous painted tiger is also featured on the cover of the book.

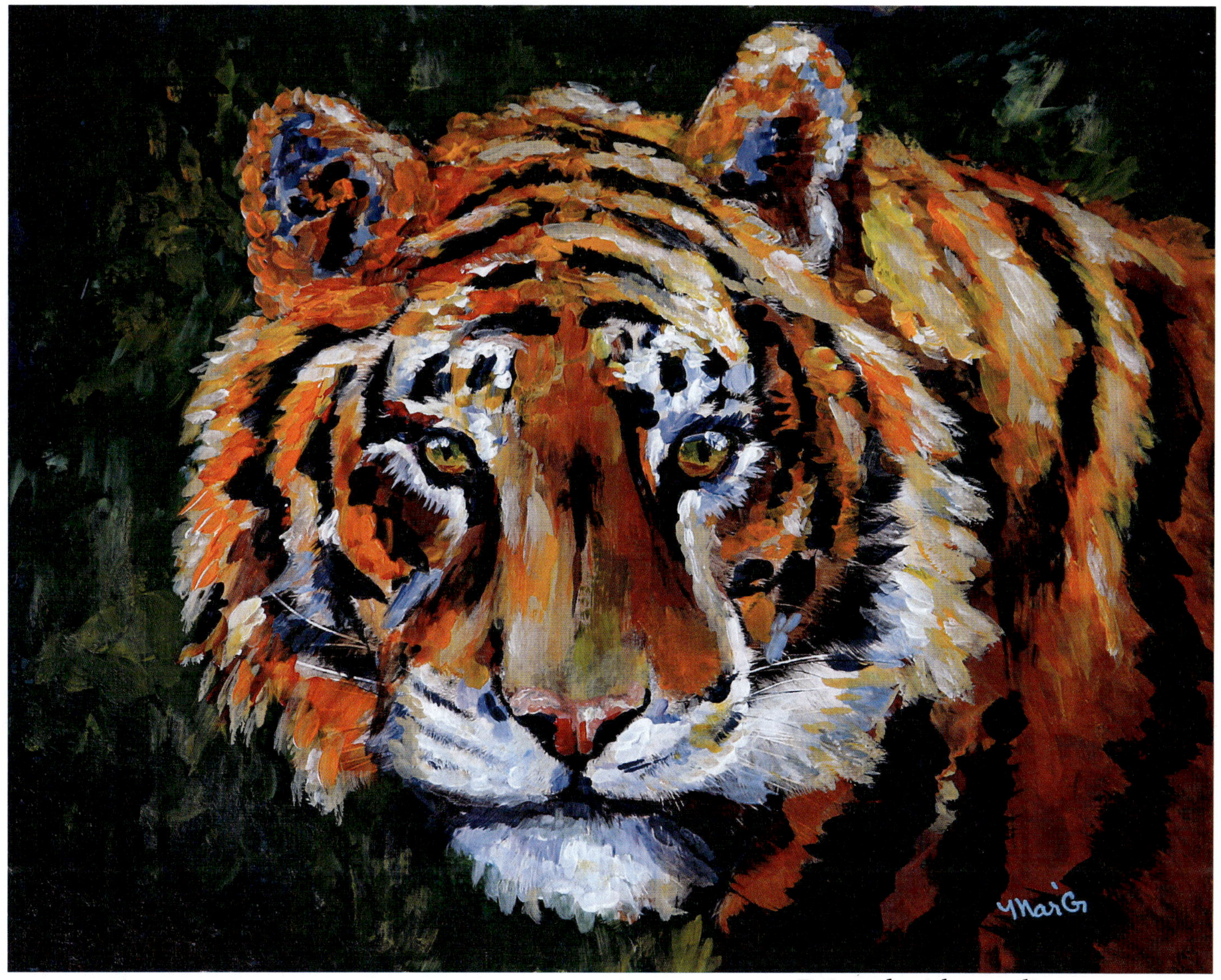

Painted with acrylics.

Linda provided me with a selection of black and white photographs printed on mixed media paper allowing me the freedom to choose whichever image I liked to paint. She then posed the question, "Which was my favourite photograph to enhance, and why?"

It was a difficult decision as I love flowers, and I love purples and rose colours, so the flower may have been my favourite image. But I am also drawn bright colours plus I'm trying to be more impressionistic at times. So Linda's photograph of the tiger was pretty awesome and I love painting eyes on animals, so it's hard to say

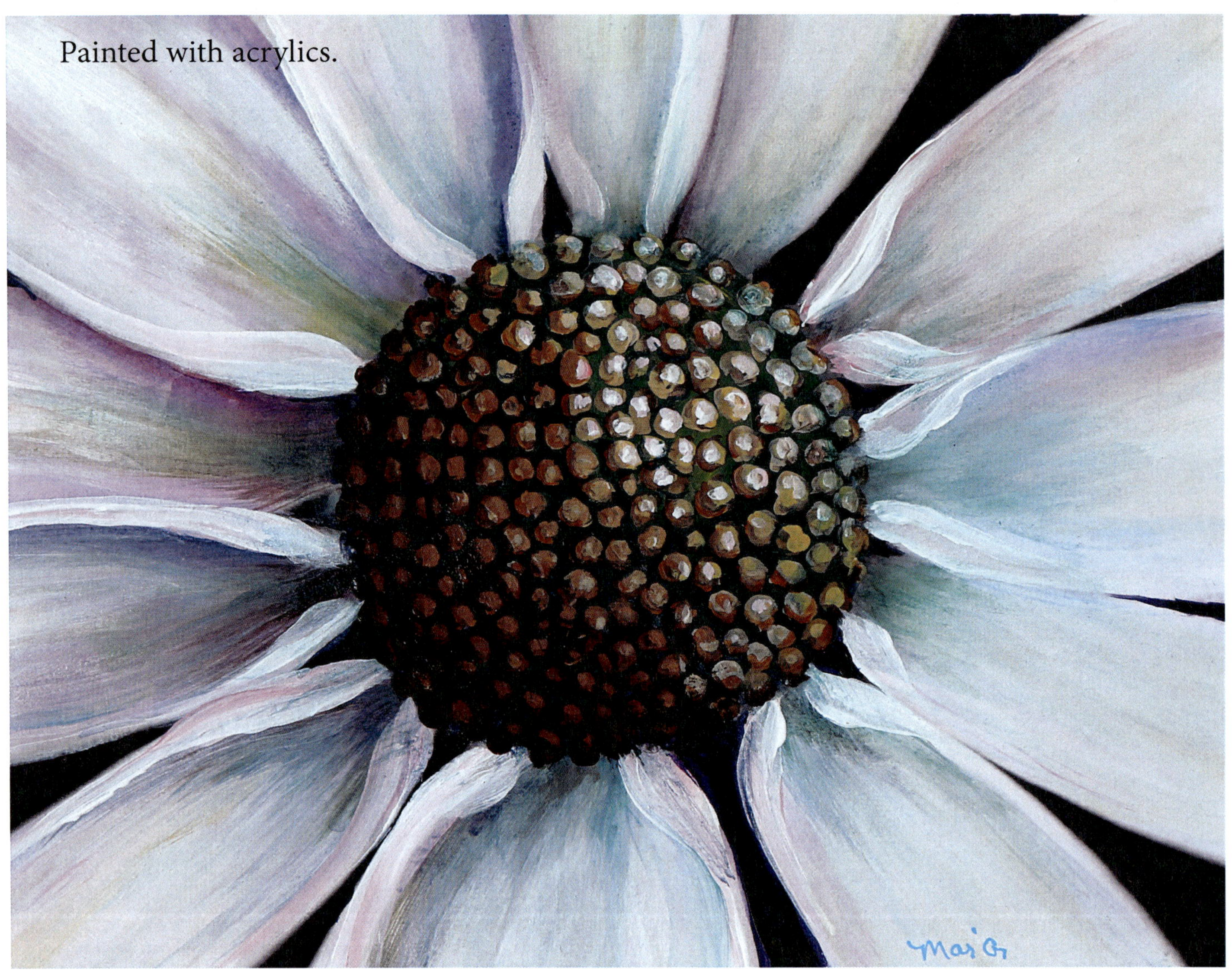

Painted with acrylics.

The most common question I get is "Have you painted all your life ?"
Without much thinking I would've said "No", however my father reminded me recently that the house I spent my teenage years in, has been up for sale, again. The real estate pictures show my old bedroom with a mural of a mare and foal that I painted 47 years ago.
I believe that creativity and art has had a place in every stage of my life. I painted sharks on basement floors and race tracks for cars for my kids when they were little. Now that I have more time I can focus on creating art that speaks to my heart, along with volunteering at church with arts and craft projects.

Who do you think this art form would be suitable for?
I can see hand tinting or painting photographs being suitable for a diverse range of ages. I have a grandson who loves to paint bricks. He would enjoy painting one of these photographs and do an amazing job of carefully painting inside the lines.
If you're that kind of person this art form will really work for you. I completed three styles, the tiger being a little more impressionistic and with impressionistic art, it doesn't matter if you slop over the lines a little. So this style would be easier for people with less than perfect motor skills.

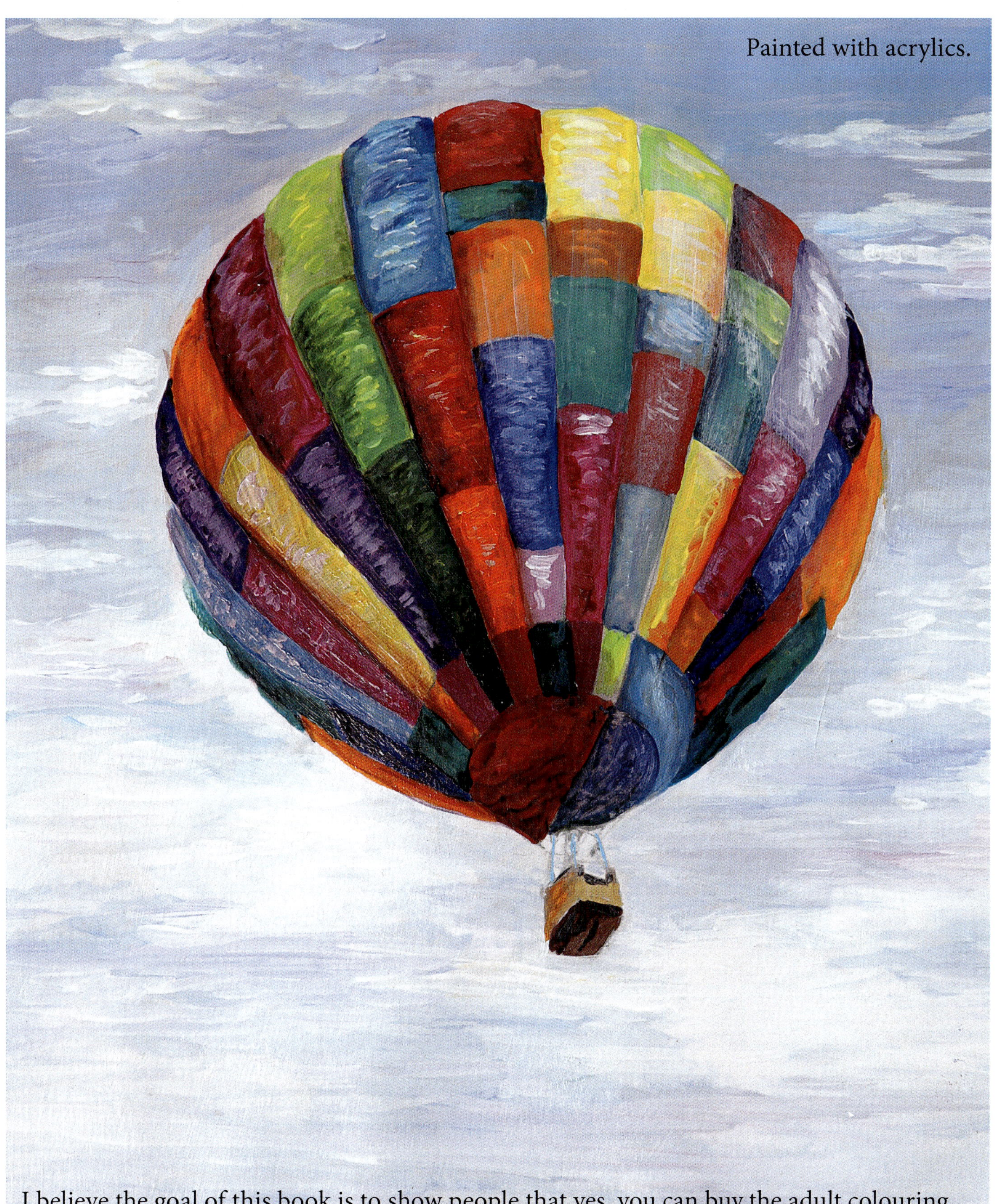
Painted with acrylics.

I believe the goal of this book is to show people that yes, you can buy the adult colouring books from Michael's and coloured pencils. But if you want to take creativity one step further you can do it on photographs as well. I think this art form will appeal to anyone who enjoys creating colourful, beautiful things.

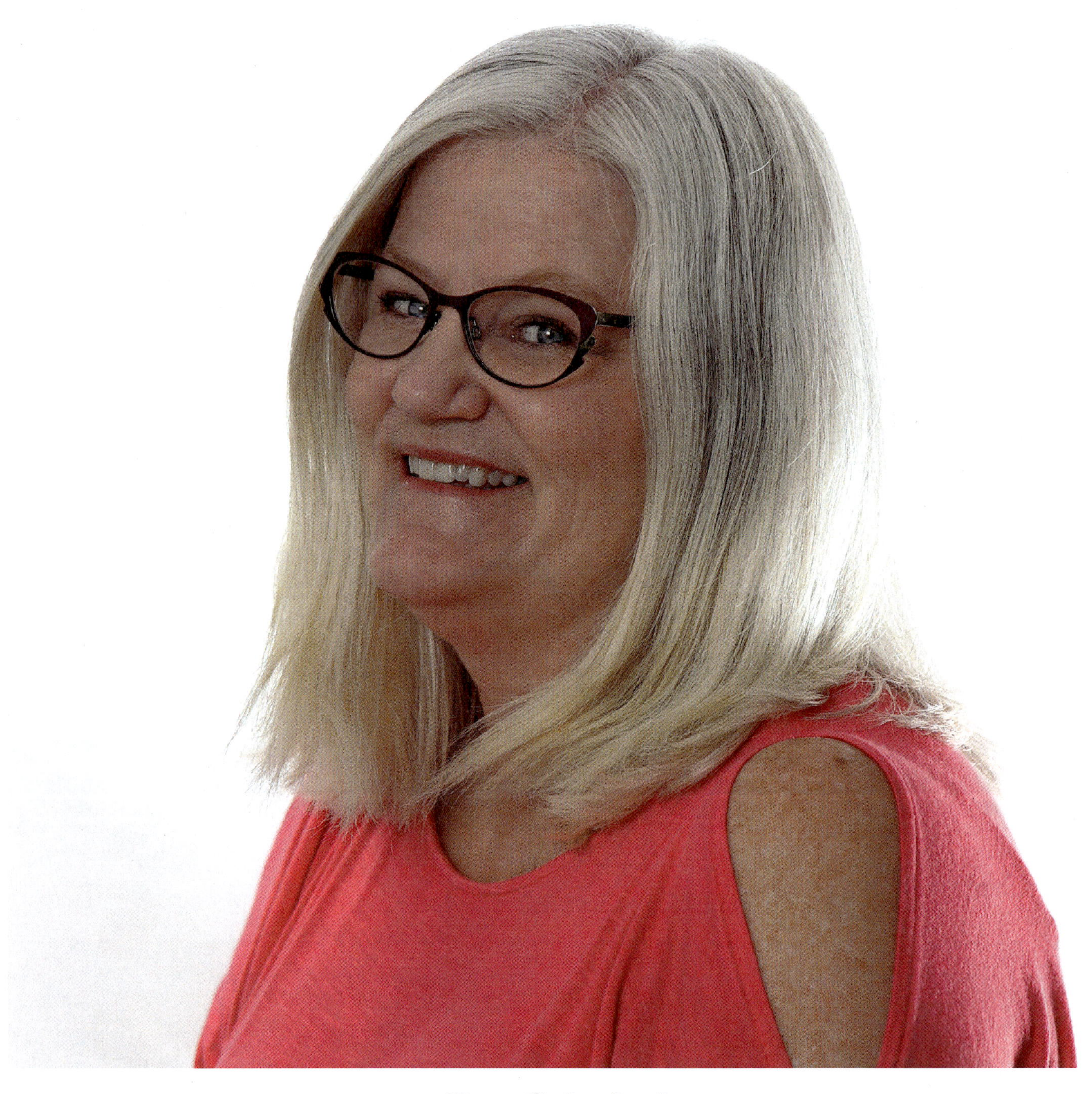

Bev Schakel

As a little girl I never really did a lot of arts and crafts. After my first child (24 years ago) I was introduced to scrapbooking through Creative Memories. Over the years this industry has exploded, and I love working with all sorts of paper. A few years ago, I met a group of ladies who introduced me to mixed media. This has opened many new doors for me, and I have only just started to explore the other types of medium that could be used to enhance my photos and papers. This experience with Linda has made me jump out of the box and just get to it!

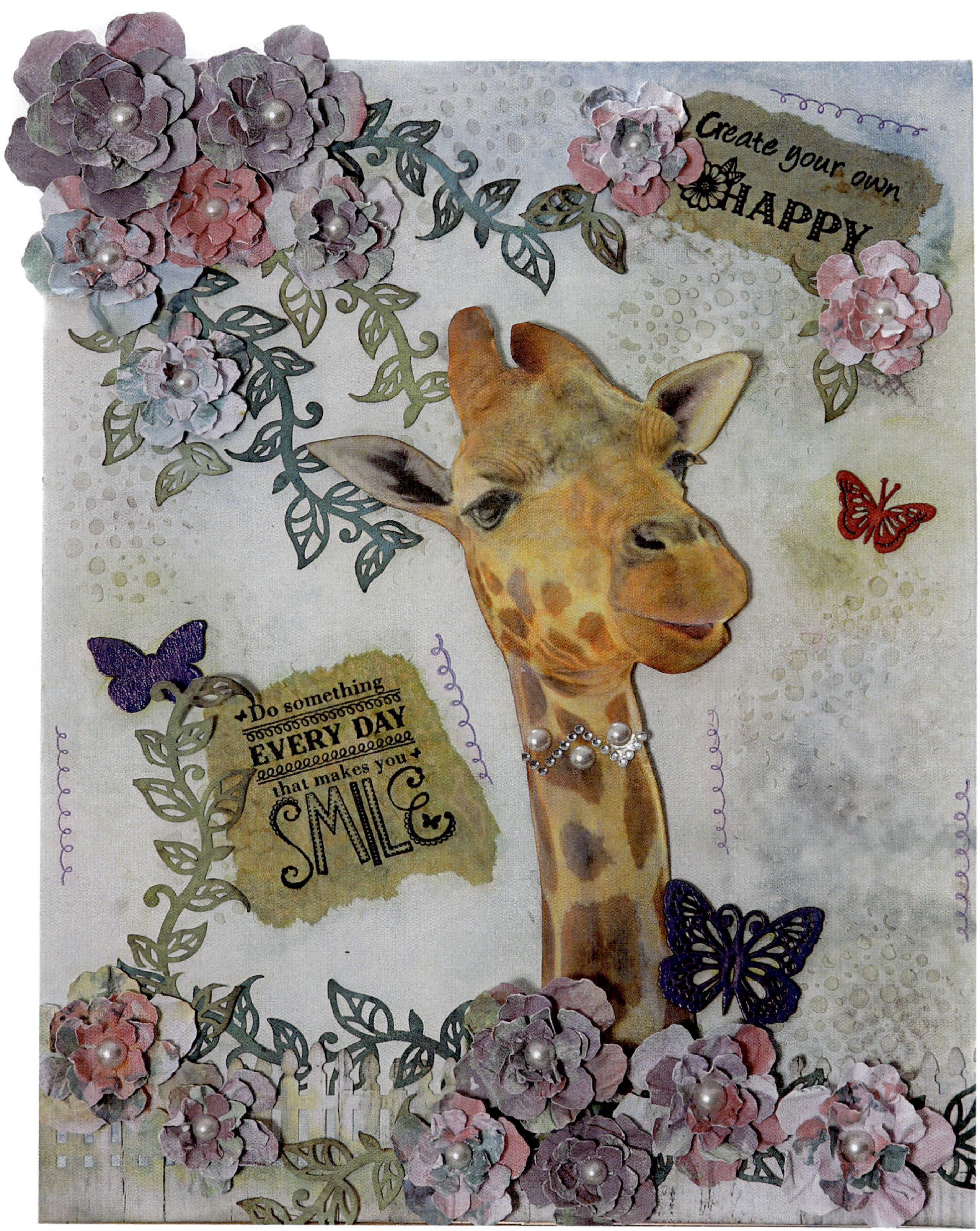

The giraffe was painted with inks.

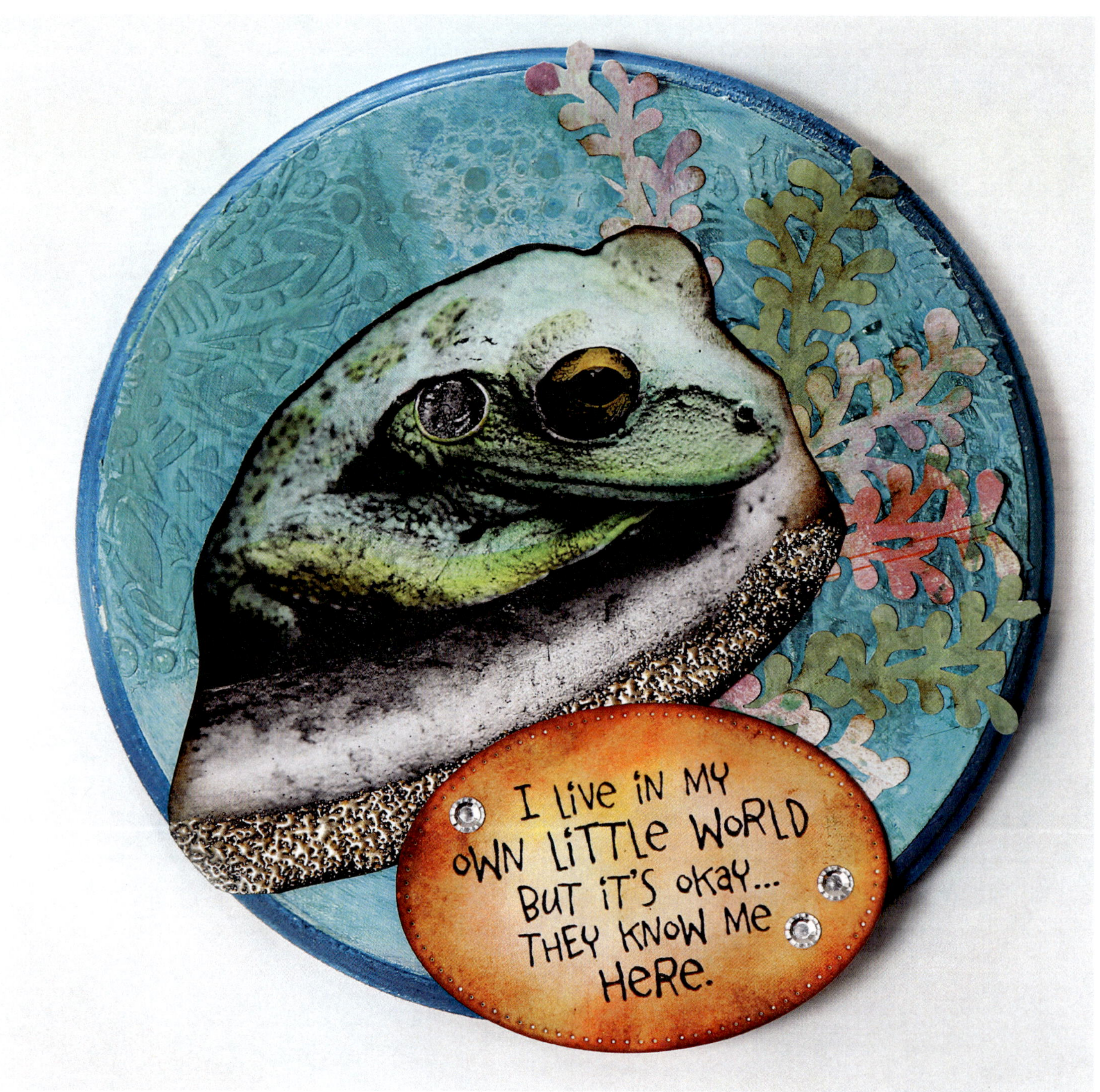

Overall Idea?
I think this is a fun way to add to the photos taken, especially if you are planning to frame it or give it away as a gift to someone.

Is this an artform?
Absolutely! The artist is adding their own touches.

I used mainly inks to colour my sample projects as that was the medium I was most comfortable with, along with my mixed media embellishments. But as I learn more, I would definitely try some other medium as well.

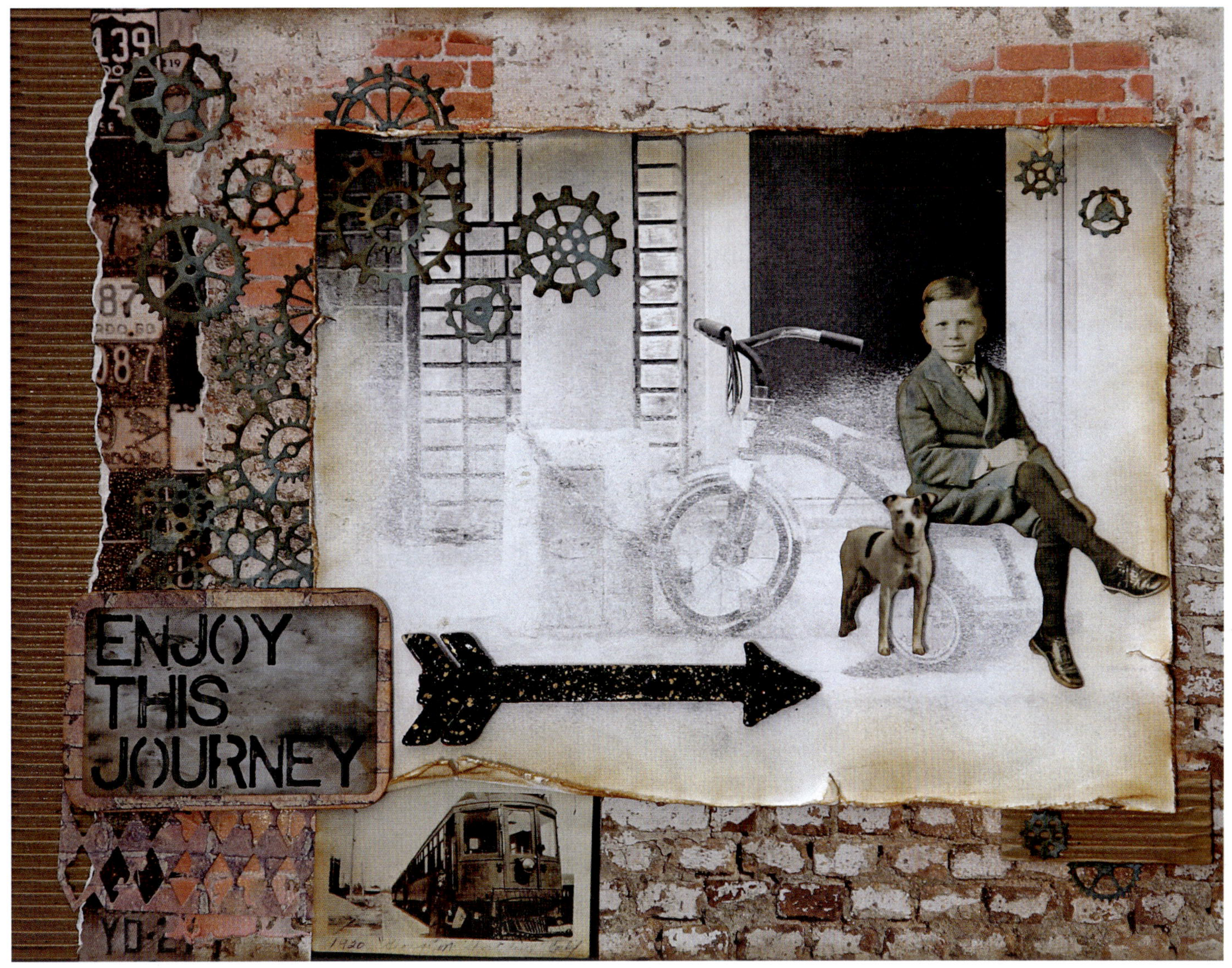

Being invited to feature in this book as a guest artist and experiment with this art form was stressful but only because I am new at this and wondered how my work compared to the others.

Who do you think this art form would be suitable for?
I think anyone. From an amateur (like me) who loves paper arts and scrapbooking to a professional artist who is looking to add more ideas and variety to their work.

This whole process was very much trial and error. I tried embossing on one photograph but that did not turn out quite right, however I was thrilled with how the stamping, stenciling and torn paper effects enhanced the finished piece.
My favorite image was the Giraffe. She pops out at you. It is my first one that I completed and I love it. This piece reminds me to just be happy and create from the heart.

Choosing the right mat

Always mat your work. This is important not only because it gives your art a nice inner frame but mats allow air to circulate around the work and put a space between the art and the glass. Acidic materials used in some mats can lead to big problems such as the mat itself becoming yellowish in colour and deteriorating the colours within the painting that is in contact with the mat over a long period of time.

Every material in contact with the painting should be acid-free or Ph neutral to prevent oxidation and aging. This also includes the tape you use to attach the painting to the mat board. Acid free tape is readily available from art stores or framers and well worth the extra few dollars.

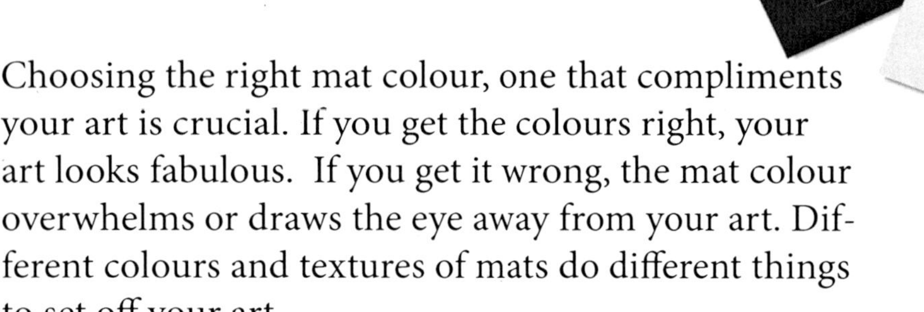

Choosing the right mat colour, one that compliments your art is crucial. If you get the colours right, your art looks fabulous. If you get it wrong, the mat colour overwhelms or draws the eye away from your art. Different colours and textures of mats do different things to set off your art.

Many artists like to choose one of the more dominant colours within the art for the mat colour. This combination draws the eye to the art rather than to the framing. If you are not sure which colour to pick from the painting, a general rule of thumb is, choose a darker mat on a dark work of art and lighter mat on a lighter coloured work of art.

Very often choosing a neutral colour for the mat will do a fabulous job of setting off the art without emphasizing any particular colours. It is just as important to consider the subject of the art and the emotion that art is trying to convey. We talked earlier about colours having temperature. Neutral colours can run the spectrum from warm to cool, from creams to greys, and they sometimes include adding texture for visual interest without adding intense colour. Sometimes white mats work as neutrals, although white mats on dark art may be too much contrast for the art.

Preserving and framing your work

There are two golden rules you must adhere to no matter what surface your finished art was created on.

The first is to avoid direct sunlight. This might sound pretty basic but sunlight breaks down the molecules in dyes and pigments used in the print and paint causing the colours to fade. Carefully choose the right place to hang your finished work. Take into account how sunlight streams into the room from windows and which walls it hits.

The second rule is also pretty obvious but is equally important avoid humidity. Hot sticky summer temperatures with high humidity will severely effect the integrity of paper regardless of how expensive the art paper was. The same is true of wet damp climates as humidity really is the enemy of all art. For this reason hanging your beautiful finished art in the bathroom would be disaster.

When your finished art has completely dried it is advisable to frame your work under glass as soon as possible. If you need to store your paintings before framing them store them flat between sheets of acid-free paper or good quality drawing paper to protect them from dirt and dust. Handle the paintings with care; do not touch the painting's surface. Pick them up by the sides with clean hands.

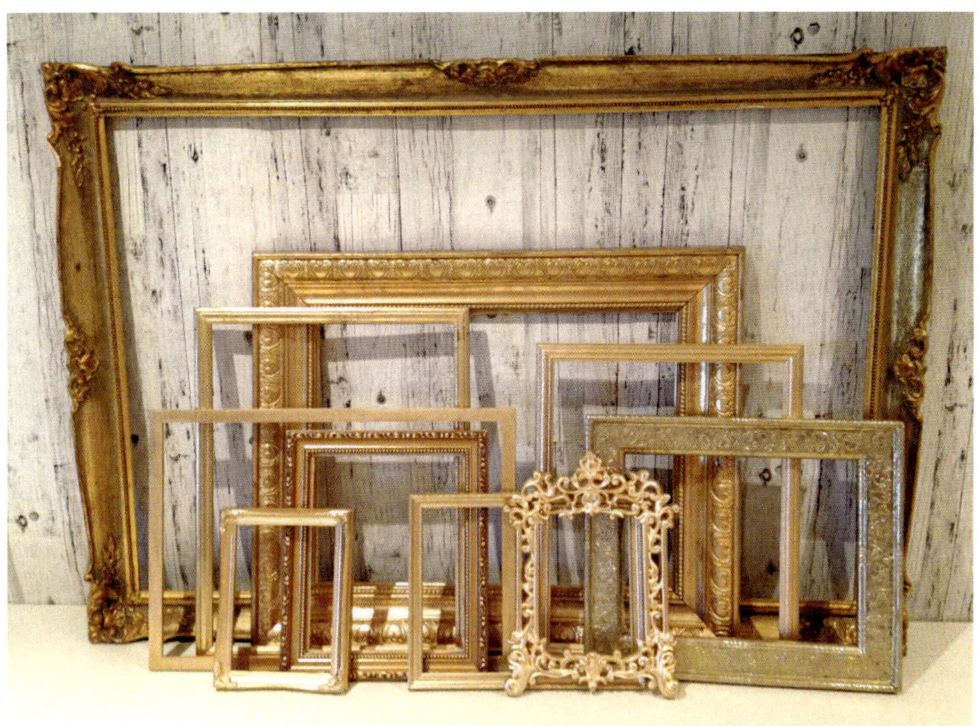

The next step is to frame your work.
Your choice of frame is very much a personal preference and may also be influenced on where you intend to hang it (room colour/aesthetic/decor, etc).
However consider the following:

Are the frame-to-painting proportions pleasing?
A frame can be too large or too small. A too-small frame doesn't give the painting the importance it deserves, which is just as bad as the overpowering effect of an oversize frame.
Does the style of the frame complement the painting?
Is the frame "too loud" or ostentatious? This makes me, the viewer, confront the frame first, not what's inside it. The painting should be the main attraction. While the frame may be beautiful in and of itself, its pairing with the painting must be harmonious.

Does the colour of the frame complement the painting?
Should a frame be gilded (gold, silver or metal leaf), painted a colour or left as natural wood? The answer isn't easy because there really are so many choices and no hard-and-fast rules. This is where your artistic ability comes into play.

Does all art need to be protected by glass?
This is the million dollar question and again there is no hard fast answer because of the variables involved, but a general rule of thumb is if the art is painted on any type of paper then the answer is "yes."

Paper is delicate and the glass will help preserve the life of the art. Oil paintings on canvas or wood panels tend to be framed without glass. But then mixed media, paintings created from more than just one type of paint or material, rocked the art world and those art pieces may be three dimensional, in which case a shadow box frame with glass would best serve to protect them.

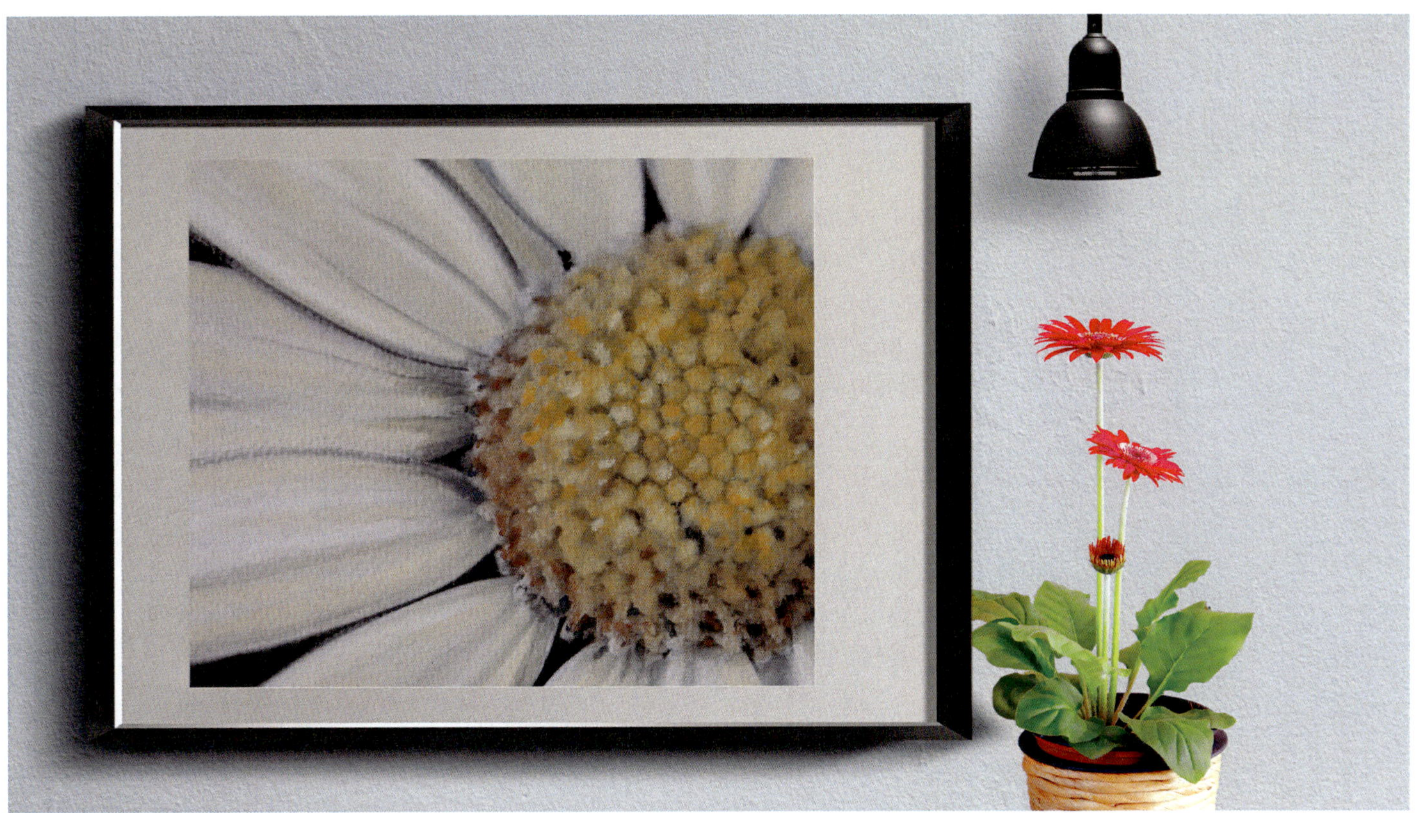

The cool neutral grey mat does not draw attention away from the art and the simple black frame means this piece of art could be hung on any wall or decor asthetic.

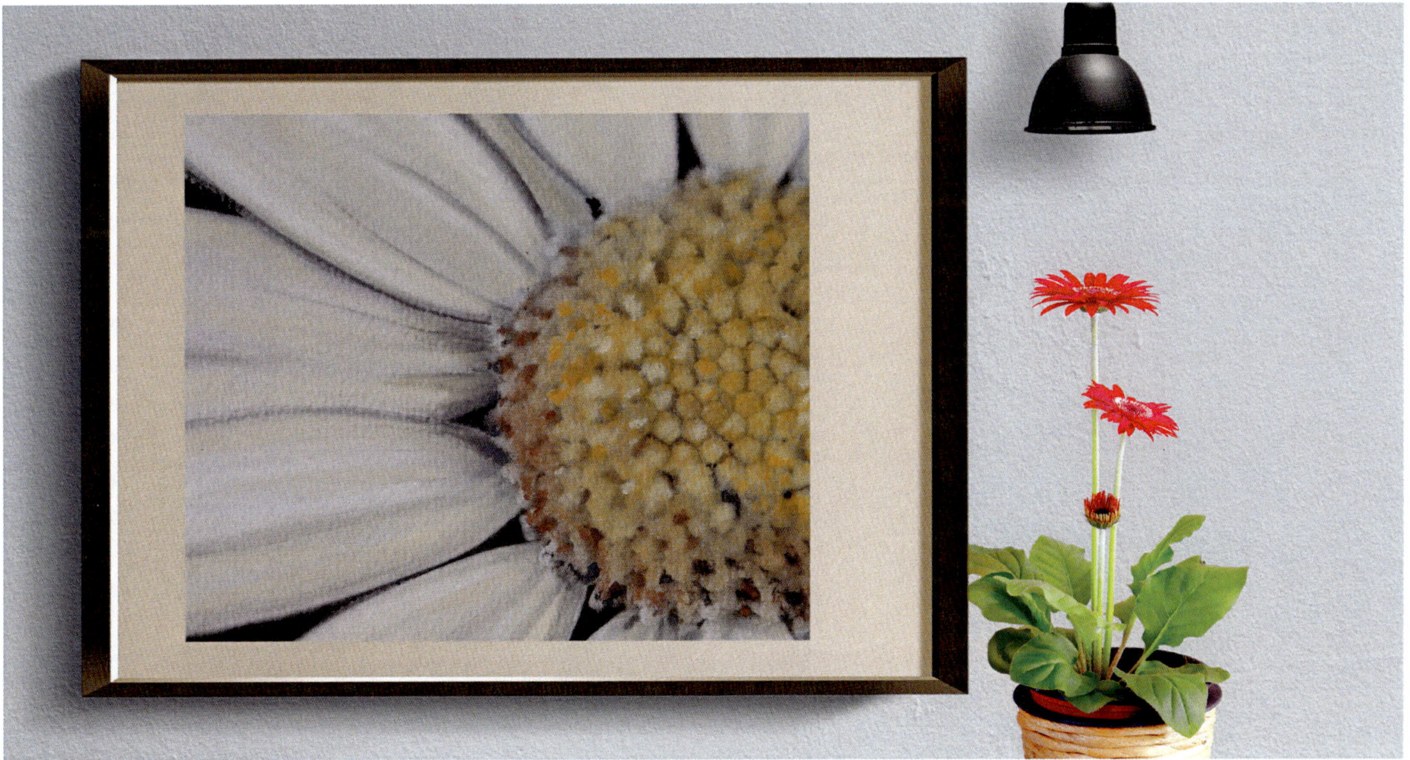

This warmer buff coloured mat and brown frame also compliments the art well.
As you can see there is no right or wrong way to mat and frame art. It is subject to personal preference and taste.

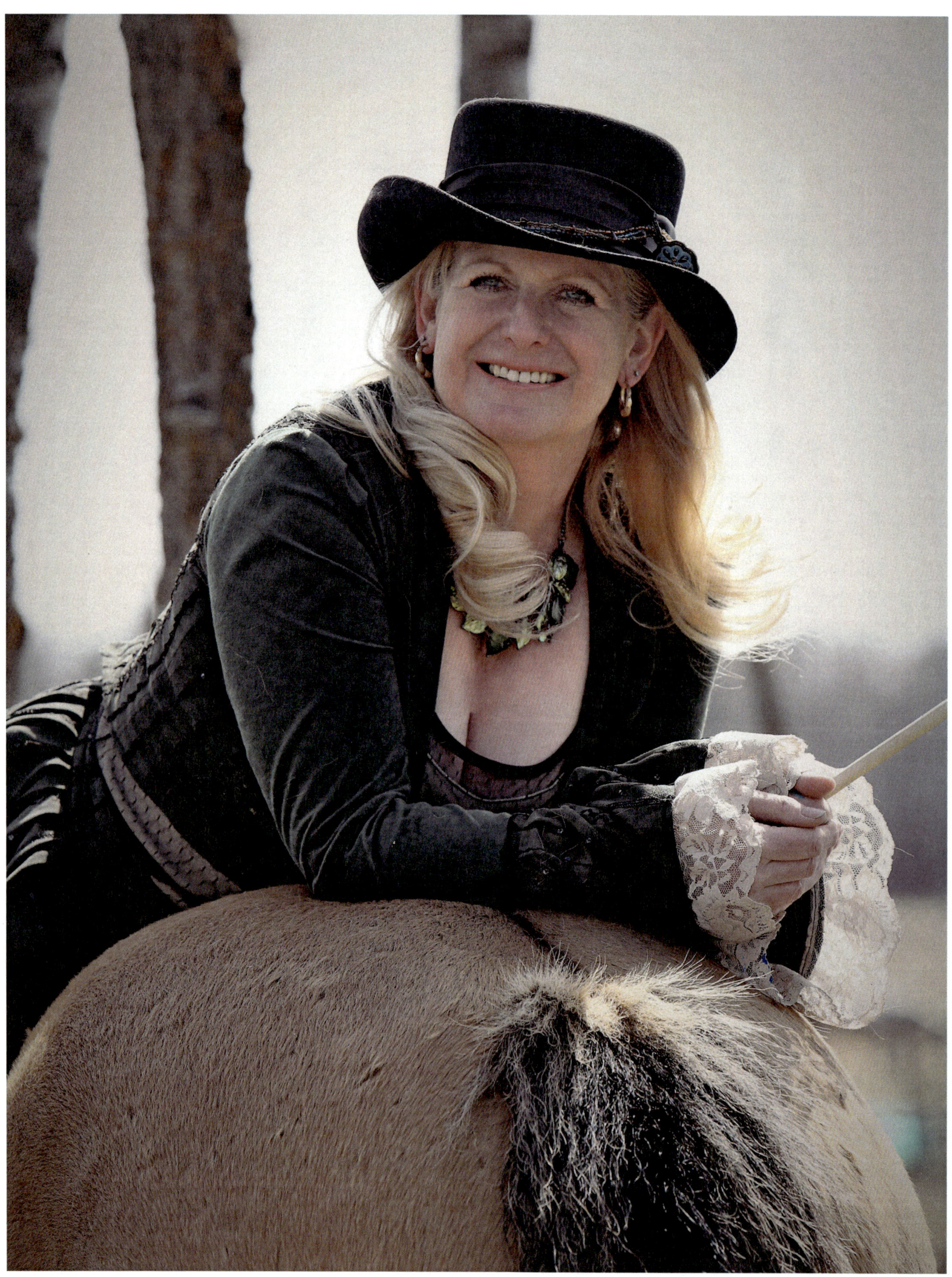

About the author

Linda Finstad
Artist / Author / Fine art photographer / Educator and all-round good egg

Linda Finstad calls herself an "Equine Artist", a description that becomes obvious when you look at her extensive body of work. Whether it's her unique "Prism-Equus" paintings, exquisite fine art photography or line-up of published books, horses are the thread that ties it all together. Finstad says "When you look at art it should evoke an emotion - and the emotion I am trying to convey in my art is joy. For myself joy comes in the shape of a horse".

Her work has been featured on several TV networks and received media attention world wide. She even received a letter of recognition from Her Royal Highness the Queen of England for her work on de-coding equine body language.

Linda loves to share her passion for art through a variety of workshops and classes. She is also a performance painter who allows people to share in the creative process as she paints on location. Using acrylic paints means there is no smell, a common problem with oil-based paints. Her use of bright colours attracts lots of attention especially from younger art enthusiasts - so she carries with her a stack of colouring pages she created to give to children so they to can join in. Linda truly believes there is an artist inside everyone just itching to get out.

"Don't think about making art, just get it done.
Let everyone else decide whether it's good or bad.
Whether they love it or hate it.
While they are deciding, make even more art".

Andy Warhol

www.LindaFinstad.com

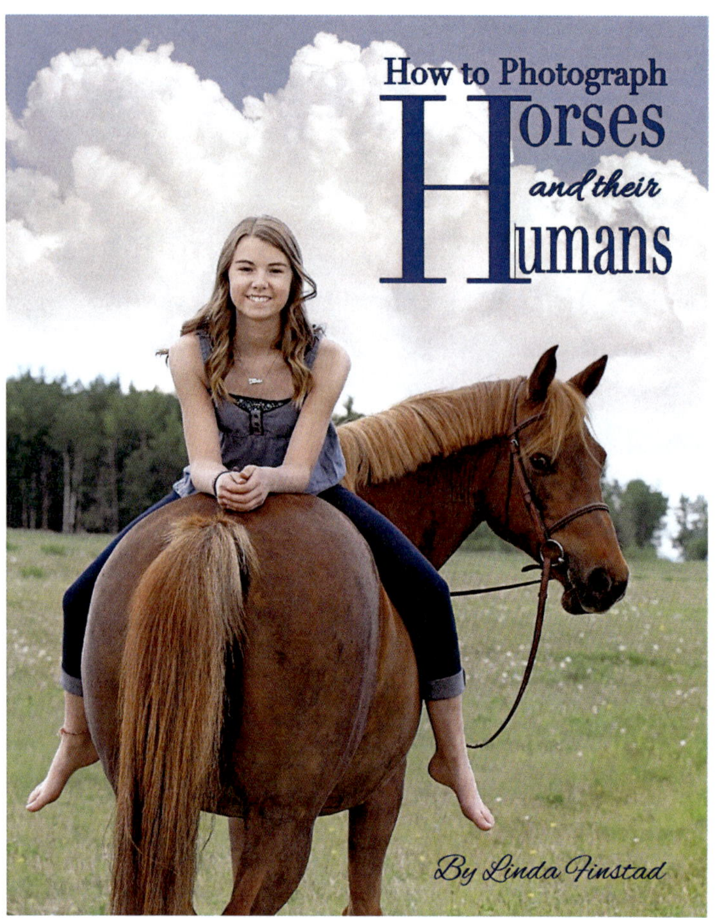

How to Photograph Horses and their Humans

This modern no-nonsense guide walks you through every step to achieving calendar-quality images of horses and their owners. In this book every age group and equine discipline is covered, from kids to cowboys. It takes an in-depth look at how to successfully move through your photo session so one pose naturally progresses to the next, making the photo experience pleasurable for everyone.

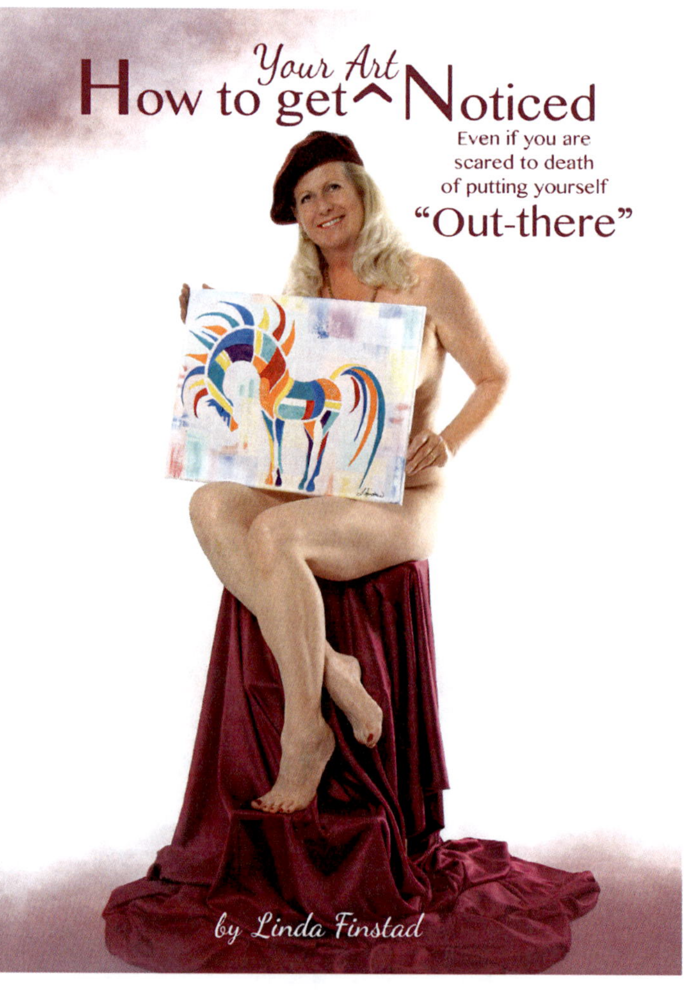

How to get Your Art Noticed

The big advice given to all artists wanting to take their art career to the next level or just sell a few pieces and make a few bucks is "You have to get your-self out-there." The author received the same ambiguous advice and decided to find out exactly where "out-there" really is. She challenged herself to paint 50 pictures in 50 different locations.

This is her story. The trails and tribulations, the rejections and humiliations plus the life-changing triumphs and amazing opportunities that came from getting out-there. This is a social experiment that anyone can replicate, whatever type of art you create.

More Books By *Linda Finstad*

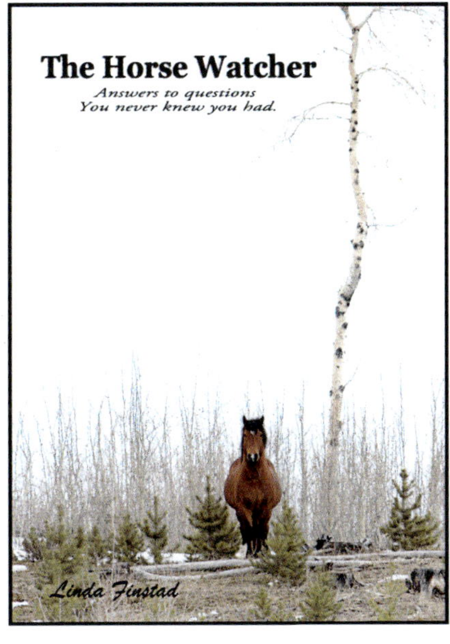

The Horse Watcher

This beautifully illustrated book answers many of the questions you never knew you had concerning equine behavior and communication. "A must read for all horse lovers." (*On The Pony Club suggested reading list.)*

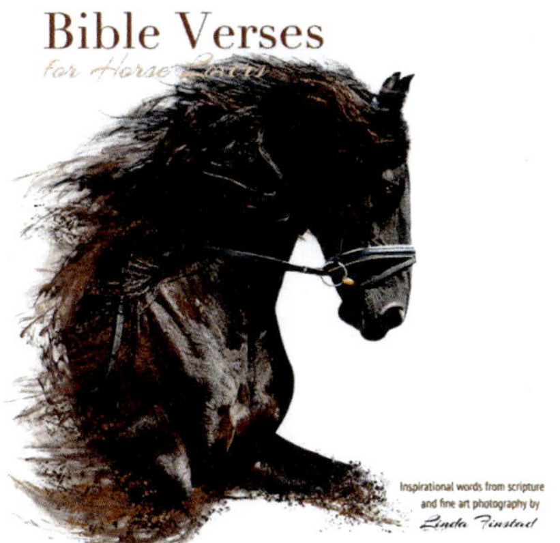

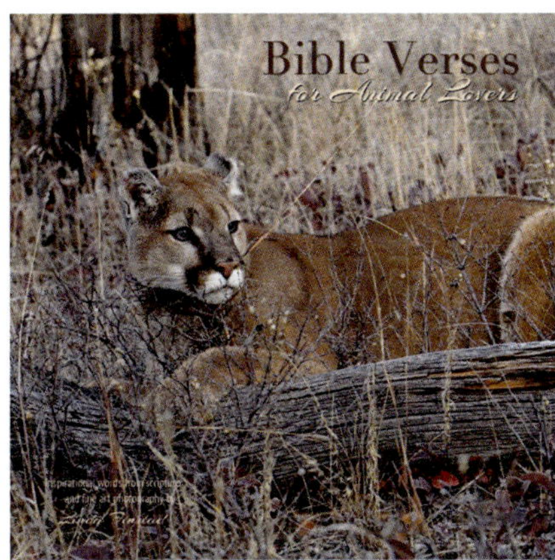

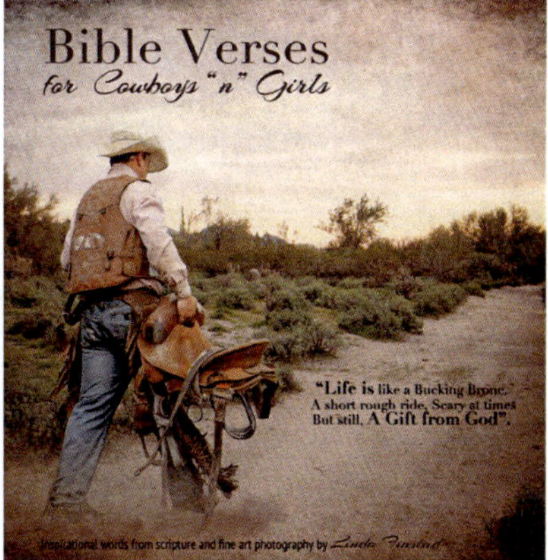

Fine art photography coupled with inspiring verses from God's word. The perfect "Gift Book" for people who "have everything", because the one thing you can't have too much of is God's word.

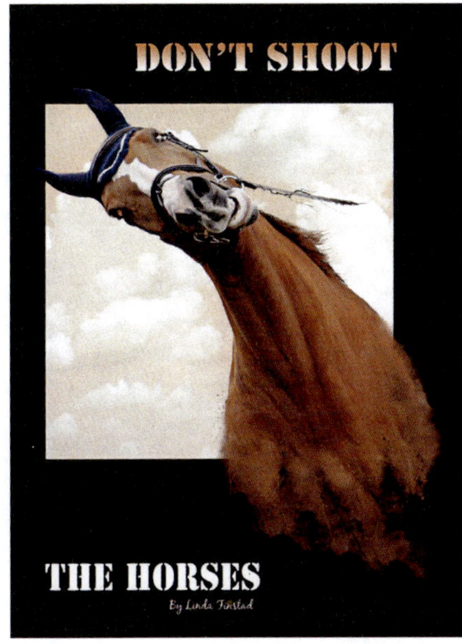

Don't Shoot the Horses

Horses are capable of many facial expressions that range from the good, the bad to the downright scary. Linda has broken the unwritten rule among equine photographers of not only capturing those moments but publishing them in her book.
Warning - *When you open these pages you will be leaving your comfort zone.*

All Linda's books areAvailable from: Amazon

References

Pg. 19 Strathmore ®
Pg. 20 Kodak
Pg. 29 Artist Loft®
Pg. 29 Golden®
Pg. 39 Golden®
Pg. 41 Dr. Ph. Martin's®
Pg. 41 Academy®
Pg. 47 PanPastel®
Pg. 48 pebeo
Pg. 48 Caran d'Arche®
Pg. 55 Grumbacher®
Pg. 57 Exablast
Pg. 57 Sargent Art®
Pg. 65 and throughout Marshall's Photo Oils
Pg. 66 and throughout Marshall's PM Solution
Pg. 66 Mona Lisa™ by Speedball®
Pg. 68 General's®
Pg. 73 Prismacolor®
Pg. 74 Sakura pigma Macron®
Throughout Q-Tips®

Made in United States
North Haven, CT
02 June 2022

19796894R00062